The Retreat of Representation

SUNY Series, Intersections:
Philosophy and Critical Theory

Rodolphe Gasché, Editor

The Retreat of Representation

The Concept of *Darstellung* in German Critical Discourse

∾

Martha B. Helfer

State University of New York Press

Published by
State University of New York Press, Albany

© 1996 State University of New York

For information, address State University of New York Press,
State University Plaza, Albany, N.Y. 12246

Production by M. R. Mulholland
Marketing by Theresa A. Swierzowski

Library of Congress Cataloging-in-Publication Data

Helfer, Martha B., 1962-
    The retreat of representation : the concept of darstellung in
German critical discourse / Martha B. Helfer.
        p.   cm. — (SUNY series, Intersections)
    Includes bibliographical references and index.
    ISBN 0-7914-2911-3 (hc : alk. paper). — ISBN 0-7914-2912-1 (pb :
alk. paper)
    1. Representation (Philosophy)   2. Idealism, German.
3. Romanticism—Germany.   4. Kleist, Heinrich von, 1777-1811—
Criticism and interpretation.   5. Novalis, 1772-1801—Criticism and
interpretation.   I. Title.   II. Series: Intersections, (Albany,
N.Y.)
BH301.R47H45   1996
141'.0943—dc20   95-18573
                                                              CIP

10 9 8 7 6 5 4 3 2 1

For my parents,
Jo and Larry Helfer

Contents

Acknowledgments

This manuscript has gone through several transformations over the past few years, and I am very thankful to the many people who have provided me with critical feedback, encouragement, financial aid, and emotional support at various stages of the project.

I am extremely grateful to David Wellbery for the keen intellect, incisive criticism, and unflagging enthusiasm with which he guided me through both graduate school and this project in its initial form. I also would like to extend a very special thanks to Kurt Mueller-Vollmer, whose critical finesse, intellectual inquisitiveness, and encouragement helped shape the contours of this investigation. I am very grateful to Russell Berman for reading an early draft of the manuscript and providing me with new perspectives on my work. Jürgen Trabant, Winfried Menninghaus, and Barbara Naumann read parts of the manuscript in its early stages, and I would like to thank them for giving me very useful feedback and direction. Thanks, too, to Glenn Kurtz for the many lunchtime conversations and editorial suggestions, to Pawel Lutomski for encouraging me to read Kant, to Gertrud Pacheco for her caring and warmth, and to Liz Wolf for her friendship and goodwill.

A grant from the Fulbright Commission supported the initial stages of this research. Further research was funded in part by a Faculty Research Grant from the University of Utah Research Committee. A Career Development Grant from the University of Utah College of Humanities provided me with leave time in which to pursue my research. I would like to thank my friends and colleagues at the University of Utah Department of Languages and Literature for their enthusiasm and encouragement over the past few years. I am especially grateful to Deborah Porter for her useful comments and suggestions for completing the technical aspects of the manuscript.

I am very thankful to Rodolphe Gasché for his strong support of this project. I also would like to thank Carola Sautter and Megeen Mulholland of SUNY Press for their help in putting the manuscript into and through production, and the SUNY Press readers for their excellent criticism.

My family has been an unwavering source of comfort and encouragement. Warmest thanks to Adam, Aisha, Rokie, Riaz, Beth, Bruce, Rebecca, Aaron, Tam, and John for their love, caring, and good humor over the years. A special thanks, too, to Cousin Frances for taking interest in my work and encouraging me to take breaks from it occasionally. My parents have provided me with an immense amount of support and love, and I am tremendously grateful to them.

Finally, I am especially thankful to Steve Nowick for his love, understanding, and friendship over the past several years.

Introduction:
Heidegger's *World Picture*:
A Space Withdrawn from Representation

In his famous essay *The Age of the World Picture* (1938) Martin Heidegger argues that the modern age is characterized by the interweaving of two events: the world becomes a picture and the human being becomes a subject. These events are actually articulations of a single phenomenon that finds its inception in the Cartesion *cogito*; namely, that representation (*Vorstellung*) has become the basis of truth and of Being: "What it is to be is for the first time defined as the objectiveness of representing, and truth is first defined as the certainty of representing, in the metaphysics of Descartes" (127).[1] By *representation* Heidegger means *vor-stellen* in the original sense of the word: to set out before oneself and in relationship to oneself (132). This process results in an objectification of whatever is, and transforms the fundamental essence of the human being, the self-proclaimed center and ground of this new worldview: "That which is, is no longer that which presences; it is rather that which, in representing, is first set over against, that which stands fixedly over against, which has the character of object (*das Gegen-ständige*). Representing is making-stand-over-against, an objectifying that goes forth and masters" (149–150). In short, the Cartesian subject masters the world by making it into a picture (*Bild* or *Gebild*), a structured visual image that it itself creates.

This modern conception of the subject is problematic, Heidegger contends, because it has no special relation to humankind and none at all to the I (128). He therefore sets out to overcome the representational paradigm of the modern age by drawing its fundamental premises into question, a

1

task that is best accomplished by reflection. "Reflection (*Besinnung*)," Heidegger writes in a definition that smacks of Kant, "is the courage to make the truth of our own pre-suppositions and the realm of our own goals into the things that most deserve to be called into question" (116). Through *Besinnung*, literally, a turning of sensible thought back on itself, the modern subject can escape the objectifying process of representation that occludes a true definition of human-kind as belonging to Being.

Having thus laid the groundwork for an incisive critique of the notion of representation that structures the modern age, Heidegger then points to a sign that portends a possible shift in paradigm: the gigantic is making its appearance everywhere. In the gigantic, Heidegger explains in an opaque analysis that bears a striking similarity to the Kantian sub-lime, quantity becomes incalculable, a feature that imbues it with a special quality: greatness. This becoming incalculable manifests itself as an invisible shadow cast around all things in the modern age. This invisible shadow performs a twofold function: it allows the world to extend itself out into a space withdrawn from representation; and it also points to the concealed essence of Being, which unveils itself first of all as Nothing. We will understand the true essence of this Being, Heidegger assures us, once we stop representing.

Heidegger suggests two ways to accomplish this feat. The first is to "track out and expose the original naming power of the worn-out word and concept 'to represent'" (132), as his own philosophical discourse purports to do. The second way for the modern subject to overcome the confines of representation and join with true Being is through crea-tive questioning and the shaping out of the power of genuine reflection (136). Hölderlin knew this, Heidegger states, citing one of his lyric verses. In other words, the transcendence of representation is best accomplished through poetry.

The Hölderlin quotation in the concluding sentences of his essay provides an oblique clue to the provenance of Heidegger's critique of representation. The obfuscating quality of his rhetoric notwithstanding, Heidegger's critique of representation is prefigured and predetermined by the critical praxis of German Idealism and early German Romanticism, the two philosophical movements that best define Hölderlin's metaphysical framework, albeit negatively. The parameters of Heidegger's baffling analysis—the critique of representation and the Cartesian subject, the role of reflection in effecting this critique, the process of visualization that structures the modern age, and the compensatory power of the poetic to redress the shortcomings of philosophical discourse—are all components of the late eighteenth century's critical preoccupation and experimentation with the notion of *Darstellung*, sensible presentation, presencing, or representation. First introduced into philosophical discourse by Kant and assigned a pivotal role in poetics by Klopstock, the notion of *Darstellung* constituted a radically new type of representation that was programmatically opposed to the various conceptions of mimetic or "objectifying" representation (*Nachahmung, Repräsentation, Vorstellung*) prevalent in late eighteenth-century critical discourse. Due in large part to Kant's elaborations of the *Darstellung* problematic in his first and third *Critiques*, this new notion of representation quickly catapulted to the center of the leading philosophical and aesthetic theories in the years between 1790 and 1810. *Darstellung* is perhaps *the* defining force of German Idealism and early German Romanticism and arguably forms the basis of our own critical consciousness today. As Lacoue-Labarthe and Nancy have asserted, we are still working within the critical framework of early German Romanticism, yet "the present period continues to deny precisely this belonging, which defines us."[2]

The ellipsis of *Darstellung* from Heidegger's analysis and his tacit indebtedness to the German Romantic tradition are expressions of this denial. If Lacoue-Labarthe and Nancy are correct in inscribing all of modernity within the Romantic paradigm, then Heidegger's claim to be the philosophical harbinger of a worldview that defines itself in "a space withdrawn from representation" would appear to be untenable, a mere repetition of the eighteenth century's critical exposition of the concept of *Darstellung*. In fact,

Heidegger's positing of a space withdrawn from representation in which the subject joins with a true Being that first reveals itself as "Nothing" is a redaction of the conceptually powerful and tremendously alluring figure of the *negative Darstellung* of the Kantian sublime. This representational link has not been lost on theoreticians like Beaufret, Derrida, Lacoue-Labarthe, and Nancy, who have recognized the significance of *Darstellung* to Heideggerian and post-Heideggerian thought and reinstated it in contemporary critiques of representation. Paradoxically, then, Heidegger's modern age reaffirms its representational roots at the same time that it tries to escape them. Heidegger's pronouncement of the advent of a space withdrawn from representation is perhaps prescient, but certainly premature. At best we can talk today about the retreat of representation within that space.

The goal of the present study is to document the inception, development, and retreat of the notion of *Darstellung* within the German Romantic paradigm. Although the importance of *Darstellung* to Kantian aesthetics, German Romanticism, and modern critical discourse has long been acknowledged in such influential and wide-ranging works as Walter Benjamin's *The Concept of Criticism in German Romanticism* and *The Origin of German Tragic Drama*, Philippe Lacoue-Labarthe and Jean-Luc Nancy's *The Literary Absolute*, Winfried Menninghaus's *Infinite Doubling*, Manfred Frank's *Introduction to Early Romantic Aesthetics*, Jochen Hörisch's *The Gay Science of Poesy*, Azade Seyhan's *Representation and Its Discontents*, Jacques Derrida's *The Truth in Painting*, and more recently in a collection of essays edited by Christiaan Hart Nibbrig, *What Does ≫Darstellen≪ Mean?* my investigation is the first to offer an extensive examination and interpretation of this dynamic notion of representation in its own discursive context. I take Lacoue-Labarthe and Nancy's lead in arguing that the notion of *Darstellung* inevitably involves the question of the relationship between philosophy and literature, and that this question is first raised by the structure of critical discourse in Kant's *Critiques*. My basic thesis is that the Idealist and Romantic theories of representation that come into being around 1800 develop as a direct response to aporiae in Kant's notion of *Darstellung*, and my study traces the genesis of the term's function in four case studies dating from the 1780s to approximately 1810, taking examples from early Idealism, Jena Romanticism, and the works of Heinrich von Kleist, whose writings present a response to Kantian philosophy that is fundamentally opposed to Idealism and Jena Romanticism. In each chapter the relationship between philosophy and literature is approached from a different vantage.

Chapter 1 examines the inception of *Darstellung* as a philosophical concept in Kant's *Critiques*, contrasts this Kantian notion of representation with other eighteenth-century aesthetic theories of *Darstellung*, and further demonstrates Kant's unwilling admission of the "poetic" into his philosophy. Kant introduces the notion of *Darstellung* into the *Critique of Pure Reason* to address three basic issues: first, how to mediate between sensibility and understanding, the two branches of knowledge that constitute all human cognition; second, how to safeguard against linguistic ambiguity in the stylistic presentation of philosophy; and, finally, the fundamental question that will determine the direction of Idealism and Romanticism in the wake of Kant, how to guarantee that the sensible subject can define itself as a moral subject of reason. In the *Critique of Judgment* the paradoxical figure of the *negative Darstellung* of the sublime functions as a panacea for the various shortcomings in Kant's elaboration of the *Darstellung* problematic, but poetic language and visual metaphors indicate the tenuousness of this rhetorical solution to Kant's representational troubles and open up the possibility of a poetization of the philosophical discourse of transcendental idealism.

Chapter 2 traces the Idealist response to Kant's crisis in representation from Karl Leonhard Reinhold's attempt to recast Kant's critical philosophy as a transcendental theory of representation (*Vorstellung*) through the critique of transcendental idealism formulated by the skeptic Gottlob Ernst Schulze to the early philosophical writings of Johann Gottlieb Fichte, which were developed as a direct response to Schulze's attack on the critical philosophy. In his little-known review of Schulze's *Aenesidemus* and his *Own Meditations on [Reinhold's] Elementary Philosophy*, Fichte defines the subject as *Darstellung* and briefly explores the efficacy of the sublime in realizing this definition, but then abandons this formulation almost immediately in favor of the model of the self-positing subject set forth in the *Doctrine of Knowledge*. In his later years, however, Fichte reintroduces this representational component into his definition of the self-positing subject, then revises his model to include an ocular component, and eventually comes to believe that this definition can only be expressed in poetic form using visual metaphors.

Chapter 3 illustrates the poetization of Fichte's Kantian definition of the subject as *Darstellung* in the works of Novalis, one of the theoreticians of the Jena Romantic Circle, a literary-philosophical movement led by the Schlegel brothers and Novalis (Friedrich von Hardenberg), who considered their "transcendental poesy" to be an extension of Kant's and Fichte's transcendental idealism. In his *Fichte-Studies* Novalis transforms Fichte's discarded definition of the subject as *Darstellung* into a theory of *Darstellung* in which the subject defines itself via a visual *poiesis*. *Klingsohr's Tale* depicts the genesis of this theory in literary form. The *Hymns to the Night*, the highest expression of Novalis's theory of *Darstellung*, incorporate a theory of the Romantic lyric that is akin to the *negative Darstellung* of the Kantian sublime.

Chapter 4 interprets the oeuvre of Heinrich von Kleist, a chronological successor of Jena Romanticism whose literary career was launched by a famous and much-disputed "Kant crisis," as a literary critique of the Idealist and Jena Romantic notions of representation. Kleist's "Kant crisis" stems from a recognition of insurmountable inadequacies in transcendental theories of representation and provides a blueprint for his poetic program. *On the Marionette Theater* couples a critique of reflection with a trenchant revision of the *negative Darstellung* of the Kantian sublime. *The Foundling*, a critical rewriting of Fichtean ego philosophy, questions the viability of transcendental theories of self-consciousness, and *The Broken Jug* presents a model of visual *poiesis* that effectively undercuts Novalis's theory of *Darstellung*. Finally, the concluding comments demonstrate that Kleist's critique of representation anticipates Heidegger's position by more than a hundred years.

A preliminary note on the English translation of the word *Darstellung*: *Darstellung* is, as Lacoue-Labarthe and Nancy have argued, a highly equivocal term that evokes a variety of meanings in various contexts[3] and has no adequate equivalent in either English or French.[4] Throughout the text I have used either "presentation" or "representation" in the English translation. Any other designation for "representation" in the original German (e.g., *Vorstellung, Repräsentation*) will be indicated in the text.

1

Kant and the Genealogy of the Romantic Notion of *Darstellung*

In the wake of Kant's *Critiques* the notion of *Darstellung* comes to the fore in German critical discourse with such force that it forms the cornerstone of all the leading theories of Idealism and early Romanticism. Fichte, for example, defines his *Doctrine of Knowledge* as "the representation of the system of human knowledge" (*die Darstellung des Systems des menschlichen Wissens*).[1] Similarly, Hegel describes the project of the *Phenomenology of Spirit* as "the representation of developing knowledge" (*die Darstellung des werdenden Wissens*),[2] and in his *Aesthetics* he defines the goal of art as "the sensible representation of the Absolute" (*die sinnliche Darstellung des Absoluten*).[3] Schelling, too, states that art is the "representation of the Absolute" (*Darstellung des Absoluten*),[4] and he defines his philosophy of art as the "representation of the universe in artistic form" (*Darstellung des Universums in der Form der Kunst*).[5] This Idealist notion of representation is central to the linguistic and aesthetic theories of Romanticism. Working together with Fichte in 1801, the linguist Bernhardi defines *language* as "a species and modification of representation" (*eine Gattung und Modifikation der Darstellung*).[6] Bernhardi's and Fichte's connections to the Jena Romantics are noteworthy, because *Darstellung* also lies at the root of the Jena Romantic enterprise. According to Friedrich Schlegel, transcendental poesy "must represent itself in each of its representations" ([*die Transcendentalpoesie*] *muss in jeder ihrer Darstellungen sich selbst mit darstellen*),[7] and Novalis

explicitly assigns this Romantic notion of representation
transcendental status: "representability, or thinkability is
the condition of possibility of all philosophy" (*Darstell-
barkeit, oder Denkbarkeit ist das Kriterium der
Möglichkeit aller Philosophie*).[8] Thus, *Darstellung* constitutes an essential point of tangency for German Idealism
and Romanticism, and the critical exposition of this Kantian
notion of representation in various disciplines results in a
tremendously productive interplay of philosophy, aesthetics,
literature, and linguistic theory in German critical discourse
around 1800.

The development of Kant's notion of *Darstellung* can
be briefly sketched as follows.[9] In Kant's critical philosophy
Darstellung is a technical term that designates the mediation
of the imagination between sensibility and understanding,
the two branches of knowledge that form human cognition:
"the making sensible of a concept" is its sensible presentation or representation, and this process can be effected
either directly, via the schematism, or symbolically, by
analogy. *Darstellung* is a crucial component of one's cognitive processes, one's self-definition, and one's psychological
well-being: the displeasure and fear associated with the
sublime result from the failure of the human faculty of
presentation (*Darstellungsvermögen*). Kant also uses *Darstellung* in its more general sense to refer to the stylistic
presentation or representation of his philosophical system.
According to Kant, only mathematics is capable of pure
presentation, and he expresses concern for the limitations
and lack of elegance in the exposition of his *Critiques*.

Darstellung proves problematic to Kant's *Critiques* in
three regards. First, Kant is unable to establish a mechanism
for the "making sensible of a concept" that stays within the
confines of his transcendental analysis, and he readily
admits the tenuousness of his primary solution to this
presentational problem, the schematism: "This schematism
of our understanding with regard to phenomena and their
mere form, is a hidden art in the depths of the human soul,
whose true workings we will likely never divine from nature

and place unveiled before our eyes" (B 180–181).[10] Hence, there is a breakdown at a crucial juncture in Kant's argument for the underlying synthetic unity of intuition and understanding in cognition. The second problem that *Darstellung* poses to Kant's analysis is related to the first. Because the synthetic unity of apperception falls beyond the limits of the transcendental *Critique*, the sensible subject cannot represent itself to itself as it really is, as a moral subject of reason. The fact that reason imposes these limits on the scope of philosophical investigation points to the third problem that Kant encounters, the problem of the rhetorical presentation or representation of his philosophical system.

These aporiae in Kant's notion of *Darstellung* determine the direction of philosophical investigation in subsequent Idealism and Romanticism. In his Elementary Philosophy Reinhold, Kant's acknowledged philosophical heir, addresses both the general problem of representation (*Vorstellung*) in Kant's transcendental idealism and the problem of the formal stylistic presentation (*Darstellung*) of the Kantian philosophical system; Fichte's *Doctrine of Knowledge* attempts to remedy the fact that the Kantian subject cannot represent itself as a moral subject of reason; and the Jena Romantic program is defined by the search for the "sensible-spiritual" representation lacking in Kant.[11] One of the ways the Romantics attempt to do this is to explore the *negative Darstellung* of the Kantian sublime by experimenting with new modes of poetic representation. In this context *Darstellung* is simultaneously a question of representation in Kant's technical sense ("the making sensible of a concept") and of rhetorical presentation or style, and the Romantics considered Kant to be the inaugurator of a new philosophical-literary discipline: Friedrich Schlegel admiringly characterizes Kant as the creator of the first philosophical art "chaos,"[12] and Novalis credits Kant's critical philosophy with transforming speculation into a "poetic instrument."[13] Although Kant himself tries to divorce artistic considerations from his *Critiques*, he resorts to metaphorical language when he reaches the limits of transcendental representation;

and Schlegel and Novalis are quite right to discern a literary level in his philosophy.

From a biographical point of view, Kant's poetic sensibility is not particularly surprising. In his precritical *Observations on the Feeling of the Beautiful and the Sublime* of 1764 Kant had explored aesthetic questions, and in the same year he was even offered a professorship in "rhetoric and poetry" at the University of Berlin.[14] From a critical vantage, however, it is doubtful that Kant would have agreed with Schlegel's and Novalis's assessments of his work as philosophical art. Kant modeled his *Critiques* on a mathematical rather than a poetic paradigm, and his writing is infused with attacks on the vagaries of human language. Nonetheless, Kant himself exploits language's poetic qualities in his own philosophical presentation, and in the years between 1781 and 1790 art becomes increasingly important to his critical philosophy. Although he had explicitly excluded the possibility of a critical discourse on art from the *Critique of Pure Reason*, in the *Critique of Judgment* Kant celebrates poetry (*Dichtkunst*) as the highest art, an art capable of creating an "indirect" or symbolic representation of the moral good. In other words, art is one of Kant's solutions to the problem of how to mediate between pure and practical reason, and as the early Romantics recognized, aesthetic representation proves to be both extremely important and extremely problematic to his critical enterprise.

There are actually two competing discourses on *Darstellung* that develop in the 1770s through 1790s and inform Romantic discourse: the first growing out of the debate on aesthetic imitation (*die Nachahmungsdebatte*) and epitomized in Klopstock's poetics; the second finds its inception in Kant's critical philosophy. It is my thesis that Kant's definition of *Darstellung* is the dominant force in the genealogy of the Idealist and Romantic notions of representation, and this chapter will situate Kant's definition with respect to the Klopstockian aesthetic tradition and then trace the genesis of the term in the *Critique of Pure Reason* and the *Critique of Judgment*.

Eighteenth-Century Aesthetic Theories of *Darstellung*

An analysis of the rich and varied semantic history of the word *Darstellung* is essential to understanding its usage in eighteenth-century aesthetic theory. Not documented in Old and Middle High German texts, the verb form *darstellen* and the noun form *Darstellung* first appear in early modern German with spatial associations. Grimm lists several examples dating from 1439 onward in which the word refers to the setting down, presenting, or representing of an object or entity at a specific place. In other early occurrences the spatial dimension is less pronounced or completely absent, and *darstellen* then refers to the naming of a person to an office or function, as well as to the presenting of a witness or the bearing witness to a truth. By the sixteenth century the word takes on additional meanings, including the production of concrete objects and the giving form to and making visible of noncorporeal entities.[15] In 1691 Kaspar Stieler's dictionary, *Genealogy and Development of the German Language*, defines *darstellen* as "to produce, offer or present (*offere*), represent (*repraesentare*), or place before the eyes (*ante oculos ponere, statuere*)," and it also lists among its examples the previously mentioned meaning of bearing witness to a truth.[16] Stieler's description of *darstellen* as both to present and to represent has an important visual dimension ("to place before the eyes") that anticipates the term's usage in late eighteenth-century aesthetic theory.

In an extensive analysis of the term's semantic development from Stieler's definition to its function in eighteenth-century critical discourse, Fritz Heuer interprets the original sense of *Darstellung* as the making present in such a manner that the object or entity being presented only comes into its true being in the process of being represented. Moreover, this process of rendering present or actual requires recognition by others.[17] Heuer argues that this dynamic definition does not come to fruition in aesthetic theory until the end of the eighteenth century. This is due in part to the conflation and confusion of the word *Darstellung* with its etymological correlate, the term *Vorstellung*. Although *Vorstellung* generally corresponds to the Latin *repraesentatio* and *Darstellung* to *praesentatio* in eighteenth-century aesthetic theory, these translations are by no means absolute, as Stieler's dictionary definitions of *darstellen* as *repraesentare* and *vorstellen* as *praesentare* attest. In fact, the semantic fields of the two terms frequently overlap, and they occasionally appear as synonyms. *Vorstellen*, popularized by the wide acceptance of the philosophies and aesthetic theories of Leibniz, Wolff, Baumgarten, and Meier, is the prevailing term throughout much of the eighteenth century. Mendelssohn, for example, states that "the essence of the fine arts and sciences consists in an artistic sensibly complete representation (*Vorstellung*) or in an artistically represented (*vorgestellt*) sensible totality."[18] In this Baumgartian usage *Vorstellung* refers to both the mind's activity in producing the representation and to the actual artistic representation. Moreover, *vorstellen* can also designate the physical process of making present, and in all three senses the term borders on the meaning of *Darstellung* as sensible presentation or representation. In the 1770s through 1790s rigorous distinctions between *Darstellung* and *Vorstellung* develop in Klopstockian aesthetic theory and in Kant's critical philosophy, thereby paving the way for the Idealist and Romantic inception of *Darstellung* as a term in its own right.[19]

Although Kant himself had tried halfheartedly to divorce his critical definition of *Darstellung* from the artistic realm, the influence of his notion of *Darstellung* on German aesthetic theory around 1800 is incontestible.[20] Sulzer's *General Theory of the Fine Arts* (1792) contains no systematic discussion of the term, but Schiller's *Kallias, or On the Beautiful* of 1793[21] and Hölderlin's "On the Workings of the Poetic Spirit"[22] emphasize the importance of *Darstellung* to Kantian aesthetics, and in 1798 the entire Jena Romantic program is defined in terms of *Darstellung*. By 1835 the Kantian notion has become so entrenched in general aesthetic theory that, in his *Aesthetic Lexicon* of 1835, Jeitteles devotes an entire article to *Darstellung*. For Jeitteles, *Darstellung* is "the particular artistic activity of bringing an object to the intuition by making it perceivable to the senses,"[23] a description that clearly reflects the Kantian definition, "the making sensible of a concept." Thus, the critical reception of the Kantian notion of *Darstellung* in post-Kantian aesthetic theory is quite clear. The question of the extent to which there is a connection between pre-Kantian aesthetic theories and Kant's use of the term is much more complex and inconclusive.

There was, of course, a tradition of aesthetic analyses of *Darstellung* prior to Kant's introduction of the word into his critical philosophy, and the relationship between philosophy and literature is frequently at issue in these theories. In what is perhaps the earliest aesthetic treatise on *Darstellung*, August Buchner's *Poet*, published posthumously in 1665, *poetry* is defined as a subform of philosophy. Because of its subsidiary status, poetry, unlike philosophy, makes no claims to present "complete knowledge." Like the painter, the poet presents only the information necessary for an external cognition of his subject matter. The goal of this deliberately incomplete representation is pedagogical: "Thus it is the poet's duty to represent an action as it is, as it should be, or as it could be, so that he simultaneously amuses and teaches, which is precisely the goal to which he should always aspire."[24] The fact that the poet presents an action rather than an object and that the representation produced is deliberately incomplete distinguishes this notion of representation from the notion of mimetic representation (*Nachahmung*) soon to become popular in the eighteenth-century debate on aesthetic imitation. Whereas *Nachahmung* aims to imitate nature as closely as possible, for Buchner *Darstellung* is clearly inventive imitation.

A similar notion of representation forms the basis of Klopstocks's aesthetics. Klopstock's definition of *Darstellung* is not only didactic, but socially edifying as well: it forms the foundation of his *German Academic Republic* (*Deutsche Gelehrtenrepublik*, 1774), the first major theory of *Darstellung* in the eighteenth century. Just as Buchner's definition involves a deliberately incomplete representation, Klopstock, too, insists on the illusory nature of the artistic process: "The goal of *Darstellung* is deception (*Täuschung*)," he writes in his dialogic essay "On Representation" (*Von der Darstellung*, 1779).[25] Like Buchner, Klopstock compares poetry to painting, and he argues that poetic representation is superior to visual representation because poetry is more deceptive. In perceiving a painting the eye rests on its object, and the observer is aware that he or she is seeing an illusion. Poetry, on the other hand, involves the perception of an action rather than an object, and the mind has less time to figure out that it is being deceived. By presenting the unexpected, producing apparent disorder, abruptly breaking off thoughts, and arousing expectations, poetry sets the soul in motion and makes it receptive. Objects that are sublime or that incorporate a lot of action or passion are most susceptible to a successful representation. Klopstock, intent on developing a dynamic poetic theory, concludes his essay with nine practical stylistic rules.

Given his notion of deception (*Täuschung*) and his reasons for valuing dynamic poetry over static painting, it is quite clear that Klopstock's argument is derived from Lessing's *Laocoon* (*Laokoon*, 1766). In the preface to this study Lessing sets out to explain what is pleasing about the illusion that poetry and the plastic arts produce, and in the course of his analysis he ranks poetry higher than the plastic arts and in fact implies that drama, as "living painting," is at the pinnacle of this hierarchy,[26] for precisely the reasons Klopstock cites. Although Lessing himself uses the term *Darstellung* roughly synonymously with the words *execution* (*Ausführung*) and *expression* (*Ausdruck*),[27] he allots *Darstellung* no special significance in his treatise.[28] With the introduction of the term into the *Laocoon* argument, Klopstock thus makes an extremely important contribution toward developing a comprehensive theory of *Darstellung*: he brings *Darstellung* into mainstream eighteenth-century aesthetics, into the debate on aesthetic imitation (*die Nachahmungsdebatte*).

As Menninghaus has argued, Klopstock does not merely appropriate Lessing's argument; he radically revises it. Whereas Lessing's illusion is derived from the logic of (re)presentation, a making present of something absent,

Klopstock's *Darstellung* is completely divorced from this representational logic, indeed, from the object itself: "For Klopstock *Darstellung* does not deceive because it stands for something else, but precisely because it does *not* stand for something else."[29] Hence, its significance lies in the act of invention, in the process of creating a poetic representation sui generis. In a prescient statement anticipating Jena Romanticism, Klopstock argues that this poetic representation contains its own theory: in comparison to the treatise (*Abhandlung*), which is "only theory," Klopstock asserts, "**Darstellung** has theory. It uses language in varying degrees of deception to make present what is absent. In both the poetic production and the impression it creates on the audience *Darstellung* involves the entire soul, the treatise only the judgment."[30] The poet overcomes the one-sided intellectuality ("the judgment") of the treatise by setting the entire soul in motion and creates what the Romantics will later call a sensible-intellectual representation. This notion of *Darstellung* as setting the audience's soul into motion, which has an important reception-theory component, will become a cornerstone of late eighteenth-century aesthetic theories of *Darstellung*.

Although Klopstock's argument is derived in part from Lessing's *Laocoon*, an important dimension of Lessing's discussion of aesthetic representation is absent in Klopstock's. *Laocoon*, subtitled "On the Borders of Poetry and Painting [*Malerei*, a term Lessing uses to refer to the plastic arts in general]," is an analysis of aesthetic representation and its limits, and Lessing's enterprise is distinguished from Klopstock's by the fact that it is self-reflexive. Lessing is just as concerned with establishing the limits of his own investigation as he is with determining the borders of poetry and the plastic arts, and he carefully prefaces his analysis with a discussion of his role as critic. Given this concern for the conditions of possibility and the limits of an aesthetic investigation, it is clear that *Laocoon* is a precursor of the Kantian *Critique*.

As Klopstock's tacit reference to the *Laocoon* debate indicates, Lessing's importance to the development of an aesthetic theory of *Darstellung* should not be underestimated.[31] It is no accident that a character from his famous drama *Emilia Galotti*, the painter Conti, who argues that Raphael would have been just as great a painter if he had been born without hands, plays a cameo role in Stolberg's "On Poetry and Representing" (*Vom Dichten und Darstellen*, 1780). In this panegyric to poetry Stolberg defines *Darstellung* as a bastardized form of poetry. Poetry refers to the almost divine spiritual condition of the artist, whereas the inferior physical process of representing a poem is its *Darstellung*. Although the poet loses his divine insight in this mundane act, compassion motivates him to "stoop to representation in order to elevate other people."[32] Stolberg does concede, however, that there may be some benefits to this spiritual debasement: "Representation provides the poet with a more initimate knowledge of the apparitions of his spirit" (379). Read against the grain, then, Stolberg's essay actually contains a dynamic definition of the subject via *Darstellung*: in the process of representing the poet gains self-knowledge, and in this sense, Stolberg, like Buchner and Klopstock, propounds its educational value.

Both Stolberg's essay and Klopstock's redaction of Lessing are indications of the proximity of the eighteenth century's discourse on *Darstellung* to its debate on aesthetic imitation. These two traditions become fused in the works of Gottfried August Bürger and Herder, who both substitute the word *Darstellung* for *Nachahmung* (imitation) in the translation of the Aristotelian notion of mimesis. In "On the Popularity of Poesy," an essay roughly contemporaneous with Klopstock's and Stolberg's,[33] Bürger gives the following curt definition: "What is *Darstellung*? The word itself says it more clearly than any explanation could." Bürger then deigns to explicate this laconic statement for the linguistically inept: "*Darstellung* is the mirror and the mirror image of the original object,"[34] a definition that capitalizes on the visual dimensions of the word. Bürger's justification of his substitution of *Darstellung* for "the miserable word *imitation* (*Nachahmung*)" clarifies the visual basis of his definition: whereas imitation presents a paltry afterimage thrown back from a dull surface, *Darstellung* produces a true image as it is embodied and animated in a shining mirror. Thus, Bürger's notion of *Darstellung* is analogous to Klopstock's "setting the soul into motion," and Bürger, like Klopstock, believes that certain immutable stylistic laws will ensure a successful poetic representation.

Bürger's argument for the animating power of *Darstellung* is very close to the attack against mimesis that Lenz launches in his "Comments on the Theater" (1774). According to Lenz, if a poet bases his work on "raw imitation" he will be a "sophomoric fool, quack, or bedwarmer" but not what he is supposed to be; namely, a "representer (*Darsteller*), poet, or creator."[35] Similarly, years later Goethe will define the poet's activity in terms of representation, rather than imitation. He states that the poet is dependent upon *Darstellung*, and that the epitome of poetic activity is reached when the representation rivals reality: "that is, when the mind animates poetic depictions so that they can be taken to be present for everyone."[36] Herder, too, advances a definition of *mimesis* as "living representation,"[37] and he adopts an Aristotelian argument for the philosophical value of art.

According to Herder, the dramatic form is *the* exemplary aesthetic representation of inner truth. Like Lessing and Klopstock, Herder argues that this artistic representation involves illusion, but he explains that this illusion is really the product of an interchange of ideas: *täuschen* ("to deceive") comes from *Tausch* ("exchange"), and the poet necessarily deceives the observer when the observer replaces his or her own thoughts with those of the poet. Herder also embraces Plato's definition of the beautiful as a representation of the good and the true, and he attacks Kant for his denial of the beautiful as the *Darstellung*, or sensible expression, of a totality.

I have been summarizing a small portion of the argument of *Kalligone*, Herder's diatribe against Kant's *Critique of Judgment*. Herder's criticism is interesting first of all because he challenges Kant on the grounds of the notion of *Darstellung*, while waffling in his own use of the term, at one time alloting it a key position in his analysis of the plastic arts and at another dismissing it as a "tropic word" that has no place in a definition of poetics.[38] But there is a much more important dimension to Herder's criticism of Kant than merely the use of the word *Darstellung*: what is at stake in Herder's challenge is nothing less than the relationship between literature and philosophy. Curiously, Herder, like the Romantics, traces the confluence of these two disciplines to Kant's *Critique of Pure Reason*, rather than to his critique of aesthetics, the *Critique of Judgment*, as one might have expected: "The *Critique of Pure Reason* transformed philosophy into something it had never been and never should have become, phantasy, i.e., bad poesy, poetic abstraction."[39] By poeticizing philosophy, Herder argues, Kant kills both philosophy and criticism. Motivated in part by personal animosity,[40] Herder's bitter condemnation, written in 1800 at the height of the Jena Romantic movement, stands in stark opposition to Schlegel's and Novalis's celebration of Kant as the inaugurator of a new philosophical-literary representation.

Most of the aesthetic theories surveyed here fall within the province of inventive imitation (Buchner, Lessing, Klopstock, Bürger, Lenz, Goethe, Herder) and share two basic components: an insistence on the value of aesthetic illusion and pragmatic stylistic injunctions against a mechanical representation that would shatter this illusion. Klopstock, who adapts Lessing's *Laocoon* and coins the first explicit theory of *Darstellung* in the eighteenth century, is undoubtedly the don of this tradition of inventive representation, whereas his loyal follower Stolberg, perhaps unwittingly, problematizes the tradition from within and creates a dynamic theory of *Darstellung*.

Unlike those of his contemporaries, Stolberg's aesthetic theory is not based on inventive imitation, but on divine inspiration. "On Poetry and Representing" addresses the problem of externalizing this inner inspiration. It is a theory of communication in which the poet gains self-knowledge via the process of representing. In this respect Stolberg clearly anticipates Romanticism. Stolberg develops this new theory of *Darstellung* at the same time that Kant imports the term into his critical philosophy, and although Kant's notion of *Darstellung* is quite different from Stolberg's, it also augurs Romanticism.

The chronology of Kant's gradual adoption and adaptation of the term is indicative of its proto-Romantic status within his oeuvre. In his precritical *Observations on the Feeling of the Beautiful and the Sublime* of 1764 there is no mention whatsoever of *Darstellung*. In 1781, one year after the publication of Stolberg's essay, the term occupies an important, albeit marginal, position in the first *Critique*, the *Critique of Pure Reason*. Although not an explicit issue in the *Critique of Practical Reason* (1788), *Darstellung* is the keystone of Kant's demonstration of the partial concretization of the idea of freedom in this second *Critique*. By 1790 *Darstellung* has become so central to the third *Critique*, the *Critique of Judgment*, that a modern-day commentator like Hans Graubner can convincingly argue that "giving a summary of Kant's conception of aesthetics means coming to terms with the Kantian notion of *Darstellung*."[41] For Kant, of course, "aesthetics" deals with sensibility and not with a theory of art per se, and it is noteworthy that he is implicated three times in the history of eighteenth-century aesthetic theories of *Darstellung*. Lessing's *Laocoon* is a kind of proto-Kantian critique, while Herder attacks Kant for poeticizing philosophy. Although Kant explicitly distances himself from this tradition of aesthetic imitation and illusion, stating that *Darstellungen* are clearly distinguished from "mere characterizations," which serve as only a means for reproducing objects (*CJ* B 255, p. 197), his notion of *Darstellung* shares with these theories both an insistence on the value of illusion, the subreption of the Kantian sublime, and a concern for stylistic representation. Finally, Kant, at the same time as Stolberg, defines the subject in terms of *Darstellung* and hence sets the stage for the entire Jena Romantic movement.

The Role of Representation in Kant's Epistemology

Genealogically speaking, however, Kant's notion of representation is completely divorced from Klopstockian aesthetic theory. Kant derives his definition of *Darstellung* from the classical discipline of rhetoric: he uses the term synonymously with the Latin *exhibitio* and the Greek *hypotyposis*, and, as Gasché has shown, the history of this rhetorical figure is essential to Kant's critical definition.[42] *Hypotyposis*, a composite word derived from *hypo*, under, below, or beneath, and *typosis*, a figure made by molding or sketching, originally meant a sketch, an outline, a pattern, or a book and is documented in this sense in Sextus Empiricus. Aristotle gives the word a specifically philosophical meaning: that which forms, shapes, or molds essence itself. Kant, however, does not adopt this Aristotelian usage but instead invokes the rhetorical tradition of the term with his equation of *hypotyposis* with *subjectio sub aspectum*; that is, visual presentation, throwing under the eyes, or exhibiting under its appearance or aspect. This visual dimension of hypotyposis, also evident in such synonyms as *enargeia, evidentia, illustratio*, and *demonstratio*, has a strong resonance in classical rhetoric. Cicero, for example, emphasizes sight in his discussion of hypotyposis, noting the effectiveness of "clear explanation and the almost visual presentation of events as if practically going on." Similarly, Quintilian, referring to Cicero's "*sub oculos subiectio*," defines *hypotyposis* as "an appeal to the eye rather than the ear."[43] "In short," Gasché summarizes, "as a rhetorical notion, hypotyposis means an illustration in which the vividly represented is endowed with such detail that it seems to be present, and to present *itself*, in person and completely by itself," and he stresses its ability to present subject matter as if it were to be beheld by the eye.[44] This visual dimension of hypotyposis is transmitted to the German philosophical tradition[45] and is also evident in Stieler's dictionary definition of the German word *darstellen* as *ante oculos ponere*, to place before the eyes. Indeed, although apparently unrelated to the classical rhetorical tradition, the original meaning of *darstellen* documented in Stieler's dictionary, to render present or actual, corresponds to the definition of hypotyposis.

Although Kant's definition of *Darstellung* is related to both the visual rhetorical sense of hypotyposis and to its original meaning of "model," "sketch," "outline," or "pattern," its rhetorical underpinnings first become evident in the *Critique of Judgment*, when Kant explicitly equates *Darstellung* with synonyms from classical rhetoric. In the *Critique of Pure Reason* the critical definition of *Darstellung* corresponds more precisely to the everyday German usage exemplified in Stieler's dictionary, to render sensibly present or actual. In addition to assigning *Darstellung* a critical definition, however, Kant also uses the term in the first *Critique* to refer to the rhetorical presentation or style of his argument, although he does so without recourse to the classical rhetorical tradition. When Kant does import terminology from classical rhetoric into the third *Critique*, he simultaneously levels an attack on the art of rhetoric, a move that is indicative of both the increasing significance and the problematic status of *Darstellung* in his critical enterprise.

To appreciate this development more fully, we must first briefly consider the epistemological framework of the *Critique of Pure Reason*. Ultimately concerned with the question of whether metaphysics as a rigorous philosophical discipline is possible, Kant sets out to examine what we as human beings can actually know. He begins by placing the subject and subjective knowledge at the center of his investigation. Objects as they really are lie outside the purview of human knowledge and are hence excluded from the realm of critical inquiry. Restated in more familiar terms, Kant argues that we cannot know things-in-themselves, but have only subjective knowledge of them. This subjective knowledge comes from two sources, sensibility and understanding, the two branches of human cognition that perhaps share a common, but to us unknown, root (B 29). Sensibility provides the mind with intuitions it receives from the senses, whereas understanding contains the concepts necessary to process this sensory information. Both forms of knowledge are necessary for all cognition.

Now, cognition (*Erkenntnis*) is quite distinct from thought in general. Although it is possible to think (*denken*) without sensory information, our concepts remain empty and no cognition has occurred: we have only "played with representations (*Vorstellungen*)" (B 195). For cognition to occur, all thought must relate, directly or indirectly, to sensibility (B 33): our concepts must be made sensibly concrete. "If cognition is to have objective reality, that is, a connection to an object," argues Kant, "then the object must be capable of being given in some manner" (B 194). "Being given," Kant indicates parenthetically, is what he means by *Darstellung*: "That an object be given (if this expression be taken, not as referring to some merely mediate process, but as signifying immediate presentation [*Darstellung*] in intuition), means simply that the representation (*Vorstellung*) through which the object is thought relates to actual or possible experience" (B 195). Here, then, is Kant's indirect definition of *Darstellung*. The representation (*Vorstellung*) through which an object is thought is its concept. The concept, however, must be presented immediately in intuition (*unmittelbar in der Anschauung* **darstellen**). Hence, the making sensible of a concept is its *Darstellung*, and all concepts, regardless of their kind, must undergo this process of sensibilization for cognition to occur (B 195).

Kant is addressing a problem that can be roughly illustrated in terms of the following example. When we see a table, how do we know that it is a table that we see? That is, how do we mediate between the sensible knowledge we receive from our bodies and the conceptual representation (*Vorstellung*) "table" present in our minds? According to Kant, what happens when we see a table is that the imagination takes the sensible information it receives from the body (e.g., brown, square, four legs, etc.) and uses the concept "table" that is given to the mind to create a sensible presentation or *Darstellung* of the table. Although the table itself as object is unknowable to the thinking subject and the concept "table" by itself is an empty representation

(*Vorstellung*), through *Darstellung* the concept "table" is rendered sensibly present or actual to the mind.

Hence, *Darstellung*, sensible presentation or representation, is clearly differentiated from *Vorstellung*, or representation, a general term that Kant never actually defines, but nonetheless uses "to designate the operation by which the different faculties that constitute the mind bring their respective objects before themselves."[46] Whereas *Vorstellung* represents a priori perceptions (intuitions, concepts, and ideas) already present *in* the mind, *Darstellung* renders a concept sensibly present or actual *to* the mind: it provides the mind with the objective reality necessary for cognition. Two components are necessary for a successful *Darstellung*. First, the imagination mediates between concept and intuition to create a sensible representation; the faculty of judgment then checks to see if the intuition really corresponds to the concept. This twofold process is crucial for all cognition.

Because *Darstellung* is the making sensible of a concept and all concepts must undergo this process, the nature of each *Darstellung* is determined by the kind of concept being sensibly presented to the mind. Three types of concepts are delimited in the *Critique of Pure Reason*, based on their various representational properties: categories, empirical concepts, and pure concepts of reason.[47] The categories, pure concepts of the understanding, form the a priori condition of possibility of all objective cognition, and the all-important and notoriously problematic process by which these categories are applied to appearances is called the schematism. Empirical concepts, concepts like "table," guarantee objective validity in cognition. Pure concepts of reason, or ideas, are concepts to which no empirical intuition, and hence no direct *Darstellung*, corresponds.

This nonrepresentability of ideas is of utmost concern to Kant. Although ideas lie outside the realm of human cognition and are accordingly not constitutive, they play an indispensable regulative role in the theoretical domain: the three "leading ideas" of God, freedom, and immortality are necessary for our determination of ourselves as moral subjects of reason. Ideas are absolutely essential to Kant's epistemology and ethics, and their nonrepresentability will form the crux of his discussion of *Darstellung* in the *Critique of Judgment.*

Kant's solution to the problematic status of the representation of ideas forms a systematic unity among the three *Critiques* that can be briefly outlined as follows.[48] Because the idea is a necessary concept of reason to which no corresponding object can be given in the senses, it cannot be presented to pure reason. However, in the *Critique of Practical Reason*, Kant sets out to demonstrate that pure reason is really practical reason. In the Preface to this second *Critique*, he argues that the idea of freedom forms the cornerstone of the whole system of pure, and even speculative, reason, and that the other transcendental ideas (God and immortality) are in fact subsumed under this one idea (A 4). Moreover, in practical reason the idea can, and indeed must, achieve partial presentation or concretization, an issue Kant addresses in a section analogous to the schematism discussion of the first *Critique*, "On the Typic of Pure Practical Judgment." The fact that this concretization is only partial is limiting to cognition, and Kant overcomes this limitation via the aesthetic idea in the *Critique of Judgment*. The aesthetic idea achieves full concretization, albeit indirect or negative, in the judgments of the beautiful and the sublime and therefore forms a bridge between pure and practical reason, a bridge between nature and freedom.

With this discussion of aesthetic ideas I have jumped far ahead of myself in my explication of Kant's notion of *Darstellung* in the *Critique of Pure Reason*. Indeed, this is not the only misleading element of my analysis thus far. Up to this point I have perhaps created the mistaken impression that *Darstellung* plays a major role in the first *Critique*. The perplexing fact of the matter is this: despite its absolute centrality in Kant's epistemology, there is no section specifically devoted to *Darstellung* in the *Critique of Pure Reason*, no overt definition, little explicit discussion, and indeed, minimal mention of the term whatsoever.[49]

Moreover, Kant's notion of *Darstellung* is characterized by an almost ironic inconsistency. As we have seen, Kant uses the term in two basic senses: in its everyday meaning it refers to the rhetorical presentation of his philosophical system; its critical definition is "the making sensible of a concept." According to Kant, these two types of *Darstellung* are related to each other, but in philosophy they cannot be identical. Nonetheless, as the Romantics were well aware, Kant tends to meld together these two uses into one, thereby undermining his own transcendental rigor and conflating criticism and art. This tendency becomes increasingly apparent as he integrates the notion into his philosophy. In the course of the *Critiques*, *Darstellung* develops from a rhetorical, to a critical, and ultimately to an aesthetic figure.

The *Critique of Pure Reason*: The Limits of *Darstellung*

The groundwork for this evolution is laid out in the *Critique of Pure Reason*. In the Introduction to the second edition of this first *Critique* (1787), Kant uses the term *Darstellung* to refer to the style or presentation of a philosophical system. That stylistic presentation should be so important to his critical enterprise should come as no surprise. The *Critique of Pure Reason* is, after all, "a treatise on method, not a system of science itself" (B XXII), and Kant's great Copernican "revolution in the mode of thinking" is a methodological one. Kant, however, struggles with the stylistic aspects of this methodological revolution. In response to criticism about the first edition of his *Critique*, he states that he has found little to change in his philosophical strategy, yet he admits that there is still much to be done in the stylistic presentation or *Darstellung* of his method (B XXXVIII). This concession should not be taken lightly, because methodology is such an essential component of Kant's enterprise that he concludes his *Critique* with a "Transcendental Doctrine of Method."

Kant introduces his definition of a priori *Darstellung* within this "Doctrine of Method." The placement of the definition within this section, an appendix to the main body of his argument, indicates the marginal importance of *Darstellung* to the first *Critique*. Indeed, just as the previous

definition of a posteriori presentation was introduced parenthetically in a discussion of *Vorstellung* (representation),
here the definition of a priori presentation is couched in an
analysis of mathematical construction and is completely
motivated by Kant's discussion of *Darstellung* as style.
Concerned with the question whether the presentation of
a philosophical system can be anything but dogmatic, Kant
contrasts philosophy with the only true a priori science of
reason, mathematics. Within the context of this comparison
Kant then defines construction as a priori *Darstellung*:
"Philosophical knowledge is the knowledge gained by reason
from concepts; mathematical knowledge is the knowledge
gained by reason from the construction of concepts. *To construct a concept means to present a priori the intuition
which corresponds to the concept (einen Begriff konstruieren, heisst: die ihm korrespondierende Anschauung a
priori darstellen)*" (B 741, emphasis mine). Kant illustrates
this definition with the example of the construction of a
triangle: "Thus I construct a triangle by presenting the
object which corresponds to the concept, either by imagination alone, using pure intuition, or on a piece of paper, empirically, in both cases completely a priori, without having
borrowed the pattern from any experience" (B 741). Because
mathematics is built on this a priori presentation of concepts,
it is capable of logical demonstration. This logical demonstration is in fact self-presentation: in mathematics "concepts
must be presented (*dargestellt*) immediately in concreto in
pure intuition" (B 739).

Therefore, mathematics is the locus of pure presentation or representation: the stylistic presentation or demonstration of a triangle, for example, is identical to its critical
definition. Philosophical proofs, on the other hand, enjoy
neither the same logical rigor nor the pure presentation of
mathematics. They are discursive proofs, "since they are
carried out using nothing but mere words" (B 763). Because
philosophy is cast in language, then, its stylistic presentation cannot be identical to its critical definition, and philosophy, unlike mathematics, cannot present itself purely.
Kant, it seems, is not particularly pleased with this conclu-

sion. On the one hand, he would like to be able to utilize the precision and elegance of mathematics for his own *Critique*, yet at the same time he realizes that this is an inappropriate desideratum: "From all this it follows that it is not in keeping with the nature of philosophy, especially in the field of pure reason, to take pride in a dogmatic procedure, and to deck itself out with the titles and insignia of mathematics, to whose ranks it does not belong, though it has every reason to hope for a sisterly union with it" (B 763). The result of this realization of philosophy's forced self-limitation is what Nancy has called Kant's *crisis* of representation.[50] Philosophy must keep stylistic and critical *Darstellung* divorced from one another. It is condemned to "indirect" representation: "Through concepts of understanding pure reason does, indeed, establish secure principles, not at all, however, directly from concepts, *but always only indirectly*, through the relation of these concepts to something altogether contingent, namely, possible experience" (B 764–765, emphasis mine). As we will see, the indirect philosophical presentation reflected in Kant's indirect definitions of *Darstellung* in terms of *Vorstellung* and mathematical construction bears a striking similarity to what Kant will later call the *indirect presentation* (*indirekte Darstellung*) of the symbol in the *Critique of Judgment*.

Even though philosophy cannot enjoy the direct presentation that mathematics does, mathematical construction does provide the criteria for its indirect presentation. In the Introduction to the first edition of the *Critique of Pure Reason*, Kant identifies two requirements for the stylistic presentation of his *Critique*, "certainty and clarity" (A XVI). Under the latter rubric he draws the following distinction between "logical" and "aesthetic" clarity: "As regards *clarity*, the reader has a right to demand, in the first place, *discursive* or logical clarity, through *concepts*, and secondly, *intuitive* or aesthetic clarity, through *intuitions*, that is, through examples or other modes of illustration in concreto" (A XVII-XVIII). "Logical clarity" (explication by means of *concepts*) and "aesthetic clarity" (explication by means of *intuitions*) are in fact the two components of the definition of a priori presentation applied to stylistic presentation ("The construction of a concept is the a priori presentation of the *intuition* which corresponds to the *concept*"). Hence, Kant draws a clear connection between stylistic *Darstellung* and his critical definition of *Darstellung*, yet for him a one-to-one correspondence between the two is impossible: "I have provided sufficiently for the first requirement [logical clarity]. This was essential to my purpose; and it thus became the accidental cause of my inability to do justice to the second requirement, which, while not as rigorous, is nonetheless quite reasonable" (A xviii). Logical stylistic presentation precludes aesthetic stylistic presentation, yet Kant admits that it is "quite reasonable" to require this aesthetic component. In the Preface to the second edition, he pointedly leaves this task "to other worthy men," stating that he believes himself incapable of combining thoroughness of insight with lucid presentation (B xliii). Thus, Kant clearly realizes that his *Critique* is marred by a deficient *Darstellung*.

According to Kant, language prevents philosophy from enjoying the same pure presentation that mathematics does. Unlike mathematics, philosophy cannot "define" its concepts, because in the strict sense of the word *to define* means "to present originally the complete concept of a thing within its own limits" (B 755). Because of linguistic ambiguity, empirical concepts can be only "explicated," but not defined: "For since we find in it [the empirical concept] only a few features of a certain kind of sensible object, it is never certain that we are not using the word, in denoting one and the same object, at one time to think of more, and at others to think of fewer features" (B 755–756). Kant repeats a similar critique of language in his discussion of why philosophy must rely on "discursive demonstrations," rather than on logical proofs: "since they are carried out using nothing but mere words" (*nur durch lauter Worte*, B 763). The phrase *nothing but mere words* indicates Kant's discontent with the fact that philosophical presentation is dependent on language. In a way, though, Kant's ostensible dissatisfaction with linguistic ambiguity is merely an expression of the representational tension that runs throughout his work: at the same time that he disparages language, he relies on its metaphorical qualities for the presentation of his own *Critiques*.

The opening paragraph of the "Transcendental Doctrine of Method" clearly illustrates how Kant capitalizes on the "mere words" of language in his critical philosophy. He begins: "If I *look at* the sum of the cognition of pure and speculative reason as an *edifice*, for which we have at least the idea in ourselves, then I can say that in the Transcendental Doctrine of Elements we have made an estimate of the materials and determined for what *building* and for what height and stability they suffice" (B 735, emphasis mine). Kant, drawing on the rhetorical tradition of a visual *Darstellung*, compares his enterprise to a building to be looked at. In the next sentence he proceeds to expand these semantic registers of construction and vision to include language by invoking the image of the Tower of Babel: "To be sure, we have found that, although we had a tower in mind which should reach to Heaven, the supply of materials sufficed merely for a habitation which was just spacious enough for our business on the level of experience, and just high enough to *overlook* it. But that bold undertaking necessarily failed for want of materials—not to mention the *linguistic confusion*, which gave rise to inevitable disputes among the workers over the plan, and at last scattered them all over the world, each to erect a separate building for himself, according to his own special design" (B 735, emphasis mine).

With the concessional "to be sure" (*freilich*) that begins this statement, the architect Kant introduces a negative semantic charge into his building imagery, a negative charge that is reinforced by the image of the Tower of Babel, traditionally a symbol of the origin of linguistic confusion in the world. Kant, however, should not just be concerned with interphilosophical linguistic confusion, but with linguistic confusion within his own work as well. If we submit his argument in transcendental fashion to his own *Critique*, we find that he himself is guilty of introducing a remarkable representational confusion into his writing. Kant's building metaphors participate in the same semantic register of "construction" that he uses a few pages later in his critical definition of *Darstellung* as a priori construction. In using the same semantic fields—construction and language—to describe stylistic presentation and define *Darstellung* in its critical sense, Kant brings the two types of *Darstellung* into close proximity with each other. As he perhaps realized, this linguistic conflation can be problematic, and he expresses his uneasiness about language with the figure of the Tower of Babel. In addition to being a symbol of the danger of language undermining the foundations of philosophy, the Babel image is also a warning against philosophical hubris: "At present, however, we are concerned not so much with the materials, but with the plan; and inasmuch as we have been warned not to venture upon a random *blind* project which could perhaps be beyond all our capacities, yet, at the same time, we cannot very well abstain from building a secure abode, we must design our building in conformity with the material which is given to us, and which is, at the same time, appropriate for all our needs" (B 735, emphasis mine). Kant repeats this warning in the visual metaphors that run throughout the paragraph. He begins his analysis with a semantically uncharged "to look at" (*ansehen*) and then expands this visual imagery with the word *übersehen*, which contains an intrinsic ambiguity. At first glance, *übersehen* would seem to mean "to take in at a glance, perceive, survey." However, *übersehen* can also mean "to overlook, omit, not see or take notice of," and Kant is so worried about the dangers of this philosophical oversight that he concludes his series of visual images with an admonition against "venturing upon a random *blind* project." This visual imagery will prove instrumental in Kant's discussion of *Darstellung* in the third *Critique*.

There is a melancholy moment in the final sentences of the opening paragraph of the "Doctrine of Method." Kant's yearning for a philosophical home or habitat (*Wohnhaus* or *Wohnsitz*) is retrospectively reminiscent of Novalis's famous Romantic dictum, "We are always going home." This connection to Novalis is, perhaps, more than coincidental. Lurking in Kant's metaphors of language and building is a conception of philosophy as *poiesis*. (The Greek word *poiesis*, from which the German *Poesie* and English *poesy* are derived, comes from *poiein*, "to make, create.")

Indeed, Kant specifically states that a complete philosophical system is an art or *Kunst*, a word that has a wide range of meanings in eighteenth-century discourse. The "Doctrine of Method," that is, the determination of the formal conditions of a complete system of pure reason, is divided into four parts: a discipline, a canon, an architectonics, and a history of pure reason. Kant explicates the third division, the architectonics of pure reason, with the following words: "Under an *Architectonic* I understand the *art* of systems" (B 860, emphasis mine). As if to underline this conception of philosophy as *techne*, Kant qualifies the description of his philosophical system with an artistic metaphor: "Under the reign of reason our cognitions must by no means be permitted to form a *rhapsody*, but must form a system" (B 860; cf. B 195). With this contrast of the *Critique* to the rhapsody—for him perhaps the paragon of literary elegance[51]—Kant introduces, *ex negativo*, the question of literary genre into his critical philosophy.

This is not the first time that art has crept into the first *Critique*. Earlier Kant had described the schematism as "a hidden *art* in the depths of the human soul, whose true workings we will likely never divine from nature" (B 180–181, emphasis mine). With this statement Kant admits that he cannot present the conditions of possibility of the schematism. Hence, he has clearly reached the limits of his transcendental critique, and at this transcendental limit art enters into his critical philosophy. Kant's stylistic presentation becomes extremely metaphorical, and within this metaphorical language he actually describes the schematism as a "hidden art." The schematism, Kant explains in the third *Critique* (B 255), is a presentation in the critical sense of "the making sensible of a concept." Thus, underlying Kant's two types of *Darstellung*—the critical definition and stylistic presentation—is a certain insistence on the value of art.

This is why both Herder and the Jena Romantics trace the poeticizing of philosophy to the first *Critique*, rather than to the third. As a "methodological revolution," the *Critique of Pure Reason* presents itself as an attempt to establish a new philosophical genre, a genre that defines itself negatively, as that which it cannot be (mathematics) and that which it should not be (rhapsody). Language prevents Kant from presenting his *Critique* as mathematics, and it also provokes him to present his philosophy as *poiesis*. Kant fights this linguistic provocation, and his struggle is played out in the development of the notion of *Darstellung* within the *Critique*. Kant uses the word as both a rhetorical term and a critical definition, and despite his intention of keeping these two types of representation distinct, they become fused in an aesthetic notion at the limits of his *Critique*.

At these limits, the notion of the "limit" itself becomes essential to Kant's notion of *Darstellung*. According to Kant, *to define* actually means "to present originally the complete concept of a thing *within its own limits*" (B 755, emphasis mine), and only mathematics is capable of this "original presentation." Nonetheless, in another curious blending of the critical and rhetorical levels of presentation, Kant applies this mathematical criterion to his own *Critique*. The *Critique* is defined as "the determination of the *origins*, as well as the extent and *limits* [of cognition]" (A XII, emphasis mine), a definition that is clearly related to the mathematical definition of *to define* ("to present *originally* the complete concept of a thing *within its own limits*"). Kant himself draws this connection between his notion of the *Critique* and his definition of *to define* by introducing this definition with the statement that "it is precisely in *knowing its limits* that philosophy consists" (B 755). The problem of *Darstellung* on both levels, then, is the staying within limits, and it is therefore noteworthy that in the course of his *Critiques* Kant *revises* the limits of his philosophy so that aesthetics, which he had explicitly excluded from critical discourse in the *Critique of Pure Reason* (B 36), falls within the province of critical inquiry in the *Critique of Judgment.* Once again, it would seem that Kant's critical philosophy, stretched to its limits, resolves in aesthetics.

In fact, the final "paradox" of presentation that is posed in the *Critique of Pure Reason* is also addressed in the *Critique of Judgment* via art. Kant's subject cannot present itself to itself as it really is: "Here is the place to explain the *paradox* which must have been obvious to everyone in our exposition of the form of the inner sense (§6): namely, how this inner sense presents to consciousness even our own selves only as we appear to ourselves, not as we are in ourselves, since we intuit ourselves only as we are inwardly affected, which seems to be contradictory, since we would then have to be in a passive relationship with ourselves" (B 152–153, emphasis mine). That the subject can present itself to consciousness only as it *appears*, rather than as it *is*, is problematic, because this dual presentation (or nonpresentation) of the subject violates Kant's requirement that all philosophy be based on a "synthetic unity of apperception" (§16). Although this issue ultimately remains unresolved in Kant's critical philosophy and in fact was of remarkably little concern to him,[52] the *Critique of Judgment* does offer a partial explanation of how the subject can present itself to itelf as it is rather than just as it appears. The beautiful and the sublime are aesthetic judgments that offer sensible presentations of the subject, yet both judgments involve a moment in which the imagination transcends sensibility and paradoxically creates a presentation of the supersensible subject. In the case of the beautiful it is an indirect presentation (*indirekte Darstellung*) of the moral good, which is "originally determining" for the subject (§59 and B 125), and for the sublime it is a negative presentation (*negative Darstellung*) of the "idea of humanity in our subject" (§27 and B 97). Given these two explications of the subject in terms of aesthetic presentation, it is clear that *Darstellung* has assumed a much more central role in the third *Critique* than it had had in the first.

The *Critique of Judgment*: The *Darstellung* of Limits

It should come as no surprise, then, that Kant has moved the critical definition of *Darstellung* from its marginal status in the *Critique of Pure Reason* to a prominent position in the Introduction to the *Critique of Judgment*. Furthermore, he has replaced his indirect, parenthetical explications of the term with a precise definition: "If the concept of an object is given, the business of the judgment in the use of the concept for cognition consists in *Darstellung* (*exhibitio*), i.e., in setting a corresponding intuition beside the concept. This may take place either through our own imagination, as in art when we realize a preconceived concept of an object which is a purpose of ours, or through nature in its technique (as in organized bodies), when we supply to it our concept of its purpose in order to judge of its products" (B XLIX, p. 29). Significantly, Kant now equates *Darstellung* with the classical rhetorical term *exhibitio*, but the stylistic or rhetorical dimension of *Darstellung* that was so important to the "Transcendental Doctrine of Method" in the first *Critique* has been incorporated into its critical definition and is no longer an explicit issue in the third *Critique*. Indeed, in §60, "Of the Method of Taste," Kant argues that methodology *cannot* be an issue here, because "there neither is nor can be a science of the beautiful, and the judgment of taste is not determinable by principles" (B 261, p. 200). Moreover, the applicability of the term *Darstellung* has been extended from the disciplines of epistemology and mathematics to the provinces of art and nature, and *Darstellung* is now related to the notion of purposiveness. *Natural beauty* is defined as "the presentation of the concept of the formal (merely subjective) purposiveness," and *natural purposes* as "the presentation of the concept of a real (objective) purposiveness," and the division of the text into a "Critique of Aesthetic Judgment" and a "Critique of Teleological Judgment" is based on this distinction (B L, p. 30). Finally, *Darstellung* assumes a central role within the "Critique of Aesthetic Judgment." The "satisfaction

with mere presentation or with the faculty of presentation"
defines both the beautiful and the sublime (B 74, p. 82).

Hence, *Darstellung* has become essential to the third
Critique, and throughout the text Kant introduces synonyms from classical rhetoric with his critical definition.
Darstellen is now equated with "to represent aesthetically"
(*ästhetisch vorstellen*, B 84), as well as with "to demonstrate, show, or exhibit" (*demonstrieren, aufzeigen, osten-
dere,* and *exhibere*, B 240–241), and *Darstellung* with *hypotyposis, exhibitio,* and *subjectio sub adspectum* (B 255).
Moreover, the rhetorical term *hypotyposis* actually takes
precedence over the term *Darstellung* in a pivotal definition,
the differentiation of "schematic" and "symbolic" presentation: "All *hypotyposis* (*Darstellung, subjectio sub adspectum*), as sensible illustration, is twofold. It is either *schematic*,
when to a concept comprehended by the understanding the
corresponding intuition is given a priori, or it is *symbolic*.
In the latter case, to a concept only thinkable by reason and
to which no sensible intuition can be adequate, an intuition
is supplied that is in accordance with a procedure of the
judgment analogous to what it observes in schematism, i.e.,
merely analogous to the rule of this procedure, not to the
intuition itself, consequently merely to the form of reflection
and not to its content" (B 255, p. 197). According to Kant,
schematic presentations contain "direct" presentations of
their concepts, whereas symbolic presentation functions
"indirectly" (B 256), by analogy. The fact that Kant draws
this distinction in the penultimate paragraph of the "Critique of Aesthetic Judgment" (§59, "On the Beautiful as
a Symbol of the Moral Good") suggests that symbolic presentation is both crucial and problematic to his argument.
The beautiful as a symbol of the moral good represents a
mediation between pure and practical reason, the bridge
between understanding and reason that Kant had announced
in the Introduction to the third *Critique*.

It is extremely curious that Kant should take recourse
to the rhetorical term *hypotyposis* at this crucial juncture
in his argument.[53] *Hypotyposis* in its classical rhetorical
usage, we recall, is a stylistic device that presents subject

matter vividly to the eye. Yet Kant does not introduce the term here as a rhetorical tool but as a synonym for the critical definition of *Darstellung*, the making sensible of a concept. Indeed, he pointedly denounces the art of rhetoric as deceptive just a few paragraphs earlier, in his discussion of the division of the beautiful arts (§51–54). Whereas poetry proceeds with honesty and candor and hence maintains the highest rank of all the arts, Kant argues, rhetoric plays with illusion and is accordingly "a treacherous art which means to move men in important matters like machines to a judgment that must lose all weight for them in quiet reflection" (B 218, p. 172). This begs the question whether Kant employs a similarly treacherous rhetorical technique when he introduces the term *hypotyposis* in §59, ostensibly as a critical definition rather than as a stylistic device. In fact, his rhetoric in this section belies his stated argument. With the words, "Now I say: the beautiful is the symbol of the moral good" (B 258, p. 198) Kant pronounces, rather than proves, his point. His identification of the *beautiful* as the symbol of the moral good is an ad hoc solution to the problem of how to unify the *Critiques*, a rhetorically deceptive *Darstellung* ex machina, as it were, whose provisional nature becomes clear when we take Kant's advice and look, "in quiet reflection," at the definitions of presentation at work in the third *Critique*.

According to Hans Graubner, two basic classes of *Darstellungen* are operative in the *Critiques*.[54] The first corresponds to what Kant here calls *schematic presentation* and consists of presentations created by the imagination when it is bound by concepts and by a determining faculty of judgment. These presentations, mediations between intuitions and pure or empirical concepts of the understanding, produce objective cognition via "schema" and "example," yet offer no possibility of spanning the gap between nature and freedom. We recall that this is one of the central problems of presentation that Kant faces in the first and the second *Critiques*: the fact that transcendental ideas, necessary concepts of reason to which no corresponding object can be given in the senses, are not presentable to pure reason, and that in practical reason the idea of freedom achieves only partial concretization. In the third *Critique* Kant attempts to solve this problem by combining a new kind of idea with a new kind of presentation, the symbolic presentation of the aesthetic idea: "By an aesthetic idea I understand that representation [*Vorstellung*] of the imagination which occasions much thought, without however any definite thought, i.e. any *concept*, being capable of being adequate to it; it consequently cannot be completely compassed and made intelligible by language. We easily see that it is the counterpart (pendant) of a *rational idea* (*Vernunftidee*), which conversely is a concept to which no *intuition* (or representation [*Vorstellung*] of the imagination) can be adequate" (B 192-193, p. 157). However, as Kant goes on to explain in §49, aesthetic ideas not only complement transcendental ideas of reason, they actually bring the entire faculty of intellectual ideas into movement. By animating the cognitive faculties, aesthetic ideas enable the mind to construct symbolic presentations of transcendental ideas.[55]

With this in mind we consider the second class of presentation that Graubner delimits, presentations created by a free imagination and a reflective faculty of judgment. These symbolic presentations, mediations between intuitions and indeterminate concepts of the understanding or ideas of reason, produce only contingent cognition or indirect presentations, but appear as sensible indications of a possible reconciliation between nature and freedom. Within this second class Graubner identifies four types of *Darstellung*: (1) the aesthetic idea or the beautiful, which appears as "the presentation of an indefinite concept of understanding" (B 75, p. 82); (2) totality in empirical intuition, which is "the presentation of an empirical concept in its teleological aspect"; (3) the sublime, which appears as "the presentation of an indefinite concept of reason" (B 75, p. 82); and (4) the symbol of the moral good, which as an aesthetic idea is the presentation of a concept of the understanding, yet is judged by analogy to be, in Graubner's words, an "indirect presentation of the nonpresentable idea of man's moral purpose."[56]

Graubner has perhaps been too quick here in his equation of the aesthetic idea with the beautiful. What Kant actually states is that the beautiful is an *expression* (*Ausdruck*) of the aesthetic idea (B 203, p. 164), and in fact, the aesthetic idea is as much an expression of the sublime as it is the beautiful. To be sure, Kant himself would no doubt deny the sublime this status, since he pointedly denigrates this type of aesthetic judgment, while at the same time arguing that the symbol of the moral good is presented by the beautiful. If we look at the categories of *Darstellung* that Graubner has delineated, however, we see that the presentation of the moral good actually *combines* the presentations of the beautiful *and* the sublime. Like the beautiful it appears to be a presentation of a concept of the understanding, and like the sublime it appears to be the presentation of an idea of reason. In other words, Kant's definition of the beautiful as a symbol of the moral good would not be possible without his definition of the sublime. Indeed, he himself concedes the point earlier in the *Critique*: "Hence it follows that the intellectual, in itself purposive, (moral) good, judged aesthetically, must be represented (*vorgestellt*) as sublime rather than beautiful". . . (B 120, p. 112). Given his statement that the beautiful is "by far" more important than the sublime and his simultaneous subordination of the sublime to the status of a "mere appendix to the aesthetic judgment of the purposiveness of nature" (B 78), it seems that this relationship between the beautiful and the sublime is a bit more intimate than Kant himself had hoped for.

In fact, Kant clearly privileges the sublime in his discussion of *Darstellung*. Despite the central position he allots *Darstellung* in both the Introduction and in his definition of the beautiful as a symbol of the moral good, the term plays a minimal role within the "Analytic of the Beautiful," appearing only once, in §17, "Of the Ideal of Beauty," where it is not at all essential to his analysis. The discussion of *Darstellung* is almost exclusively within the "Analytic of the Sublime," and Kant actually introduces his presentational definition of the beautiful within this section (B 75). In §23, "Transition from the Faculty which Judges of the Beautiful to that which Judges of the Sublime"—a section of tremendous interest in that it is marked as a "transition" in a text about borders—Kant goes to great lengths to identify the differences between the beautiful and the sublime and to argue for the primacy of the beautiful over the sublime. Contrary to his own argument, however, it is clear from Kant's rhetoric that he considers the presentational potential of the sublime to be much more dynamic than that of the beautiful.

According to Kant, the satisfaction of presentation itself or with the faculty of presentation is the common denominator between the beautiful and the sublime, yet the two are distinguished by the different types of presentation ascribed to them in aesthetic judgments: "The beautiful in nature is connected with the form of the object, which consists in having *boundaries*. The sublime, on the other hand, is *also*[57] to be found in a formless object, so far as in it or by occasion of it *boundlessness* is represented (*vorgestellt*), and yet its totality is also present to thought. Thus the beautiful seems to be regarded as the presentation of an indefinite concept of the understanding, the sublime as that of a like concept of reason" (B 75, p. 82, emphasis mine). In comparison to the beautiful, which is associated with only formal limitation, the sublime is "also" found in formless objects. In other words, like the beautiful, the sublime can be found in formal limitation, yet it is distinguished from the beautiful in that it can also be judged to be a presentation of the limitless, of an infinity that, paradoxically, has a totality attributed to it.[58] Hence, the sublime incorporates, but goes beyond, the presentational limits of the beautiful.

The dialectical relationship between limitation and limitlessness played out in these definitions of the beautiful and the sublime is essential to Kant's notion of *Darstellung*. Whereas the problem of presentation in the first *Critique* is how to stay *within* the limits of *Darstellung*, what is at issue in the third *Critique* is the figure of the limit itself. The demarcation of this limit is a recurring motif that runs throughout the text on the sublime, and if we trace the development of this motif, we find that the sublime is interesting to Kant precisely because its *negative Darstellung* marks—and transcends—the limits of presentation.

First, as we have seen, the sublime marks the borders of the beautiful, and its transcendence over the beautiful is illustrated in the language Kant uses to explicate the presentational definitions of the beautiful and the sublime cited previously. Whereas the beautiful is presented by a "playful imagination," the role the imagination plays in the presentation of the sublime is "not a game, but serious" (B 75, p. 83). What makes the sublime more serious than the beautiful is the fact that it involves the staking of life. While the beautiful fosters a direct feeling of furthering life, the sublime intensifies this feeling of life "indirectly," via a momentary checking of the life forces that results in an increased vitality (B 75, p. 83). This momentary checking (*augenblickliche Hemmung*; literally, a stoppage for a blink of the eye) presents a visible limit to the sensible subject, and at this sublime limit the subject perceives itself as a moral being.

This transition from the sensible subject to the moral subject of reason is the second border that the sublime marks. In the sublime judgment, sensibility is unable to process the sensory data it receives; and the imagination, rather than producing a direct schematic presentation, races to infinity. The subject feels threatened by this failure of the faculty of presentation (*Darstellungsvermögen*, B 76, p. 83) and is afraid. Reason, however, violently imposes a claim of totality on the imagination, and following a "certain subreption" (B 97, p. 96), this process results in "the awakening of the feeling of a supersensible faculty in us," "the idea of humanity in our subject" (B 97, p. 96). This theory of the moral subject that the sublime produces is presented by a subset of indirect presentations that Kant calls *negative Darstellung*.

This paradoxical negative presentation is the crux of the Kantian sublime. Kant explains: "We need not fear that the feeling of the sublime will lose by so abstract a mode of presentation—which is quite negative in respect of what is sensible—for the imagination, although it finds nothing beyond the sensible to which it can attach itself, nonetheless feels itself unbounded precisely by this removal of its limits; and thus that very separation is a presentation of the Infinite, which can never be anything but a mere negative presentation, yet which nonetheless expands the soul" (B 124, p. 115). It is noteworthy that Kant states that in the sublime judgment the imagination "feels" unlimited because of the doing away of the limits of sensibility, because this "feeling" suggests that the imagination is nonetheless grounded in sensibility, and it only *appears* that the limits of sensibility have been abolished. In fact, in another description of the same process, Kant does not talk about the "doing away" of these limits. Rather, he states that the imagination is "stretched to its limits" in the sublime judgment (B 116, p. 108). In the preceding quotation (B 124, p. 115), Kant qualifies his description of the "removal of limits" by stating that this whole process is an *Absonderung*, a separation, which is also a marking of a limit. According to Kant, this separation is a presentation of the Infinite, a presentation that can only be negative, yet that paradoxically expands the soul (*die aber **doch** die Seele erweitert*). Thus, *negative Darstellung* seems to be composed of two related components: a drawing of limits or a drawing into question of limits and an expansion of the "soul"; that is, of morality.

Kant gives two concrete examples of what this negative presentation—which is in fact a presentation—might look like. The first, which is introduced in the next sentence of the same passage and clearly illustrates these two components, is the Old Testament injunction against the creation of graven images: "Perhaps there is no sublimer passage in Jewish law than the command: 'You shall not make any graven image for yourself, nor the likeness of anything which is in heaven or on the earth or under the earth,' etc." (B 124, p.115). In stating that it is wrong to make an image or a likeness of God (or of what is presented here as a negative presentation of God), the commandment defines the limits of presentation negatively, and Kant interprets this nonpresentation of the Absolute as analogous to the "representation (*Vorstellung*) of the moral law and the predisposition to morality in us" (B 125). The second example of *negative Darstellung*—which, incidentally, serves as an illustration of the aesthetic idea and is thus further evidence that the aesthetic idea is rooted in the sublime rather than the beautiful—is identified as the epitome of the sublime: "Perhaps nothing more sublime was ever said and no sublimer thought ever expressed than the inscription on the Temple of Isis (Mother Nature): 'I am all that is and that was and that shall be, and no mortal has lifted my veil.'" (B 197, p. 160).

It is noteworthy that this most sublime thought is expressed in poetic language. If we compare the two examples, we see that both contain a commandment, an imperative utterance of the Absolute (not unlike Kant's almost imperious pronouncement that the beautiful is a symbol of the moral good), and that both contain an important visual component: "You shall not make graven images"; "You shall not lift my veil." Both commandments make a limit visible: an image that must not be made; a veil that must not be lifted. This limit can, but must not, be crossed. The result of a transgression of the limit would be idolatry or fanaticism (*Schwärmerei*) in the first case; death in the second. Thus, negative presentation lays down a moral law for the subject: it is a kind of categorical imperative that *compels* the subject to think: "We may describe the sublime thus: it is an object (of nature) the representation (*Vorstellung*) of which *compels the mind to think* the unattainability of nature as a presentation (*Darstellung*) of ideas." (B 115, p. 108, emphasis mine). Or again, more emphatically, *negative Darstellung* "*forces* us to think": "This effort—and the feeling of the unattainability of the idea by means of the imagination—is itself a presentation of the subjective purposiveness of our mind in the employment of the imagination for its supersensible destination and *forces us*, subjectively, *to think* nature itself in its totality as a presentation of something supersensible, without being able objectively to arrive at this presentation" (B 115–116, p. 108, emphasis mine).

Negative Darstellung forces the subject to think the supersensible—the idea—without actually producing an objective presentation of this idea. Thus, it presents nothing except the process—the striving or effort (*die Bestrebung*)—of *Darstellung* itself. It is self-presentation or *Selbstdarstellung* in the Romantic sense of the word, and it is no coincidence that the notion of "negativity" becomes constitutive for Idealism and Romanticism. Indeed, Kant himself indicates the applicability of his theory of the sublime to artistic production: "Even the presentation of the sublime, so far as it belongs to beautiful art, may combine with beauty in a tragedy in verse, a didactic poem, or in an oratorio; *and in these combinations beautiful art is even more artistic. . .*" (B 213–214, p. 170, emphasis mine). Given this clear recognition of the artistic applications of the sublime, one has to wonder why Kant not only does not draw the same conclusions from his own theory that the Romantics do, but in fact actively squelches its productive potential.

The key to the reason for Kant's hesitance vis-à-vis the sublime is contained in his explication of *negative Darstellung*. In Kant's critical philosophy *negative Darstellung* is a control mechanism whose function is to keep reason within its borders:

> This *pure*, soul-uplifting, merely negative presentation of morality brings with it, on the other hand, no danger of fanaticism, which is *an illusional belief in our capacity to see something beyond all bounds of sensibility,* i.e. of dreaming in accordance with fundamental propositions (or of going mad with reason); and this is so just because this presentation is merely negative. For *the uninvestigatability of the idea of freedom* completely cuts it off from any positive presentation, but the moral law is in itself sufficiently and originally

determinant in us, so that it does not *permit* us *to look around* at any ground of determination external to itself. (B 125, p. 116, emphasis mine)

Negative Darstellung, grounded in a moral law that does not allow us to question its validity, safeguards against fanaticism and keeps reason from running amok by not letting it disregard the limits of sensibility. The demarcation of this limit is reflected in the process of presentation itself: positive presentation is "completely cut off by the uninvestigatability of the idea of freedom"; that is, it is limited by the limits of Kant's transcendental investigation. *Negative Darstellung* transcends the limits of positive presentation, indeed, of the *Critique* itself. Thus, *negative Darstellung* is not just one aspect of the critical definition of *Darstellung*; it is also a stylistic device, an extension of the rhetorical presentation that was so important in the first *Critique*. Hence Kant's constant equation of *Darstellung* with synonyms from classical rhetoric. *Negative Darstellung* is a self-reflexive rhetorical figure: its enunciation is simultaneously its critical presentation. It is an analogue of the pure mathematical presentation defined in the first *Critique*.

As if to substantiate this conclusion, Kant actually describes *negative Darstellung* as "pure" or *rein*, and this designation is extremely revealing, given his repeated insistence that the sublime is an a posteriori aesthetic judgment (see, for example, B 99). If "pure" means that sensibility is excluded from sublime presentation, as it generally does in Kantian parlance, then this "pure negative presentation" is indeed nothing less than the pure presentation that was lacking in philosophy in the first *Critique*. According to the parameters that Kant himself establishes, this pure, negative philosophical presentation would be poetic, because poetry, the highest expression of the aesthetic idea (B 194), "adds to a concept much ineffable thought" (B 197, p. 160). This is clearly the conclusion the Romantics draw from the *Critiques*, and it is a conclusion, Nancy has suggested, that Kant was aware of, but avoided.[59] If this is the case, then the final limit that *negative Darstellung* demarcates is the border between critical discourse and poetry.

Summary

The *Critique of Pure Reason*: The Limits of *Darstellung*

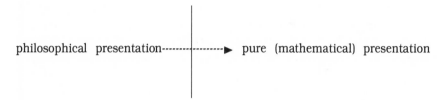

The *Critique of Judgment*: The *Darstellung* of Limits

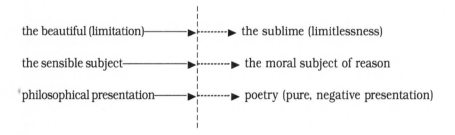

> A work is formed when it is sharply delimited everywhere, but within these limits limitless and inexhaustible, true to itself, the same everywhere, and yet sublimely elevated above itself. (Friedrich Schlegel, KA II: 215, #297)

> Criticism shows precisely the necessity of limitation—determination, stopping—points to a specific goal—and transforms speculation into a useful, and indeed poetic, instrument. (Novalis, *Schriften*, vol. 3, p. 442, #906)

Novalis is quite right to point to a speculative level in Kant's critical philosophy. There is a remarkable textual obscurity, if not a fictional character, to Kant's "Analytic of the Sublime" that merits interpretation. Despite its central importance to his *Darstellung* discussion, Kant identifies the "Analytic of the Sublime" as a "mere appendix" to his study, and there is a tentative tone to his rhetoric throughout the text. Kant invariably chooses expressions like *as it were* and *as if* to explicate his definitions, and his entire discussion of *Darstellung* is predicated on the notion of illusion or appearance (*Schein*): "Thus the beautiful *seems to be regarded* as the presentation of an indefinite concept of the understanding, the sublime as that of a like concept of reason" (B 75, p. 82, emphasis mine). Kant avoids a simple declarative statement here, repeats the formulation verbatim later in the same paragraph when he states that the imagination in the sublime judgment "*seems to be regarded* as emotion," and employs another conjectural definition in his discussion of *Darstellung* in the Introduction to the third *Critique*: "yet we thus ascribe to nature, *as it were*, a regard to our cognitive faculty according to the analogy of a purpose. *Thus we can regard* natural beauty as the presentation of the concept of the formal (merely subjective) purposiveness, and natural purposes as the presentation of the concept of a real (objective) purposiveness" (B L, p. 30, emphasis mine). The tentative nature of these assertions, as well as Kant's subordination of the sublime to the beautiful when so much of his argument speaks for the priority of the sublime, raises the question whether the "certain subreption" (B 97, p. 96) that the sublime effects is in fact the narrative principle of Kant's own text.[60]

In concluding, I want to suggest that this is indeed the case at a crucial juncture in Kant's discussion of *negative Darstellung*. *Darstellung* in general has an important visual dimension. As a classical rhetorical term it refers to a "making visible via words," and Kant incorporates this visual dimension into his critical philosophy.[61] In the first *Critique* Kant is repeatedly concerned with overcoming or avoiding blindness: witness the visual metaphors in the "Transcendental Doctrine of Method," the famous formulation that "thoughts without content are empty, intuitions without concepts are *blind*" (B 76, emphasis mine) and the description of the imagination as a "*blind* yet indispensible function of the soul" (B 103, emphasis mine). In the third *Critique*, however, Kant suppresses sight in his paradoxical notion of *negative Darstellung*, thereby effectively opposing the classical rhetorical definition of *Darstellung* as the "making visible via words." The two examples of *negative Darstellung* that he provides—the Old Testament injunction against the creation of graven images and the taboo against lifting the veil of the image of the goddess Isis—derive their forcefulness from a repression of the visual. Indeed, if we return once again to Kant's explication of this paradoxical rhetorical figure, we find that doing away with sight is absolutely central to *negative Darstellung*. *Negative Darstellung* is a moral imperative that guards against the "illusional belief in our capacity to *see beyond* all bounds of sensibility. . . . it does not *permit* us to *look around* at any ground of determination external to itself" (B 125, p. 116, emphasis mine). The reason why Kant imposes an artificial blindness here is clear: he is trying to safeguard against fanaticism in his own philosophy. A few years later in an essay on "The Newly-Elevated Refined Tone in Philosophy" (1796) he will repeat this formulation almost verbatim. *Negative Darstellung* always carries with it a certain danger: the danger of succumbing to fanatic vision, which is the death of all philosophy.[62]

Given this suppression of sight in the third *Critique*, it is remarkable that post-Kantian theories of *Darstellung* capitalize on the visual, a fact noted by Jean Paul as early as 1804: "If style is to be the tool of *Darstellung*—not of mere expression—it can only do so by means of sensibility, which can only appear as plastic, i.e., through form and movement, either real or in pictures—*since only the fifth sense, the eye, is to be used at the writing desk in Europe*."[63] Fichte, who considered himself a true Kantian disciple, develops a visual definition of the subject that it is grounded in *Darstellung*. Like Fichte's, Schelling's definition of intellectual intuition involves an Ego seeing itself. The notion of the gaze is also essential to Romanticism. E. T. A. Hoffmann uses an eroticized gaze as a narrative technique in *The Sandman* and *The Golden Pot*. In *Godwi: or The Petrified Image of the Mother*, Brentano defines *the Romantic* as "a looking glass, or rather the color of the lens and the definition of the object by the shape of the lens."[64] Similarly, Friedrich Schlegel states that romantic poesy should be "a mirror of the whole surrounding world; a picture of the age,"[65] and Novalis develops a theory of visual-verbal *Darstellung*.

The following chapters will trace the evolution of Kant's notion of *Darstellung* in Idealism and Romanticism, focusing on the visual semantics that structure these various theories. Chapter 2 demonstrates the derivation of Fichte's visual definition of the subject as *Darstellung*. Chapters 3 and 4 then examine the critical reception of Kant's and Fichte's visual theories of *Darstellung* in the oeuvres of Novalis and Kleist, writers whose works incorporate opposing reactions to Kantian aesthetics and who are therefore representative of two distinct philosophical strains of Romanticism.

2

The Idealist Response:
From Reinhold to the Romantics

Chapter 1 followed Lacoue-Labarthe and Nancy in reading Kant's critical philosophy through Romantic eyes, as it were, to illustrate the exigencies in Kant's discussions of *Darstellung* that prompted the Romantics to formulate a literary response to transcendental idealism. This Kantian derivation of Jena Romanticism departs from most other interpretations of the movement, which focus primarily on Fichte's 1794 *Doctrine of Knowledge* (*Wissenschaftslehre*) as the programmatic text of the Romantics, without considering the true provenance of Fichte's ego philosophy or analyzing sufficiently Kant's contributions to the Romantics' transcendental poesy. There can be little doubt that the Romantics read Fichte, were profoundly influenced by his *Doctrine of Knowledge*, and liberally incorporated his thought and terminology into their own writings, but the real impetus for their poetic program, Lacoue-Labarthe and Nancy argue, lies in Kant's critical philosophy.

The genealogy of Idealism from Kant through Fichte to the Romantics is a good deal more complex than is generally acknowledged in most literary studies of Jena Romanticism, which tend to see Fichte's ego philosophy as a direct outgrowth of Kant's *Critiques* and regard the *Doctrine of Knowledge* as a template for Jena Romanticism. Strictly speaking, neither of these derivations is completely correct, and the purpose of the present chapter is to trace the development of post-Kantian Idealism from the critique of Kant leveled by his acknowledged successor, Karl Leonhard Reinhold, through the skepticism that transcendental idealism inspired in Gottlob Ernst Schulze to the early philosophical writings of Fichte, which were developed as a direct response to Schulze's attack on Reinhold. In these early writings Fichte advances a definition of the subject as *Darstellung*, a definition that the Jena Romantic Novalis adopts in this early form, but one that Fichte discards almost immediately in favor of the model of the self-positing subject formulated in the *Doctrine of Knowledge*. My aim in delineating this history is to demonstrate that a fundamentally Kantian notion of representation informs Jena Romanticism.

Reinhold's Elementary Philosophy: Recasting Kant's First *Critique* as a Theory of Representation

Strange though it may seem to us today, Kant's now canonical "Coperican Revolution" in philosophy did not enjoy immediate success when the *Critique of Pure Reason* first appeared on the German intellectual scene in 1781, a state of affairs that frustrated its middle-aged author, who tried in vain to draw attention to his magnum opus. In fact, the man who popularized and gained acceptance for Kant's critical philosophy was Karl Leonhard Reinhold (1758–1823), an Austrian ex-monk turned Protestant who was grappling with questions of faith.[1] As a young man Reinhold had risen through the ranks of the popular philosophers, an eclectic and loosely associated group of German intellectuals comparable to the French *philosophes* whose aim was to make Enlightenment philosophy practical and applicable to everyday life, as Reinhold put it, "to break down the barriers between philosophy and life, speculation and action, so that the principles of reason were not locked away in an ivory tower, but practiced by church and state."[2] The popular philosophers appealed to common sense in evaluating all philosophy, a criterion that frequently led to skepticism with regard to the metaphysical models of their contemporaries. Because philosophy could not prove its assertions empirically, they argued, it could not claim universal validity unless it were to discover a new scientific model on which to base its claims.[3]

In 1785 Reinhold became increasingly skeptical of his own religious convictions because he could not found them rationally and was faced with an intellectual crisis of faith: although he wanted to believe in the existence of God, providence, and immortality, reason led him to doubt these Christian tenets. His curiosity piqued by an excerpt of the *Critique of Pure Reason* he had seen in one of the leading literary newspapers, the *Allgemeine Literatur-Zeitung*, he then studied Kant's book, found in it a new scientific model for metaphysics, and became an immediate convert to the critical philosophy. He was so taken by what he had read that he decided to popularize and espouse this "gospel of pure reason," and in a series of *Letters on Kantian Philosophy* published beginning in August 1786 in the eminent Enlightenment journal *Teutsche Merkur*, Reinhold began to explicate Kant's convoluted and cryptic system in elegant, understandable terms, focusing on Kant's doctrine of practical faith.[4] The *Letters* were an overnight success, and Reinhold, Kant, and the critical philosophy were all plunged into the limelight. Reinhold sought and easily gained Kant's public endorsement of the *Letters*, and in 1787 the reformed popular philosopher was appointed to the newly established chair of transcendental idealism at the University of Jena.

At first happy to serve as a spokesman for the critical philosophy, Reinhold began to hold lectures expounding the *Critique of Pure Reason*, but Kant's acknowledged philosophical heir soon started to criticize and revise his mentor's system. In a series of writings published between 1789 and 1794 Reinhold laid out his meta-critical critique of Kant and established a new form of transcendental idealism, which he dubbed the *philosophy without a nickname*, the so-called Elementary Philosophy.[5] Like other philosophers before him, Reinhold argued, Kant had not been self-critical enough in laying the foundation of his epistemology: he had not defined many of the basic terms in his system; he had relied on numerous presuppositions in his deductions; and he had not established a true critical method. If epistemology were to succeed as a "strict science," philosophers could not take its very existence for granted, but must

ground its possibility in a single incontrovertible fundamental principle from which the rest of the system would
then be derived.[6] The building blocks of this "strict science"
were contained in Kant's *Critique*, Reinhold thought, and
by eliminating unwarranted presuppositions, establishing
rigorous definitions of its basic components, and formu-
lating a fundamental principle that was both universally
valid and universally accepted,[7] Reinhold was convinced
that he could establish a solid base on which to construct not
just a metaphysics, but a science of all human knowledge.

Now, the fundamental principle or *Grundsatz* of this
epistemology must be a description of a fact of consciousness that is self-evident or *elementar* in the Kantian sense
of the word, that is, not derivable from any other principle,[8]
and here, Reinhold thought, was where Kant had not been
sufficiently thoroughgoing in his analysis. Kant had assumed
that the critical philosophy must investigate the conditions
of possibility and the limits of knowledge, but knowledge,
Reinhold argued, was predicated on representation (*Vorstellung*): the various forms of knowledge that Kant delineates—
the intuitions of sensibility, the concepts of the understanding, and the ideas of reason—are all forms of representation,
but Kant had neglected to define or sufficiently investigate
this pivotal term.[9] Consequently, Reinhold's Elementary
Philosophy is nothing less than a transcendental theory of
representation, and the basic principle that forms the keystone of his critical philosophy is representational in nature.

This fundamental proposition was not to be a definition
but was to describe a self-evident fact of consciousness,
because, as Reinhold saw it, not even a skeptic could deny
that he or she was conscious, that he or she had representations: "*Consciousness* forces everyone to agree that to every
representation there pertains a representing subject and a
represented object, *both* of which must be distinguished
from the *representation* to which they pertain."[10] This statement, Reinhold thought, was completely self-evident: the
term *representation* (*Vorstellung*) simply refers to what
occurs in our minds when we are conscious; no one would
deny that he or she is conscious; and no one would deny

that there is a distinction between subject and object.[11] Here, then, was the universally recognized self-evident proposition of consciousness, *der Satz des Bewusstseins*, the grand first principle of all philosophy: "In consciousness the subject distinguishes the representation from the subject and the object and relates it to them both." This statement is in essence, as Beiser has pointed out, a witting expansion of Kant's principle of the unity of apperception: whereas Kant had merely stated that the "I think" must be able to accompany all my representations, Reinhold's proposition of consciousness seeks "to specify *the manner* in which the subject must be able to be self-conscious of his representations."[12]

Starting from this rather vague proposition of a representing consciousness, Reinhold's transcendental theory then proceeds to investigate the necessary conditions of possibility of representation in general, a task Reinhold allocates to the first part of his Elementary Philosophy, the "Theory of the Faculty of Representation." Kant's failure to demonstrate the existence of a "common root" to his two branches of human cognition, sensibility and understanding, had forced him, Reinhold thought, to present his epistemology in unrigorous and unconvincing terms. Hence, the stated goal of Reinhold's "Theory of the Faculty of Representation" is to derive the common root of all knowledge from the fundamental proposition of consciousness, and he sets out to prove that "*space, time, the twelve categories*, and the *three forms of the ideas* are originally nothing but properties of *mere representations*."[13] Having demonstrated the representational common root of all knowledge to his satisfaction, Reinhold then derives the faculty of knowledge from the faculty of representation, and in the "Theory of the Faculty of Knowledge" he deduces the main doctrines of the *Critique of Pure Reason* based on the results of his previous analysis of representation. The final section of the Elementary Philosophy, the "Theory of the Faculty of Desire," attempts to prove the priority of practical reason over theoretical reason.[14]

But how does Reinhold define the cornerstone of his system, the notion of representation (*Vorstellung*)? According to his analysis, representation simply describes what happens in our consciousness when we are conscious. Moreover, all representation is predicated on an essential duality, one that is implicit in the fundamental proposition: "In consciousness the subject distinguishes the representation from the subject and the object and relates it to them both." Since a given representation must be related to and distinguished from both the subject and the object, Reinhold argues, it must have two components: form, which relates it to and distinguishes it from the representing subject, and content, which relates it to and distinguishes it from the object represented. But Reinhold's thesis, as his skeptical critic Schulze soon demonstrated, is logically unsound: although the representation stands in distinct relation to the subject and the object, it does not follow that it itself must have distinct components.[15] For all his talk of a necessary first principle, Reinhold's Elementary Philosophy rests on a weak foundation.

Indeed, this is not the only logical fallacy that Reinhold is guilty of, Beiser argues: "In assuming that the objective content of a representation corresponds to its object, in postulating an active subject and object that are the causes of representation, and in applying the category of cause to the thing-in-itself, Reinhold commits himself to assumptions which are not verifiable within consciousness itself."[16] His real undoing, however, Beiser contends, is the faculty of desire. As a true Kantian, Reinhold wants to maintain the primacy of practical reason over theoretical reason, and hence argues that the faculty of desire actually produces all representation. If this is the case, then his entire epistemology founders: representation was to be its most fundamental principle, and now Reinhold is forced to argue that desire is even more fundamental than representation. It seems, then, as Fichte realized, that Reinhold should have based his system on the faculty of desire and not on the faculty of representation, that he should have started with an investigation of practical rather than theoretical reason.[17] This, of course, is the path that Fichte will pursue in the *Doctrine of Knowledge*, and through a quirk of fate Fichte soon replaced Reinhold, both figuratively and literally, as the spokesman of the critical philosophy: in 1794 Reinhold retired to Kiel and was succeeded by Fichte at Jena; and in 1797 Reinhold, who was known for his mercurial philosophical allegiances, renounced his own Elementary Philosophy and enthusiastically endorsed Fichte's system, albeit for a short time.[18]

It is not my intent here to provide a thoroughgoing analysis of Reinhold's epistemology but merely to indicate its relevance to the genealogy of the Idealist and Romantic notions of *Darstellung*. Historically speaking, Reinhold's foregrounding of the concept of representation (*Vorstellung*) in the Elementary Philosophy is indebted to Christian Wolff's rationalist philosophy: according to Wolff, the mind consists of a single force, the *vis repraesentativa* or power of representation. Kant had vehemently opposed this single-faculty doctrine as being dogmatic, and in this sense Reinhold might be seen as taking a step backward in his attempt to further the critical philosophy by reverting to Wolffian epistemology.[19] Nonetheless, his theory of representation was to prove extremely productive in the development of Idealist theories of *Darstellung*. Compared with Kant's dichotomous definition of *Darstellung* as sensible representation and rhetorical presentation and his expansion of these definitions in the "Analytic of the Sublime," Reinhold's theory of representation might at first glance seem reductionist, but being reductive was of course Reinhold's goal: he wanted to construct a clear and rigorous exposé of the critical philosophy, and in this sense Reinhold vitalized Kant's rhetorical or stylistic definition of *Darstellung*. There was clearly no need to include Kant's critical definition of *Darstellung* in the Elementary Philosophy: for Reinhold sensible representation (*sinnliche Vorstellung*) is simply a subset of the general genus representation (*Vorstellung*). Although this reduction undoubtedly simplifies Reinhold's model of the mind, it does so, as Fichte clearly realized, by sacrificing the representational potential inherent in Kant's elaborations of the *Darstellung* problematic. As we will see, Fichte will reintroduce the Kantian

notion of *Darstellung* in his critique of Reinhold's fundamental proposition of consciousness: in his *Own Meditations on Elementary Philosophy* Fichte develops a definition
of the subject as *Darstellung.*

    Although Reinhold's success was short-lived and his
theory of representation untenable, his recasting of the
foundation of the critical philosophy was to have profound
consequences for the development of German Idealism.
Even though subsequent philosophers did not agree on the
nature of this foundation, Reinhold's demand for a meta-
critical epistemology forms the basis of the post-Kantian
speculative systems of Fichte, Schelling, and Hegel.[20] Paradoxically, Reinhold's programmatic insistence on the critical
evaluation of epistemology was to allow the skeptic Schulze
to launch a compelling attack against Reinhold and Kant,
an attack that created the impetus for Fichte's evolution of
the *Doctrine of Knowledge.*

Schulze's *Aenesidemus*: Meta-Critical Skepticism

    The downfall of Reinhold's Elementary Philosophy was
precipitated by a philosophical tractacte published anonymously in 1792, *Aenesidemus, or Concerning the Foundations of the Elementary Philosophy Propounded in Jena
by Professor Reinhold, Including a Defense of Skepticism
against the Pretensions of the Critique of Pure Reason.*
True to its expansive subtitle, the book launched an in-depth
assault on Reinhold and Kant, arguing that any true critical
philosophy must necessarily end in skepticism. Though by
no means its first critic, the author of *Aenesidemus* presented such a strong case against the transcendental idealism
of Kant and, especially, Reinhold that many in the philosophical community doubted that the critical philosophy
could withstand this attack. In fact, *Aenesidemus* was taken
seriously by everyone except Reinhold himself, who asserted
that his anonymous critic had intentionally misunderstood
him. A year or so after its publication, the author of the book
emerged in the figure of Gottlob Ernst Schulze (1761–1833),
a little-known professor of philosophy at the University of

Helmstedt whose one claim to fame, as Beiser puts it, was to be *Aenesidemus*.[21]

Schulze takes as his title character a first-century champion of skepticism who anticipates his own position vis-à-vis the critical philosophy. The historical Aenesidemus had attacked academic skeptics who dogmatically taught that knowledge is impossible, and he himself had propounded instead a skepticism that consisted in the assertions that sensibility cannot provide objective knowledge of things-in-themselves and that the concept of cause is unreliable.[22] These tenets are reflected in the self-proclaimed Humean Schulze's definition of *skepticism*, which he describes as the view "that in philosophy nothing can be decided on the basis of incontestably certain and universally valid first principles concerning the existence or nonexistence of things-in-themselves and their properties nor concerning the limits of man's capacity for knowledge."[23] Schulze argues that the critical philosophy has violated both these propositions by making an illicit move from the subjective to the objective, by going beyond mental representations and logical laws to claim that both objective knowledge of the thing-in-itself and the transcendental I are thinkable. Schulze also contends that nothing in the critical philosophy supports its thesis of the priority of practical reason.

Schulze's meta-critical skepticism is made all the more compelling by the fact that he takes Kant's starting point as his own: Schulze's guiding principle is the assertion "that all our beliefs must submit to free and open examination of reason."[24] Although he supports many of the propositions of transcendental idealism and even claims to admire it as "philosophical art,"[25] Schulze argues that submitting the critical philosophy to its own critique necessarily results in skepticism. Schulze garners support for this thesis by systematically going through the Elementary Philosophy and pointing out inconsistencies in Reinhold's logic. For example, although he agrees with Reinhold's insistence on founding philosophy on a first principle grounded in representation (*Vorstellung*), he argues that Reinhold's fundamental proposition of consciousness is riddled with linguistic ambiguities, a claim he then easily substantiates. Moreover, Schulze contends that Reinhold's proposition of consciousness is subsumed under the principle of contradiction, and hence cannot be the fundamental principle of all philosophy. Reinhold does provide an explanation that arguably overrides this remonstration, but he has no answer to Schulze's further assertion that his dichotomous division of representation into subjective and objective components is fallacious.

Schulze effected his critique of Reinhold with such finessse that the Elementary Philosophy soon toppled, even though many of his objections to the critical philosophy were grounded in a psychologizing of transcendental idealism that ultimately proved indefensible. Initially, however, Schulze's meta-critical skepticism presented a serious threat indeed to the critical philosophy, and the young Kantian Johann Gottlieb Fichte, who considered *Aenesidemus* to be "one of the most remarkable products of the decade,"[26] felt compelled to counter this challenge. As Fichte put it in a personal letter to his friend Stephani, *Aenesidemus* "has overthrown Reinhold in my eyes, has made me suspicious of Kant, and has overturned my whole system from the bottom up. . . . It cannot be helped; the system must be rebuilt." Dovetailing this statement is Fichte's somewhat immodest proclamation that he has discovered a new foundation for transcendental idealism "from which it will be easy to develop the whole of philosophy,"[27] a derivation that he then publishes in his review of *Aenesidemus*.

Fichte's *Own Meditations on Elementary Philosophy* and the *Aenesidemus* Review: Defining the Subject as *Darstellung*

Like Reinhold, Fichte was attracted to Kant by the moral and religious dimensions of his critical philosophy and had been propelled to fame in 1792 when his *Attempt at a Critique of All Revelation*, a treatise he had written to introduce himself to the grand master of Königsberg, was published anonymously and taken to be the work of Kant. After the smoke had cleared and Kant had expressed his approval of this new contribution to the critical philosophy, the aspiring young Fichte was invited to become a reviewer for the prestigious *Allgemeine Literatur-Zeitung*. The first book he chose to evaluate was Schulze's recently published *Aenesidemus*. Fichte, profoundly disturbed by both a caustic review of his own book that he suspected Schulze of writing and by the challenge Schulze's skepticism presented to the critical philosophy, took the better part of a year to complete the review, compiling copious notes for the project, his *Own Meditations on Elementary Philosophy*, and its attendant *Practical Philosophy*, which contains a nascent aesthetic theory. These rambling, exploratory texts, written in 1793–94 but first published in their entirety in 1971, have only recently received due attention in Fichte research: together with the 1794 *Aenesidemus* review and its four extant prepublication drafts, they clearly demonstrate the dialogical evolution of Fichte's ego philosophy as a response to Schulze's criticisms of Reinhold and Kant and form an unmistakable blueprint of the 1794 *Doctrine of Knowledge*.[28]

Fichte develops his definition of the subject as *Darstellung* in his notes on the Elementary Philosophy and in the early drafts of the *Aenesidemus* review. This unpublished definition marks a curious juncture in the history of the *Darstellung* problematic: Fichte reintroduces Kant's notion of *Darstellung* into Reinhold's epistemology to counter Schulze's skepticism, only to abandon this definition almost immediately in favor of his model of the self-positing subject, yet Novalis revives Fichte's abandoned definition in his Romantic redaction of transcendental idealism. Our first task, then, is to examine Fichte's *Own Meditations on Elementary Philosophy* in tandem with the various drafts of the *Aenesidemus* review to determine the circumstances of Fichte's brief attraction to the Kantian definition of *Darstellung* and then to consider what motivated the Romantics to resurrect Fichte's discarded definition.

The most basic charge in *Aenesidemus* that Fichte had to contest was Schulze's assertion that transcendental idealism inevitably spawns skepticism. Schulze, we recall, had substantiated this claim in large part based on his reading of the Elementary Philosophy. Although he agrees with Reinhold that philosophy must be based on a self-evident first principle that is grounded in representation (*Vorstellung*), Schulze objects to the fact that Reinhold's proposition of consciousness transcends the limits of subjective knowledge by positing a causal relationship between subjective representations and objective knowledge. Because no such relationship can be established between the thing-in-itself and subjective knowledge, Schulze argues, the Elementary Philosophy necessarily results in skepticism. In the *Aenesidemus* review Fichte concurs with Schulze on this point: even though both Kant and Reinhold retain the notion of objective knowledge in their philosophies, it is obvious to Fichte that the thing-in-itself must be abandoned if transcendental idealism is to avoid charges of skepticism. Reinhold's proposition of consciousness unwittingly requires recourse to objective knowledge and therefore clearly cannot be correct, Fichte asserts. Fichte thus sets out to formulate a new fundamental principle that describes a consciousness that is not derived from empirical knowledge, but is grounded internally in the subject.

The logical solution to this problem, Fichte suggests in his *Own Meditations on Elementary Philosophy*, is Kant's definition of mathematical construction or a priori representation (*Darstellung*).[29] Kant, as we saw in Chapter 1, had introduced this definition in a section of the *Critique of Pure Reason* specifically designed to refute charges of dogmatism, the "Transcendental Doctrine of Method." His philosophical method, Kant argues in this appendix, is patterned after mathematics, the one true a priori science: "Philosophical knowledge is the knowledge gained by reason from concepts; mathematical knowledge is the knowledge gained by reason from the construction of concepts. *To construct a concept means to represent a priori the intuition which corresponds to the concept*" (*einen Begriff konstruieren, heisst: die ihm korrespondierende Anschauung a priori darstellen*, B 741, emphasis mine). For example, Kant explains, we construct a triangle, either on a piece of paper or in our heads, by representing the object that corresponds to the concept, but in both cases without having borrowed the pattern from any experience. Kant explicitly states that only mathematics is capable of this a priori construction, since philosophical knowledge is necessarily grounded in experience.

Fichte was intrigued by this passage, and in some notes taken while reading the *Critique of Pure Reason* he cites Kant's definition of mathematical intuition, commenting: "A mathematical intuition can be given a priori; and is thus not much different from a simple pure concept.—On this I will build my idea of constructing principles of pure understanding through empirical experience."[30] With this plan to apply the concept of construction to empirical experience, Fichte, however, does not intend to fall back into the dogmatism that Kant had sought to avoid when he specifically excluded philosophy from the province of a priori mathematical construction. As Stolzenberg has argued, Fichte's concept of "empirical experience" does not correspond to Kant's here, but rather to a concept of "inner experience" that Fichte derives from Reinhold's notion of intellectual intuition. If he could use the Kantian notion of construction to demonstrate that there was an inner intuition that would explain and prove representation or self-consciousness a priori, Fichte thought, then Schulze's objections to the Elementary Philosophy would be refuted. After giving the matter extensive consideration, however, Fichte reluctantly concludes that Reinhold's theory of intellectual intuition is itself predicated on recursion: because Reinhold's concept of representation a priori requires recourse to experience, it merely describes a factual but not a necessary reality.[31] He therefore abandons the idea of applying the notion of mathematical construction to philosophy, commenting wryly that it would be bad if such a program were in fact practicable, because philosophy then would be transformed into mathematics,[32] a state of affairs that presumably would portend the demise of his own profession.

Adding to Fichte's considerations was Salomon Maimon's critique of transcendental idealism,[33] a critique Kant

himself had praised as profoundly penetrating and subtle.[34]
Fichte, too, lauds Maimon in the Preface to his contemporaneous *Concerning the Concept of the Doctrine of Knowledge* (1794): together with Schulze's *Aenesidemus*, Maimon's
excellent skeptical writings have provided the impetus for
the development of his own philosophy, Fichte maintains.[35]
Maimon had argued that Kant had created such an unbridge-
able gap between sensibility and understanding in his
epistemology that the fundamental question of the transcendental deduction in the *Critique of Pure Reason*, namely,
how synthetic a priori concepts apply to experience, is
unanswerable in Kantian terms.[36] In effect, Fichte had
attempted to answer this fundamental question by applying

the Kantian notion of construction to Reinhold's theory of
intellectual intuition, only to find that he, too, was caught
in a vicious circle: the only way he could prove consciousness a priori was by resorting to empirical knowledge. The
solution to the problem of the transcendental deduction,
Maimon had asserted, is to postulate the idea of an infinite
understanding that is present in our finite understanding
and that creates both the form and the content of experience.[37] Fichte clearly takes this argument to heart in his
revision of Reinhold's theory of consciousness: he decides
to devise a new model of the mind grounded in an infinite
understanding, the absolute subject or God, that creates or
posits the necessary reality of finite consciousness a priori,
and in this revised description of consciousness Fichte
replaces the Kantian notion of mathematical construction
with the more general Kantian notion of *Darstellung*.

Fichte's move from a description of the mind grounded
in Kant's notion of construction and Reinhold's notion of
a priori representation (*Vorstellung*) to a description of the
mind grounded in *Darstellung* is a move from a second-
order (derived) to a first-order (constitutive) description of
consciousness. Although Reinhold clearly thought his fundamental proposition of consciousness *was* constitutive, in
the *Aenesidemus* review Fichte demonstrates the second-
order nature of Reinhold's theory, arguing that Reinhold's
notion of *Vorstellung* is necessarily derived from a posteriori

knowledge: "If everything that is to be discovered in the mind is an act of representing (*Vorstellen*), and if every act of representing is undeniably an *empirical* determination of the mind, then the very act of representing, along with all of its conditions, is given to consciousness only through the representation of representing. It is thus *empirically* given, and empirical representations are the objects of all reflections concerning consciousness. . . . Consequently, the principle of consciousness, which is placed at the summit of all philosophy, is based upon empirical self-observation and certainly expresses an abstraction,"[38] as Schulze had correctly claimed.

Reinhold was led astray into thinking that *Vorstellung* is the most basic component of consciousness, Fichte continues in the *Aenesidemus* review, because he incorrectly assumed that the fundamental proposition must describe a *fact* (*Thatsache*) of consciousness. As the word *Sache* ("object" or "thing") indicates, Reinhold's notion of *Vorstellung* describes a mind in stasis, a receptive consciousness being acted upon by some outside force or object. But the fundamental proposition can also, Fichte asserts, describe an *act* (*Thathandlung*) of consciousness. This neologism, Fichte explains elsewhere, describes "an activity which presupposes no object, but itself produces it, and in which, accordingly, the *acting* (*Handlung*) immediately becomes the *deed* or *fact* (*That*)."[39] In the early drafts of the *Aenesidemus* review and in his *Own Meditations on Elementary Philosophy*, Fichte then proceeds to equate the *Thathandlung* or acting of the mind with the term *Darstellung*.

In short, Fichte effects a linguistic critique of Reinhold's notion of representation in order to revise Reinhold's fundamental proposition of consciousness: just as he had replaced the static word *Thatsache* with the active word *Thathandlung*, Fichte now replaces the static term **Vorstellung** with the active term **Darstellung** in his description of a priori consciousness.[40] In so doing, he invokes the Kantian meaning of *Darstellung* as a rendering present or actual to the mind in such a manner that the object or entity being presented

comes into its true being only in the process of being represented, or as Fichte puts it in his definiton of the synony-
mous word *Thathandlung*, "an activity which presupposes
no object, but itself produces it, and in which, accordingly,
the *acting* (*Handlung*) immediately becomes the *deed* or
fact (*That*)." The object that this representing activity produces in Fichte's theory is nothing less than self-consciousness: "The subject is active; it is independent: it
therefore has power [*Kraft*].—The subject is (for itself) by
virtue of its being:—This happens through a being active,
this being active is the source of being, and is also its effect;
this activity is called (*Darstellen*) positing itself as self in
existence; and the power, *Darstellungskraft* [the power or
force of representation]."[41] Fichte is quite consciously working with the Kantian definition of *Darstellung* here, and he
goes on to state that the subject's self-positing is realized
through the schematism.[42] With this said, we are now in
a position to see how Fichte uses the Kantian notion of
Darstellung to revise Reinhold's theory of consciousness.
Whereas Reinhold's fundamental proposition describes a
passive consciousness that constructs representations (*Vorstellungen*) a posteriori, Fichte's fundamental proposition
posits an acting consciousness that creates itself schema-
tically as its own object a priori. Consciousness is no longer
described in *terms of* representation, as it was in Reinhold's
theory. For Fichte the subject *is Darstellung*, and *Darstellung*
is the fundamental principle of all philosophy.

In the final prepublication draft of the *Aenesidemus*
review and in the published version of the text, Fichte takes
his linguistic critique one step further and replaces the term
Darstellung with the word *Setzen* or positing: he translates
his model of the self-presenting or the self-representing subject into the now more familiar form of the self-positing
subject, a form he would retain and revise in the various
versions of the *Doctrine of Knowledge*. Before examining
the probable motivation behind this final transformation,
however, we must first examine Fichte's definition of the
subject as *Darstellung* in more detail.

According to Fichte's reading of the Elementary Philosophy, empirical knowledge determines both consciousness and representation (*Vorstellung*), but this schema leaves Reinhold's epistemology vulnerable to Schulze's charges of skepticism. To counter this claim, Fichte sets up a new model of the mind, arguing that the a priori "I" must be the fundamental proposition of all philosophy. The subject must be *self*-determining in its inception: the I must determine itself a priori *as* an empirical subject. Because the empirical subject as intelligence is also determined by objective knowledge that produces both representations (*Vorstellungen*) and consciousness in the empirical subject, it is quite distinct from the originating a priori subject I and is also to some extent unknowable to the I. Because the empirical subject is both determined by and to some extent unknowable to the a priori subject I, the a priori subject I posits the empirical subject as a "Not-I."

To summarize, Fichte defines *Darstellung* as the a priori activity of consciousness that consists in representing the empirical subject as *Vorstellung*: "positing of the I is called *Darstellung*: positing of the Not-I as real,—*Vorstellung*.—Everything which enters into empirical consciousness is *Vorstellung*; *Darstellung* never enters into empirical consciousness; but it alone constitutes pure consciousness." Fichte then goes on to describe *Vorstellung* as a limitation of *Darstellungskraft* (the representational force); however, he explicitly states it is not a type of *Darstellung* but rather its exact opposite or complement (*Gegentheil*).[43]

Now if the I (*das darstellende Ich*) and the Not-I (*das vorstellende Ich*) are not two but are one and the same substance, Fichte continues, then this is conceivable only as a relationship of striving (*Streben*) between the I and the Not-I: the I (*das darstellende Ich*) must strive to make the Not-I conform to itself, and it must also strive to realize all the conditions under which such a concordance is made possible. And this, Fichte concludes, is what the expression *reason is practical* means:[44] reason is not practical in either the pure I or in the empirical I, but only in its attempt to unify the two through striving.[45] The subject posits itself as a being that, through its very self-determination, determines all that is not itself. This is tantamount to saying that it determines itself as God, Fichte claims: more precisely, the subject posits itself as an autonomous moral being striving to become God. Although this goal is unrealizable for the empirical subject, belief in this goal will be perpetuated in eternity through the striving of the pure subject to become the absolute subject, God, who is the only subject who can say: *I am.* With this argument Fichte has incorporated Kant's three "leading ideas," God, freedom, and immortality, into his model of the self-positing subject and is therefore in a position to assert that his epistemological model is in complete accordance with Kant's moral theology, even if Kant himself did not express it in these terms. Hence, Fichte concludes, he has clearly refuted Schulze's misguided claim that theoretical reason has priority over practical reason: the resolute Kantian Fichte's self-positing subject is clearly grounded in practical reason.[46]

Fichte's *Practical Philosophy* and Beyond: The Aesthetic Transformation

Fichte's *Aenesidemus* review does much more than merely revise Reinhold's proposition of consciousness and refute Schulze's skepticism: Fichte's ethically grounded model of the self-positing subject provides a solution to one of the fundamental aporiae in Kant's transcendental enterprise, the fact that the subject can represent itself to itself only as it appears, as a sensible subject, and not as it really is, as a moral subject of reason. As we saw in Chapter 1, Kant offers provisional solutions to this problem in the *Critique of Judgment* in the form of the indirect *Darstellung* of the beautiful as a symbol of the moral good and, more compellingly, in the paradoxical figure of the *negative Darstellung* of the sublime. In the sublime judgment, we recall, the mind is unable to process the sensory information it receives from the body, and the imagination races to infinity. The subject feels threatened by this breakdown of its ability to present (*Darstellungsvermögen*), and is afraid.

Reason, however, then imposes a claim to totality on the imagination and compels it to create a *negative Darstellung* that awakens "the feeling of a supersensible faculty in us," "the idea of humanity in our subject" (B 97). *Negative Darstellung* forces the subject to think of itself as a moral subject of reason, without producing an objective representation of this idea, and hence represents nothing but the striving (*Bestrebung*) of *Darstellung* itself (B 115–116). Fichte, of course, had read Kant's third *Critique*, and although there is no overt indication in his own writings that he accorded Kant's notion of *negative Darstellung* any attention whatsoever, his *Practical Philosophy* suggests that he, too, realized the representational potential of the sublime for his own model of the self-positing subject, and his tentative explorations of aesthetic theory in this fragmentary accompaniment to his *Own Meditations on Elementary Philosophy* contain many parallels to Kant's argumentation in the third *Critique*.

The primary focus of the *Practical Philosophy* is the empirical subject as striving (*Streben*), that is, the process by which the empirical subject tries to become the absolute subject, and a large portion of the manuscript is devoted to an examination of aesthetic strategies for effecting this transformation. Fichte provisionally defines striving as the relationship of subject to object as source to effect, which, however, is not recognized as source to effect. Striving cannot be defined positively but only negatively, through contradiction, and hence cannot be thought but only felt (183).[47] As a logical figure Fichte's negative definition of striving has a profound affinity to Kant's self-referential notion of *negative Darstellung*. In Kant's theory the empirical subject becomes a moral subject through negative presentation, but negative presentation represents nothing but the process (*Bestrebung*) of *Darstellung* itself. For Fichte the subject *is* striving, and in his aesthetics striving is self-referential, as it is in Kant's theory: it strives to represent itself or at least to be represented (206). Because everything that enters into empirical consciousness is *Vorstellung*, the exact opposite or complement (*Gegentheil*) of *Darstellung*, which can never enter into empirical consciousness (89–90), the striving of Fichte's empirical subject is, to coin a word, a Not-*Darstellung*, in effect equivalent to Kant's *negative Darstellung*.

The Fichtean empirical subject strives to become a pure subject by representing *Darstellung* (*durch Vorstellung der Darstellung*, 171), a feat that in itself cannot be achieved empirically but perhaps, Fichte postulates in the *Practical Philosophy*, aesthetically, through illusion. Like Kant, Fichte at first emphasizes the beautiful as a means for bringing about this transformation: the ultimate and unattainable aesthetic goal of striving is to realize the beautiful in its original form (*das Urschöne*, 207). Fichte, however, then goes on to assert that all definitions in Practical Philosophy are relative (213), and he toys with the idea of setting up a typology of the beautiful, the sublime, and a form that would combine both the beautiful and the sublime, the "mixed" form (219). He then attempts a perfunctory classification of the various art forms (e.g., music, painting, dance, landscaping, and pantomime) according to this typology, but devotes most of his attention to poetry (*Dichtkunst*). Completely in line with the eighteenth-century aesthetic theories of *Darstellung* discussed in Chapter 1, Fichte argues that the goal of true poetry is the deception of the senses, a goal best realized in lyric poetry (223). Moreover, citing Kant's denigration of the art of rhetoric, Fichte states that rhetoric is in fact almost more valuable than poetry in this regard, because it deceives "with visible eyes" (*weil sie mit sichtbaren Augen täuscht*, 222). Aesthetic deception is important to Fichte for precisely the same reason that it is for Kant: the goal of aesthetics is to effect the transformation of the sensible subject to the absolute subject, a goal that can be achieved only by dulling or deceiving the senses.

In Kant's theory this deception is epitomized in the "certain subreption" that the *negative Darstellung* of the sublime effects (B 97), and like Kant's, Fichte's theory culminates in an implicit valorization of the sublime: in perceiving the sublime the human being does not feel limited by either time or space and is hence, in a certain sense, an absolute subject or God (230). Unlike Kant, Fichte, however, does not try to exclude the sublime from his aesthetic theory: he recognizes the existence of sublime poetry (232), he accords the sublime the same status as the ideal beautiful form (*das Urschöne*) in the realization of the absolute subject (238), and he later argues that the sublime actually provides the most effective strategy for realizing the idea as a totality (246). Fichte's *Practical Philosophy* hence constitutes a significant reversal in the status of the sublime in Kantian aesthetic theory.

Fichte, however, never completed the manuscript of the *Practical Philosophy*, and the aesthetic theory that he outlines in it is rudimentary at best. The fact that he did not include this aesthetic component in the 1794 *Doctrine of Knowledge* suggests that he either was unable to formulate an aesthetic theory that was in accordance with the rest of his theory or he had decided that aesthetic theory was of limited value to his overall project. The latter conclusion is clearly untenable, because Fichte did actually sketch out a new aesthetic theory in *On the Spirit and Letter of Philosophy in a Series of Letters*,[48] a fragmentary essay he submitted to Schiller's journal *Die Horen* in 1795. Schiller, correctly interpreting the contribution as a critique of his own *Aesthetic Letters* and further miffed by Fichte's implied contention that Goethe was a better poet than he was, refused to print the essay, a circumstance that may explain Fichte's resultant lack of interest in aesthetic theory at the time. Fichte was extremely offended by this sleight, and eventually published the first three letters of the unfinished essay in his own journal in 1800.

Contrary to its misleading title, the primary emphasis of this ill-fated essay is the role of art and the artist in society; and Fichte begins the essay's second letter, which forms the theoretical core of his argument, by outlining a communicative model of art. For all the self-positing subjects in a society to coexist and to communicate, Fichte asserts, they must share certain points of union (*Vereinigungspunkte*), and the artist, who willingly sacrifices his or her own individuality for the good of the community, is instrumental in uncovering these shared points and in creating new ones through artistic representation (*Darstellung*). This communicative theory of art as bringing together isolated individuals in a society anticipates the Jena Romantic program laid out in the opening sentences of Friedrich Schlegel's *Conversation on Poesy* (1800).[49]

But the artist, Fichte continues, has to conform to and build on the individual subject's self-activity or *Selbstthätigkeit*, and he then sketches out a model of the mind that illustrates the efficacy of art for the subject's self-determination. Fichte characterizes the representing empirical subject in terms of three interrelated drives (*Triebe*) that are all manifestations of the one basic drive that defines the human subject as a representing being (*ein vorstellendes Wesen*): the cognitive drive, whose goal is knowledge (*Erkenntnis*); the practical drive, which aims at defining, changing, and developing objects to bring them into conformity with the empirical subject; and the aesthetic drive, which is completely divorced from objective knowledge and strives to represent representation (*Vorstellung*) for its own sake. The aesthetic drive is solely a mental activity that produces an image (*Bild*) in the soul; any physical realization of this aesthetic representation, say, through art, falls within the province of the practical drive. The goal of the aesthetic drive is to transcend the limits of reality and ultimately to allow the empirical subject to define itself as an autonomous being. The empirical subject must be educated, however, before it is able to make this transition, and art plays an essential role in this pedagogical process: it creates a representation (*Darstellung*) of the aesthetic image in the real world; and this illusion helps the practical subject cultivate its aesthetic sense, which in turn helps it to refine its cognitive drive and eventually allows the subject to define itself spiritually as a free being. *Darstellung* has thus clearly assumed a new meaning in Fichte's terminology: it no longer refers to the a priori self-positing of the I, but to artistic presentation or representation.

It is now time for us to return to Fichte's earlier writings to examine the motivation behind this linguistic transformation. In his *Own Meditations on Elementary Philosophy, Practical Philosophy*, and the early drafts of the *Aenesidemus* review, Fichte defines the activity (*Thathandlung*) that constitutes the fundamental proposition of consciousness as *Darstellung*. In the final prepublication draft and the printed version of the *Aenesidemus* review Fichte then drops the term from his definition: where the a priori subject had previously presented itself or represented itself (*sich darstellen*), it henceforth posits itself (*sich setzen*) in Fichte's ego philosophy. Fichte offers no reason for this terminological modification, but his *Own Meditations on Elementary Philosophy* does suggest a probable explanation. Right after he introduces his definition of *Darstellung* as the subject positing itself as self in being, Fichte asks, "Couldn't that be made more clear? . . . . that's called *Darstellung*[.] I want another word: *Darsetzung*—it should be contained in the *Dar*: it is." In a note written under the main body of the text Fichte then comments that he should use the word *Darlegung* to describe this activity, because"—the analyzing [*zergliedernde*] philosopher *legt dar* [expounds]: the poet painter sculptor *stellt dar* (the products of his fantasy, his creations.—)."[50] It seems that in Fichte's mind *Darstellung* was inextricably associated with artistic activity. To avoid undo confusion and, perhaps, to enforce a strict separation between philosophical and aesthetic discourse, he therefore dropped the term from the final versions of the *Aenesidemus* review and the 1794 *Doctrine of Knowledge*.

Fichte, however, would soon regret the loss of the representational component of his model of the self-positing subject, and in his later philosophy he not only reintroduces the notion of representation into his definition, he actually invests it with an increasingly poetic dimension. Dieter Henrich has outlined three stages in the development of this definition in the various versions of the *Doctrine of Knowledge*. In the 1794 *Doctrine of Knowledge* Fichte expresses self-consciousness with the formula: "The I posits itself." In the 1798 *Doctrine of Knowledge* Fichte revises this formulation: "The I posits itself as self-positing," where the *as* indicates representation. In 1801 Fichte, frustrated by the

linguistic limitations of his philosophical rhetoric,[51] aug-
ments this representational component with a visual metaphor that he first entertained in 1798 and that harks back
to the rhetorical tradition of *Darstellung* as a "placing before
the eyes": self-consciousness is now defined as "an activity
in which an eye is inserted." This visual definition of the
subject fascinated Fichte; and he expanded this ocular
imagery in his later philosophy, a philosophy he eventually
expressed in poetic form in three sonnets dating from
1805,[52] which arguably constitute the most complete formulation of his philosophy.[53]

The first of these sonnets describes a despondent
narrator who has lost his divine inspiration. In the second
sonnet Fichte describes overcoming this desperation and
the source of his present spiritual calmness and philosophical inspiration: hopelessly lost in the confused web of
time and space he looked into the eye of Urania, the muse
of astronomy:

> Since then this eye rests in my depths
> and *is* my being—the eternal One
> *lives* in my life, *sees* in my seeing.[54]

In the third sonnet, Fichte then reports that God is "nothing,"
and the only thing separating him from God is the veil that
is man. With this metaphorical definition of the empirical
subject becoming one with God via an unveiling, Fichte's
sonnet constitutes a poetic instantiation of the *negative
Darstellung* of the Kantian sublime, and the veil imagery
used to express this negative definition of the Fichtean
subject obliquely invokes the figure that Kant had identified
as the epitome of the sublime in the third *Critique*, the
injunction against lifting the veil of the goddess Isis at Saïs.

With this poetic transformation Fichte in a certain
sense returns to his early *Practical Philosophy*, the aesthetic
theory of the striving empirical subject, which he did not
and perhaps could not complete, at least not without trans-
cending the limits of transcendental idealism, as his sonnet
clearly does. Like Kant, Fichte comes to recognize the limita-

tions of this philosophical discourse; and at the limits of his own theory, he, too, concludes that transcendental idealism resolves in poetry, thereby tacitly confirming his contemporaries' negative and positive assessments of this brand of philosophy as "poetic abstraction" (Herder), "an artwork of the philosophical spirit" (Schulze), the first true "philosophical art chaos" (Friedrich Schlegel), "a poetic instrument" (Novalis). Fichte, like Kant, decides to refine his transcendental theory of representation using visual and poetic metaphors, but he departs from Kant in his implementation of this theory. Whereas Kant represses the visual and poetic dimensions of *Darstellung* in his *Critiques*, in his later years Fichte actively pursues both of these aspects, but not before the Romantics pave the way for him: Fichte's definition of the self-positing subject as *Darstellung* forms the starting point of the transcendental theory of poesy that Novalis outlines in his *Fichte-Studies* of 1795, a theory that anticipates Fichte's visual definition of the subject through poetry by approximately ten years.

3

Novalis: The Jena Romantic Poetization of *Darstellung*

Chapters 1 and 2 argued that Kant's and Fichte's elaborations of the *Darstellung* problematic inevitably lead to an admission of the poetic into philosophical discourse and that the Jena Romantics recognized and actively promoted this literary transformation. As Novalis puts it, "Critical Idealism—is already poetic or moral criticism" (III: 419, #778),[1] and in his famous Romantic dictum Friedrich Schlegel emphasizes the centrality of the notion of *Darstellung* to this critical idealist poetics: "transcendental poesy must represent itself in each of its representations" (*die Transcendentalpoesie muss in jeder ihrer Darstellungen sich selbst mit darstellen*, KA II: 204, #238). Both Schlegel and Novalis credit Kant, rather than Fichte, with instigating this poetic revolution in philosophy, and the present chapter will demonstrate that the Fichtean framework that structures the Jena Romantic poetization of the notion of *Darstellung* is ultimately informed by Kant's critical philosophy, a derivation obliquely acknowledged by Novalis himself: "Kant founded the possibility, Reinhold the reality, and Fichte the necessity of philosophy" (II: 143, #69). Although the Jena Romantics make no explicit mention of Kant's discussions of *Darstellung* per se,[2] the "sensible-spiritual representation" that defines their own poetic program can be understood as the logical successor of Kant's critical and rhetorical definitions of *Darstellung*. Indeed, as Menninghaus has pointed out, Schlegel's characterization of the poetic work as a "constant battle to represent the unrepresentable" (KA XVI: 241, #115) would be unthinkable without Kant's third

77

Critique.[3] Although Schlegel and Novalis both devote considerable attention to the *Darstellung* complex, the poetization of the Kantian definition is more pronounced in Novalis's philosophical fragments and literary writings than in Schlegel's, and the following analysis will explore the evolution of the notion of *Darstellung* in Novalis's oeuvre. In particular, I will argue that in his theoretical writings Novalis revises Fichte's abandoned definition of the subject as *Darstellung* using visual metaphors to redress shortcomings in transcendental theories of reflection, and in so doing he develops a theory of *Darstellung* as visual *poiesis*. When Novalis translates this theory into literary form, the resultant poesy incorporates an implicit instantiation of the *negative Darstellung* of the Kantian sublime.

Simply stated, Novalis's theory of *Darstellung* extends transcendental idealism into the poetic. According to Novalis, the real achievement of Kant and Fichte is methodological, a regularization of genius (III: 445, #921). Nonetheless, he adds a few fragments later, their philosophical presentation or *Darstellung* is deficient in that it is not malleable enough: "Fichte's and Kant's method is still not represented (*dargestellt*) completely and exactly enough. Both still don't know how to experiment with ease and diversity—not at all *poetic*—Everything is still so stiff, so timid. . . .One has to be able to present truth everywhere—to *represent* (*repraesentieren*) it (in the active, productive sense)" (III: 445, #924, emphasis on *experiment* mine). By extrapolation, Novalis's theory of *Darstellung* might be described as a poeticizing of Kant's and Fichte's methodologies. For Novalis, however, the "poetic" is a broad category encompassing literature, philosophy, mathematics, music, religion, and politics; and the key term that describes his own methodology here is the word *experimentation*. When Novalis states, "One could think of a most instructive series of specific representations of the Fichtean and Kantian systems, e.g., poetic, chemical, mathematical, musical, etc." (III: 336, #464), he is, in a certain sense, describing his own poetic program. Novalis's writings are experiments in revising and representing some of the basic tenets of transcendental idealism in various semantic registers, in the "universal, encyclopaedic critique" that Kant had initiated (III: 336, #463), and Novalis explicitly assigns *Darstellung* transcendental status in this Kantian enterprise: "Representability or thinkability, is the criterion of possibility of all philosophy" (II: 217, #305). In accordance with his plans for this universal Kantian critique Novalis concludes that "The representer must want and be able to represent everything" (II: 422, #26).

The word *Darstellung* occurs frequently in a wide variety of Novalis's writings, ranging from the cryptic statement in a pseudo-philosophical context in a letter to his brother Erasmus in 1793 that "No person gives more than he knows and than he can represent" (IV: 117), to the various fragment collections and literary texts, as well as to the political tract *Belief and Love*, which "is based on Representative Belief" (*beruht auf Repraesentativen Glauben*, III: 421, #782). Although Novalis does occasionally introduce synonyms like *Repraesentation* for the word *Darstellung* (see, for example, III: 246, #49), the latter designation is by far the most common in his philosophical fragments, suggesting its programmatic significance for his nascent Romantic theory. The following sections will examine the inception of the term *Darstellung* in Novalis's philosophical system in the *Fichte-Studies*; its evolution as a literary notion in *Klingsohr's Tale*, which, together with surrounding passages from the fragmentary novel *Heinrich von Ofterdingen*, form a discourse on *Darstellung*; and finally the application of *Darstellung* as "practical philosophy" (III: 666, #605) in the *Hymns to the Night*, "the highest, truest prose, the lyric poem" (II: 536, #51). My choice of texts is motivated by a logical development in the status of the notion of *Darstellung* in Novalis's philosophical and literary texts, and there is a slight chronological inaccuracy in my treatment of *Heinrich von Ofterdingen* as a precursor to the *Hymns*: Novalis worked on the two texts simultaneously in 1799–1800, but completed the *Hymns* first, and then continued, but never finished, writing the novel. My misordering of the two texts is, in a very real sense, negligible, in that the various writings under consideration in this chapter all were produced during the short time span of the six years between 1795 and 1801; and since Novalis never completed most of them, it is difficult to talk about a strictly chronological development within his oeuvre.

The *Fichte-Studies*: The Necessary Deception of *Darstellung*

It is common knowledge that the philosophical framework that informs Novalis's poetics is attributable much more to Fichte than to Kant. Statements like "Wonderful artworks can originate here—once one begins to Fichticize artistically" (II: 524, #11) or "I = Not-I—highest principle of all philosophy and art" (II: 542, #83) are quoted so frequently that they have become hackneyed. Nonetheless, Fichte's influence on Novalis's poetics is incontestible, and it is from the "producing viewer, visual creator" Fichte (II: 646, #469) that Novalis derives his theory of *Darstellung*, a theory, I will argue, of visual *poiesis* (as the Romantics were well aware, the Greek word *poiesis*, from which the German *Poesie* and the English *poesy* are derived, means "to produce or create"). Novalis's *Fichte-Studies* of 1795–96 document the development of this theory of visual *poiesis* from Fichte's early definition of the subject as *Darstellung*, a definition that Fichte probably discarded and Novalis probably revived precisely because of its poetic overtones.

The primacy of the notion of *Darstellung* to Novalis's philosophy is indicated by his introduction of the term in the first fragment of the *Fichte-Studies*, in an analysis of the Fichtean First Principle, "A = A": "In the sentence a is a there is nothing but a positing, differentiation, and conjoining. It is a philosophical parallelism. In order to make a more clear A is divided. *Is* is formulated as general content, *a* as specific form. The essence of identity can be formulated only in an apparent sentence (*Scheinsatz*). We leave the identical in order to *represent* it (*Wir verlassen das Identische um es **darzustellen**)*" (II: 104, #1, emphasis on *darstellen* mine). Novalis's use of the word *darstellen* here is noteworthy, because the term does not appear in this context in the 1794 version of the *Doctrine of Knowledge*, the text, it is commonly thought, that forms the basis of the *Fichte-Studies*.[4] Nonetheless, Novalis's seemingly unmotivated introduction of the notion of *Darstellung* is a direct adoption of Fichte's own terminology. As we saw in Chapter 2, Fichte formulates the self-positing of the pure Ego in terms of the Kantian notion of *Darstellung* in his *Own Meditations on Elementary Philosophy*, which although unpublished at the time, dates from 1793–94: "The subject is (for itself) by virtue of its being: it is itself source and effect of its being: This happens by means of a being active, this being active is the source of *being*, of which it is also effect; this action is called (representing [*Darstellen*]) positing itself as self in being; and the force: the *representational force (Darstellungskraft)*" (GA II, 3: 89).

Novalis's statement "We leave the Identical in order to represent it" (*Wir verlassen das Identische um es darzustellen*) shows a clear affinity to Fichte's definition of *Darstellung* as the subject "positing itself as self in being" (*sich selbst als selbst im Daseyn setzen*). Although it is uncertain that Novalis read the text in question, he did in fact meet with Fichte and Hölderlin in May 1795 to discuss philosophy[5] and began writing the *Fichte-Studies* in the fall of the same year. Novalis's explication of this notion of representation suggests he was acquainted with another definition that Fichte introduces in this earlier text, the differentiation of *Darstellung* as the a priori positing of the I and *Vorstellung* as the a posteriori positing of the Not-I, as well as with Fichte's statement that *Darstellung* alone constitutes pure consciousness and cannot enter into empirical consciousness (GA II, 3: 89–90). Novalis concludes from this assertion that any attempt to represent pure consciousness empirically must be predicated on illusion, and hence expressed as an "apparent sentence" or *Scheinsatz*: "The essence of identity can be formulated only in an apparent sentence (*Scheinsatz*). We leave the *Identical* in order to represent it (*darstellen*)— Either this happens only apparently—and the imagination leads us to believe it—what *happens*, already Is—naturally through imaginary separation and bringing together—or we represent (*vorstellen*) it via its not-being, via a non-identical—sign" (II: 104, #1). No doubt Novalis's Fichtean differentiation of the terms *Darstellung* and *Vorstellung* in the subject's self-positing is more than a happy terminological coincidence, because he goes on to comment on two other facets of Fichte's definition, the description of the subject as an activity (*Thätigkeit*) and the notion of a representational force or *Darstellungskraft* (GA II, 3: 89–90): "Is there a special representational force—that represents only in order to represent—representing in order to represent is a *free* representing. This suggests only that not the object as such, but the *subject* as the source of the activity should determine the activity" (II: 282, #633). Thus, Novalis's use of the word *Darstellung* here can be read as strong evidence of a direct genealogy of the notion from Kant through Fichte to the Romantics. If nothing else, my interpretation offers a plausible explanation of *why* Novalis introduces the term *Darstellung* here in the first place, a question, it seems, that no one has bothered to ask, much less answer.[6]

The appearance of the word *Darstellung* in both Novalis's and Fichte's texts is all the more interesting in light of the fact that Novalis effects an incisive critique of Fichte based on this notion of representation, a critique that Manfred Frank has called the most significant philosophical contribution of the early Romantics.[7] According to Frank, Novalis recognizes that Fichte is caught up in a vicious circle in what is supposed to be the one incontrovertible principle that forms the basis of his entire philosophical system, the statement "I am I." Novalis argues that the fact of self-consciousness cannot be derived from the reflexive act of self-positing, because reflection, by definition a mirroring, always results in a reversal or inversion in representation: "The image is always the inverse of Being" (*Das Bild ist immer das Verkehrte vom Seyn*, II: 142, #63). If we reflect on this reflection—*ordo inversus*—we come to the conclusion that the pure, prereflexive self, which Novalis, following Fichte, calls a *feeling* (*Gefühl*), is not accessible to the empirical, reflecting, Ego (II: 115–116, #19). Novalis explains: "In this sphere deception of the imagination, or of reflection, is unavoidable—in the representation—since you are trying to represent nonreflection via reflection, and can hence never get to nonreflection using these means" (II: 122, #125). To derive the fact of self-consciousness, then, it is precisely the nonrepresentability of this pure Ego that must be represented. Novalis explains: "If the character of a given problem is unsolvability, then we solve it by representing its unsolvability" (III: 376, #612). Moreover, the representation of the nonrepresentability of the pure Ego has a regulatory function: it is a "necessary fiction" (II: 179, #179). Hence, Novalis concludes: "The highest principle must not be something given, but something made freely, something *poetically composed*, something *thought*, in order to establish a general metaphysical system that begins and ends with freedom" (II: 273, #568). In other words, poesy, which "represents the unrepresentable" (III: 685–686, #671; cf. Schlegel's formulation, KA XVI: 241, #115), is the highest principle of philosophy (II: 590, #280).[8]

In summary, proceeding from the Fichtean definition of the self-positing subject as *Darstellung*, Novalis uses the visual dimension of the notion of reflection to prove that any empirical representation of this self-representing subject must necessarily be illusory. To circumvent this necessary deception of *Darstellung*, he then develops a scheme for representing the unrepresentable, the pure Ego, via poesy. Thus, Novalis concludes, "Being a complete subject is an art" (II: 294, #659; cf. II: 559, #153), and the goal of his aesthetic program is the construction of a poetic system in and through which this complete subject can represent itself as *Darstellung*.

As the paradoxical phrase "representing the unrepresentable" (*Darstellung des Undarstellbaren*) indicates, Novalis departs from his philosophical mentor in his implementation of Fichtean ego philosophy. Whereas Fichte had dropped the term *Darstellung* from his definition of the self-positing subject and later used the word to refer only to artistic presentation or representation, Novalis retains both senses of *Darstellung* in his poetic program, and will actually equate the two in a Kantian move in his literary writings, using poetic *Darstellung* to prove that the empirical ego and the absolute Ego are One (II: 134, #45), that the unrepresentable pure Ego can indeed represent itself, albeit negatively, via poesy.

In the course of the *Fichte-Studies* and other philosophical fragments, Novalis then experiments with different strategies for effecting this aesthetic transformation. Given the rambling, disjointed nature of these fragments, it would be impossible to do justice to the intricacies and implications of the different aspects of his discussion in a short space, and I will present its more important features in outline form.

The first strategy for constructing a new philosophical-poetic system capable of representing the unrepresentable, the pure Ego, is to examine the limitations of conventional methods of representation in the two discourses; that is, to examine the limitations of language: "Critique of language—preparatory work for the Scientist of Knowledge" (III: 384, #635). After considering various aspects of language like signification, speaking, and writing (II: 108, #11), Novalis concludes that "Language is for philosophy what it is for music and painting, not the right representational medium" (III: 573, #124; cf. II: 672–673). Accordingly, he will develop a new kind of poetic-philosophical representation, one that I will characterize as a visual *poiesis*.

It is logical that Novalis would incorporate a visual dimension into this new theory to counteract the mirroring nature of reflection that is the source of illusion in the subject's self-representation. Hence, Novalis explores a variety of methods for creating a nonillusory visual-verbal representation throughout his writings. Novalis, who devotes his short literary career to honing his "talent to represent, to watch exactly" (II: 420, #22), concludes that the science he seeks "must be a representation of the fact that occurs in the quickest blink of the eye" (*Darstellung der allaugenblicklichsten Thatsache*, II: 228, #346).

A third area of investigation for this new theory of representation is the nature of illusion in the subject's self-representation or *Selbstdarstellung*, and Novalis's stance on this point is entirely in line with the Klopstockian tradition of *Darstellung*, which, as we saw in Chapter 1, is grounded in a programmatic deception or *Täuschung*. Novalis argues that the belief in true, complete representation (*Repraesentation*), in the identity of the image (*Bild*) and the original, is the source of all error and superstition in human knowledge (II: 397, #685). He therefore insists that illusion is an essential component of truth (III: 372, #601) and emphasizes the importance of representing it as such: "True representation (*Darstellung*) of error is an indirect representation (*Darstellung*) of truth" (III: 382, #633).

Novalis incorporates these three parameters, the critiques of language, vision, and illusion, into the cornerstone of his theory of *Darstellung*, the artistic construction of the subject. Implicitly invoking the Kantian rhetorical tradition of *Darstellung* as a "setting before the eyes," Novalis argues that the poetically created subject must include a visual dimension that is clearly rhetorical in nature: he speaks of the subject's "hieroglyphic" power (II: 107, #8),[9] its status as "metaphor" (II: 561, #174), and its definition as a "complete trope of the mind" (II: 564, #197). Novalis's rhetorical definition of the subject as *Darstellung* shares a further affinity with the Kantian notion of *Darstellung* as a rendering present or actual in such a manner that the object or entity being presented or represented (in this case, the "complete" subject) first comes into being in the process of representing.

The artistic construction of the "complete" subject must also contain a corrective for the necessary deception of *Darstellung*, and Novalis provisionally resolves this problem via the Fichtean notion of hovering or oscillating (*Schweben*): "All being, being in general is nothing but free being— *hovering* between extremes, which must be unified and separated. . . . Subjectivity or productive imagination, *hovering*—determines, produces the extremes between which the subject hovers—This is a deception, but only in the province of the common understanding. Otherwise it is something completely real, since hovering, its source, is the source, the mother of all reality, reality itself" (II: 266, #555). This Fichtean notion of hovering or oscilliating, which con-

tains an important emphasis on polar opposites or "extremes,"
will become constitutive for Novalis's literary works.[10]

Finally, Novalis's new theory of *Darstellung* incorporates
the Fichtean notions of the subject as an activity or striving
(II: 204, #303), as a reciprocal determination of feeling and
reflection and of *Darstellung* as "an expression of the inner
condition, of internal changes" (II: 283, #637). *Darstellung*,
however, is not to be construed as a passive expression of
an active subject. As an activity in its own right, it is "determined determiningly" (*bestimmt bestimmend*, II: 207,
#291), and there is a reciprocal determination or *Wechsel-
bestimmung* between it and the subject.

Novalis summarizes his Fichtean theory of *Darstellung*
in a long fragment located near the end of the *Fichte-Studies*,
which begins by emphasizing the efficacy of art in the subject's self-definition:

> We set this activity [the subject's self-positing] into
> motion by giving it stimulating material./ The subject
> must posit itself as representing./ The essence of
> representing is—what the coessence (*das Beywesent-
> liche*) of the object is/ Is there a special representing
> force that represents only in order to represent—repre-
> senting in order to represent is a *free* representing.
> Which is only to say that not the object as such, but
> the subject, as source of the activity, will determine the
> activity. By these means the artwork receives a free,
> independent, ideal character—an impressive spirit—
> because it is a *visible* product of a subject. (II: 282,
> #633).

Proceeding from the Fichtean definition of a self-representing,
self-positing subject, Novalis first characterizes *Darstellung*
as a reciprocal determination of subject and object and then
assigns art, a visible product of the subject, an essential role
in this process of self-definition. Two things are noteworthy
about his argument. The first is the primacy of art as a
visual entity to his definition of the subject as *Darstellung*.
The second is that Novalis is quite clearly working with a

two-tiered notion of *Darstellung*: the term refers simultaneously to the subject's self-representing and to the formal
representation of the philosophical-artistic system in and
through which the subject posits itself as *Darstellung*.

In the continuation of the same fragment Novalis then
implies that these two levels should be identical in a true
Darstellung. In a detailed and somewhat convoluted analysis that explicates this assertion, Novalis states that the
representing, infinite subject posits itself as a free, determined, representing subject and that the object, that is, the
artistic representation of the infinite subject produced by
the finite subject, can be only the core, the model, or the
ground through which the formative power develops the
beautiful whole creatively. "Expressed differently," Novalis
explains, "the object should determine us as a product of
the subject, not as a mere object" (II: 282, #633). Because
the object or artwork is a visual product of subject, and the
subject represents itself via this object, the subject represents itself as *Darstellung*, as a visual product or creation
of the subject: the subject represents itself in and as visual
poiesis.

Novalis's conjoining of the rhetorical and critical dimensions of his definitions of *Darstellung* is reminiscent of Kant,
and the Kantian derivation of his Fichtean theory becomes
even more pronounced in the final section of the fragment.
In a completed representation, Novalis argues, an exchange
of spheres (*Sfärenwechsel*) is necessary: "the sensible must
be represented spiritually and the spiritual must be represented sensibly" (II: 282, #633). In effect, the sensible-
spiritual representation that Novalis proposes here is a
solution to the three problems that plague Kant in his various discussions of *Darstellung*: how to mediate between
sensibility and understanding, how to transcend the limits
of sensibility to define the subject as it really is, and how
to unify the rhetorical and critical definitions of *Darstellung*.
Kant had solved these problems by introducing the paradoxical figure of *negative Darstellung* into the third *Critique*; and Novalis, following Kant, will eventually develop a
poesy of the sublime.

Novalis, however, must first figure out how to translate his theory of *Darstellung* into poetic form. He therefore concludes his fragment with a rudimentary outline detailing what the formal artistic construction of the subject would entail in practice, such as regular time intervals, verbal economy, and a compositional balance between parts and whole such that the parts express the whole and the whole expresses the parts. He also notes the differences between oral, written, and musical representation, all of which he will incorporate into his new theory of representation. Finally, Novalis asserts that "we are now only at the beginning of the art of writing" (II: 283, #633). This statement contains an implicit critique of writing in its status quo, a critique he will embody in the character of the Writer in *Klingsohr's Tale*.

Before turning to *Klingsohr's Tale*, I must first say a few words about the relationship between philosophy and literature in Novalis's poetic program. Whereas Kant had actively tried to suppress the poetic dimension of *Darstellung* in his philosophy and Fichte had abandoned his definition of the subject as *Darstellung* because of the artistic connotations of the word, in the course of the *Fichte-Studies* Novalis tries to prove that poesy is a natural outgrowth of the limitations of transcendental idealism. He identifies poesy as "the key to philosophy, its goal and its meaning" (II: 533, #31) and calls poesy the *hero* of philosophy (II: 533, #31): "Poesy is the hero of philosophy. Philosophy elevates poesy to the fundamental principle. It teaches us to know the value of poesy. Philosophy is the *theory of poesy*" (II: 590, #280). Novalis considers this resolution of philosophy in poesy to be paradigmatic for all scientific evolution: "Every science becomes poesy—after it has become philosophy" (III: 396, #684); "the philosopher becomes poet" (III: 406, #717).

Poesy, however, does not supplant philosophy in Novalis's aesthetic program: "Without philosophy the poet is incomplete—without philosophy an incomplete thinker-judger" (II: 531, #29). The two disciplines must determine each other reciprocally without losing their distinctive properties. Hence, in a short programmatic statement dubbed "The Poet's Realm," Novalis differentiates between the poetic and philosophical elements in poesy (III: 693, #705 and V: 9–10), and he defines *transcendental poesy* as a *mixture* of philosophy and poesy that contains the transcendental proper (II: 536, #47).

Finally, for Novalis the poetic is not an ethereal foil of reality, but "true, absolute reality itself. This is the core of my philosophy" (II: 647, #473; cf. III: 384, #634). Poesy must strive to create this "true, absolute reality" by making the abstract sensible and the sensible abstract (III: 299, #331). Novalis calls this "true" philosophy *realistic Idealism or Spinozism* (III: 671, #611). This equation is an important reminder not only of the enthusiastic revival of Spinoza in German critical discourse at the end of the eighteenth century, but also, perhaps, of the Dutch philosopher's profession as lensmaker: "The poet's realm should be the world forced into the focus of his time" (III: 692, #705 and V: 9).

Klingsohr's Tale: "Prophetic Representation"

In my reading of the *Fichte-Studies*, I argued that Novalis's theory of *Darstellung* is based on an analysis of the illusory mirror imaging of reflection in the Fichtean subject's self-positing or *Selbstdarstellung* and that his poetic program is defined by the search for an artistic construction of the pure Ego that would correct the shortcomings in this Idealist model of self-consciousness. I then used Novalis's critique of Fichte to derive several parameters that delimit his own theory of *Darstellung*: poetic representation must contain verbal, visual, and illusory components that are incorporated into the artistic construction of the subject, and vision in particular is essential to aesthetic self-definition. Furthermore, poetic representation is also defined by the Fichtean notions of the subject as an activity, a striving, and a hovering or oscillating between, as well as a reciprocal determination of, subject and object. Finally, this theory of representation is operative on two levels in Novalis's philosophical fragments. *Darstellung* refers to both the self-representing of the Fichtean subject and to the formal representation of the philosophical-poetic system in and through which the subject represents itself as *Darstellung*, and Novalis suggests that these two levels are identical in true artistic representation. When Novalis translates his theory of *Darstellung* into practice in his literary writings, he combines these various components into a theory of visual *poiesis*.

Novalis depicts the genesis of his theory of *Darstellung* in *Klingsohr's Tale*, the famous fairy tale from his fragmentary novel *Heinrich von Ofterdingen*. This is a logical text to analyze as an example of how Novalis expresses this theory in literary form, because he considers the fairy tale to be the quintessential unit of all poesy (III: 377, #620; cf. III: 449, #940), and he actually defines the genre in terms of *Darstellung*: "The *real fairy tale* must be simultaneously *Prophetic representation*—ideal representation—absolutely necessary representation. The real fairy tale writer is a seer of the future" (III: 281, #234). Given this programmatic statement, it is not surprising that Novalis explicitly casts *Klingsohr's Tale* and its accompanying texts as a discourse on *Darstellung*. In the chapter that introduces the fairy tale, Klingsohr discusses the limits of poetic representation. The fairy tale itself, structured around a central tension between the evil Writer and his archenemy, the child Fable—that is, between writing and the nascent fairy tale—effects the critique of traditional forms of writing that Novalis had identified as a necessary stage in the development of a new theory of *Darstellung*: "Writing . . . dealt with in writing yields the science of writing. . . . The Critique of Writing is preparatory for this science" (III: 283, #244). Finally, Astralis's song, which immediately follows the fairy tale and introduces the fragmentary second part of *Heinrich von Ofterdingen*, predicts an ideal future in which "Each thing represents itself in everything" (*Jedes in Allen dar sich stellt*, 319).[11] Thus, *Klingsohr's Tale*, together with these accompanying texts, (re)presents the development of Novalis's literary notion of *Darstellung*.[12]

Klingsohr's discussion of poesy in the chapter preceding the fairy tale contains important indications about what the construction of an ideal, all-encompassing poetic representation will entail. In response to Heinrich's query whether some objects are too effusive for poesy Klingsohr answers: "To be sure. Only in principle one can't say for poesy, but only for our earthly means and instruments. . . . there is a certain limit of representability beyond which representation cannot maintain the necessary conciseness and form, and loses itself in an empty, deceiving impossibility" (285). The poet is faced with certain representational restrictions, yet, exercising prudence, he can learn to expand his poetic instruments, and thereby extend the limits of *Darstellung.* Perfecting poetic representation is the goal of all art, though elsewhere Novalis is concerned that this poetic perfection could be boring (III: 435, #682). Hence, Klingsohr offers the following practical advice for achieving formal excellence and keeping the audience's rapt attention: chaos should undermine the superficial order of the poetic composition, and the representational techniques of music and painting should be blended in the poetic. Klingsohr will incorporate these various elements into his own fairy tale, a tale, he warns, that carries "clear traces" of the poetic immaturity of his youth (286–287).

Klingsohr's program for a poetic transcendence of the limits of representation shares an intellectual affinity with Kant's notion of *negative Darstellung,* and in the *Hymns to the Night* Novalis will actually develop a poesy of the sublime. In both texts, the artistic construction of the subject is at issue, and there is a logical maturation in the theory of *Darstellung* that will effect the transformation from empirical subject to pure subject: *Klingsohr's Tale,* introduced as an experiment in creating a new poetic representation, depicts the genesis of the lyrical, visual *poiesis* that will be realized in the *Hymns.*

In *Klingsohr's Tale* the development of this theory of *Darstellung* takes place in two stages, thereby fulfilling Novalis's requirement that the fairy tale be "simultaneously *Prophetic representation*—ideal representation—absolutely necessary representation" (III: 281, #234). In the first stage, the prelude in King Arctur's court (p. 290, line 24–p. 293, line 29), the fairy tale presents an ideal representation that has been fragmented both on the natural level, in a description of the cosmos, and on the character level, in the depiction of King Arctur. Arctur, traditionally identified as "the once and future king" or a Christ figure in mythology, has been separated from the wise Sophie and is introduced as a fragmented king: "alone I am not King" (308–309). This fragmentation sets into motion the "necessary representation" of the fairy tale: the prelude predicts the reconstruction of a new, unfragmented representation, and the main body of the fairy tale (p. 293, line 30–p. 315, line 24), the conflict between the Writer and Fable, functions as a redemption story, a binding together or etymological *religio* of old and new. My thesis is quite simple: the fairy tale (re)presents the genesis of a lyrical, visual *poiesis*, and at the risk of offering what at first glance seems to be little more than a plot summary, I will retell the tale, emphasizing those features which mark it as a theory of *Darstellung*.

In the first section of the fairy tale, the prelude in King Arctur's court, the fairy tale presents itself as representing, as *Selbstdarstellung*, and the representation that is developed in these opening paragraphs is clearly visual in nature. The tale begins with a long night falling over the monarch's dark, frozen realm. The old hero hits his shield three times, and the sound resonates in the desolate streets of the town. Then the windows of the palace slowly illuminate: "The whole region became visible now, and the reflection of the figures, the clashing of the spears, the swords, the shields, and the helmets, which bowed down to the crowns appearing here and there, and finally these disappeared and made room for a plain green wreath, and formed a wide circle around it: this was all mirrored in the motionless sea that surrounded the mountain on which the town stood, and the distant ring of mountains surrounding the sea was also covered halfway with a gentle reflection" (290–291). The reflection of the fighters and the turmoil of the war implements blend together in a chaotic acoustic-visual image, which is then mirrored in the sea and on the mountains. This unified picture, reflected in the circle imagery—the wreath, the circle, and the ring of mountains—illustrates Novalis's dictum that "The idea of a whole must rule and modify an aesthetic work through and through" (II: 277, #587). The amalgamation of sight, sound, and mirroring runs throughout the fairy tale in three semantic registers, and the prophetic representation of the fairy tale will be realized through the repetition and modification of these images.

The development of this theory of *Darstellung* is presented in condensed form when the same chaotic fusion of sight, sound, and mirroring is repeated in another description of the same area: "One couldn't distinguish anything clearly, but heard a wonderous din, as if from a distant vast workshop. In contrast, the town appeared bright and clear. Its smooth, transparent walls reflected the beautiful rays, and its beautiful orderliness came into sight" (291). As if to underline the importance of this specular "coming into sight," the mirror image is repeated yet a third time, this time in modified form: "The multiplicity and elegance of the figures and the vivacity of the lights and colors offered the most magnificent spectacle, whose splendor was completed by a tall frozen fountain in the middle of the garden" (291). In contrast to the first two descriptions of reflecting mirrors, the third mirror, formed by a frozen liquid geyser, does not *reflect*, but actually "completes" this most magnificent spectacle, a detail that is noteworthy in light of Novalis's discussion of the necessary deception of reflection in the *Fichte-Studies*. A liquid mirror that reflects truly will play an important role in the conclusion of the fairy tale, and the repeated descriptions of a coming into sight portend the development of this nondistorting visual *poiesis*.

The prelude continues with an extensive explication of this new sight. The old hero opens the gate with a soft "clang" (291), and holding his shield in front of his eyes, he approaches the king's daughter, Freya. He takes her hand, and "his armor rang . . . his eyes flashed" (291–292). Arctur comes in, interrupting this amorous optical interchange, and he and his daughter engage in a wondrous stellar constellation game that consists of selecting and arranging cards "on which stood holy, profound signs composed of nothing but constellations" (292). The goal of the game, in which the spectators participate "as if each had an invisible instrument in his hands" (293), is the chance construction of "a beautiful harmony of the signs and figures" (292), a formula for representation that, true to Klingsohr's description, is composed of chaos and order, tone and vision: the stars, accompanied by music produced by their own movements, form an ever-changing series of constellations "bound together by one simple theme" (293). The star game anticipates Astralis's song in which "each thing represents itself in everything"—Astralis's stellar name emphasizes this connection—and like her song, the star game is a form of prophetic representation: the king continues to play until he suddenly cries out joyfully, "All will be well" (293). He then orders the old hero, who "also had eagerly pursued his invisible business up until now" (293), to throw his sword into the world as a harbinger of peace, and the sword's trajectory describes a brilliant synthesis of vision and sound: "It flew like a comet through the air, and appeared to break up on the ring of mountains with a resounding sound, since it fell in a shower of sparks" (293). The glowing iron shards from the old hero's sword, described in the last sentence of the introductory section, fall into the world of the fairy tale, where they will initiate the construction of a visual *poiesis*. Thus, the "formed, regularly executed imagistic language" (III: 339, #469) of the prelude, the chaotic mixing of mirroring, sight, and sound, is transmitted to the main body of the text, where it will be incorporated into the theory of *Darstellung* developed in the conflict between the Writer and Fable.

The opposition between these two characters is set up in the opening paragraph of the second section (p. 293, line 30–p. 315, line 24). The child Eros lies slumbering in his cradle, while his nursemaid Ginnistan nurses his half-sister Fable. Ginnistan has spread her scarf over Eros's cradle so that the Writer's light will not bother him. The Writer writes assiduously, interrupting his work occasionally to throw a disgruntled look at the children. Their father comes in constantly to dictate to the Writer, whose writing is therefore in some sense predetermined. When the Writer has completed his transcription, he hands the written page to the noble, godlike Sophie, who dunks the paper in a baptismal gesture into a dark bowl filled with clear water. If some of the writing withstands this water test, a verification of true *Darstellung*, Sophie hands the sheet back to the Writer, who puts it into a large book. Frequently, however, all of the writing is erased in the bowl, and the Writer is annoyed because of his wasted efforts. Sophie also uses her water to illustrate the representational properties of the Writer and his adversaries: "From time to time the woman turned to Ginnistan and the children, dipped her finger into the bowl, and sprayed some drops on them. As soon as the drops touched the nursemaid, the child, or the cradle, they dissipated into a blue mist that formed a thousand strange images that gathered around them and changed continuously. But if one of the drops happened to hit the Writer, a multitude of numbers and geometric figures fell. He assiduously collected them on a thread, which he hung around his skinny neck as an adornment" (294). In other words, Fable and her family personify a representation composed of ever-changing visual images, whereas the Writer, frequently glossed as the "Petrifying and petrified understanding" that Novalis mentions in one of his letters,[13] incorporates a static, fetishized representation composed of numerals and geometric figures. Sophie's water test is an important indication that true representation is related to fluidity, and the water from her bowl will play an integral role in the development of the fairy tale's plot; that is, in the genesis of a new, visual *Darstellung*.

   The construction of this visual *poiesis* is set into motion when a fragment from the fairy tale's prelude is introduced into the household. The father comes in with an iron rod, a splinter from the old hero's sword, that he has found in the courtyard. The Writer attaches it to a thread, and the shard points to the north. Ginnistan then takes the rod into her hand, plays with it, and the fragmented iron changes into a snake that bites itself in the tail, forming a circle, a "prophetic representation" of the unity soon to be recreated. The Writer soon tires of looking, a detail that will prove significant in light of the visual thematics being developed in the text. He jots down his findings on a sheet of paper, but his writing does not survive Sophie's water test. Hence, there is a representational tension set up here between what might be called an abortive vision and the preemptive written word.

Meanwhile, Ginnistan continues to play with the snake, and when it accidentally touches his cradle, the baby Eros wakes up, grabs it, and drinking deeply from Sophie's water bowl, is spontaneously transformed into a young man. The members of the household react to this event in various ways. Eros's mother comes in and embraces him. His father, taking advantage of this opportunity, embraces Ginnistan, and the two retreat to the privacy of the chamber. Sophie leaves the room. The Writer also disappears, and in his absence Fable picks up his quill and begins to write. After a while everyone returns, and the Writer chases Fable away from his place. He hands Sophie the pages Fable has written, fully expecting them to be wiped clean in her bowl. When Sophie returns them to him completely intact, this produces an extreme animosity in the Writer, no doubt because his own writings apparently never have come through the test in pristine condition (294). Thus, Fable is established as the new, true representer of the household.

The Writer, however, does not relinquish his position without a fight. When Ginnistan and Eros depart on their quest to find the king, he begins to plot against Fable: "The Writer was happy that they were leaving, especially since Ginnistan gave him her diary, which detailed the household schedule; but Fable remained a thorn in his eye, and he would have liked nothing better for his peace and satisfaction than to count her amoung the departing travelers" (296). Although Ginnistan's detailed diary will allow him to take control of the household, the Writer will not regain his status as "representer": the diary, described as *aufge-*

zeichnet, that is, written in a figurative sign language, is another indication of his own inadequacy as a representer; and he frequently has to ask Ginnistan for help when he is writing (296). Moreover, his deficient *Darstellung* is once again linked to sight: Fable, a "thorn in his eye" (296), threatens his vision.

The fairy tale continues with a description of a new, visual representation. Ginnistan and Eros head to the Moon, Ginnistan's father, who allows her to put on a wonderful play for Eros. The spectacle, reminiscent of the constellation game of the introductory section, ends with a prophetic vision of the future: "The scenes changed continuously and finally flowed together into one grand, mysterious representation (*Vorstellung*)" (299), an ideal representation of the sensible *Darstellung* being constucted in the tale. This prophetic visual representation is then followed by an illustration of Novalis's theory that deception is an essential component in the genesis of true *Darstellung*. Ginnistan withholds Sophie's water from Eros, and without this test for true representation, Eros, "sweetly deluded" (300), is seduced by the nursemaid, who has taken on his mother's form.[14]

Meanwhile, back home, the Writer instigates a revolution. He and his followers take the mother and father prisoner, but much to his dismay, Fable escapes to the dark realm of the Fates, where she finds the three old sisters spinning. They give her thread and put her to work, expecting that she will make a mistake and the thread will strangle her. Fable, however, proves to be a talented spinner, and as she works, countless little lights appear, forming terrible creatures that terrify the Fates. The Writer comes to their rescue wielding a mandrake root, and after warding off the visual representation Fable has produced with her spinning, he tries to take revenge, but Fable, previously described as a "thorn in his eye," once again threatens his eyes: "If your beautiful head of hair and your clever eye are dear to you, then watch out: think of my nails, you don't have much more to lose" (304). This warning succeeds in thwarting the Writer, who then tries to retaliate by making her catch tarantulas for the Fates. His plan, however, backfires: when Fable gathers the spiders, the Writer and his cohorts are caught in their webs, and they begin to dance crazily. The text does not indicate that the spiders actually kill the Writer, and his fate remains unknown. Fable then skips off with her tarantulas to the Fates, who are also dancing crazily. Following a complicated scheme that she concocts, the spiders, who are now referred to as "cross spinners" (*Kreuzspinner*) rather than "tarantulas" (308), wrap the three sisters in their webs and consume them.

Fable then goes to Arctur and announces the imminent arrival of eternal peace, which is described, once again, as a spectacle: "The curtain will soon go up and the play will start" (310). This visual prophecy is then actualized. After using Sophie's water to resurrect Atlas, Fable returns home, where she finds Ginnistan watching over the sleeping father. Sophie praises Fable for her deeds, grants her immortality, and tells her to wake the father. Gold, one of Fable's companions, fills the vessel in which he lies with a glowing liquid metal. As Ginnistan leans over the father, her necklace touches the liquid, and she puts her hand over his heart: "He woke up and pulled his enchanted bride to his breast. The metal solidified and became a bright mirror. The father stood up, his eyes flashed, and as beautiful and distinguished as his form was, his whole body nonetheless appeared to be a fine, constantly moving fluid . . ." (311). This scene, a literary instantiation of Novalis's definition of the object as a "solidified liquid" (*ein Geronnenes*) and the subject as a "fluid" (*ein Flüssiges*, III: 441, #900), describes the construction of the subject in a liquid mirror. Given Novalis's previous preoccupation with the mirror imaging of reflection in the subject's self-positing, it should come as no surprise that this is not an ordinary mirror: "The happy couple approached Sophie, who spoke words of consecration over them and warned them to consult the mirror diligently; it always reflected everything in its true form, destroyed all illusions, and held the original image eternally" (311–312). The liquid mirror containing "the original image" (*das ursprüngliche Bild*) defeats the necessary deception of *Darstellung* that Novalis had identified in the *Fichte-Studies*: "The image is always the inverse of Being" (*Das Bild ist immer das Verkehrte vom Seyn*, II: 142, #63). It tests for true representation and, like the water that Sophie tests writing in, destroys all false images.

This new visual representation evolves organically from the previous verbal one, and fluidity plays an integral role in this development. In addition to testing for true representation, Sophie's water contributes to the narrative cohesion of the text, thereby ensuring that a true *Darstellung* will be constructed in the tale: Eros drinks Sophie's water after he has been transformed into a young man; Fabel uses it to revive Atlas; Ginnistan withholds it to seduce Eros; and the liquid miror in which the father is reborn will replace Sophie's water as the guarantor of true representation. Immediately following the creation of the nondistorting mirror, Sophie takes the ashes of the mother, who has been burned by the Writer, and dissolves them in the water. Each of the characters drinks from this mixture, literally incorporating the mother in a sacred rite of Communion. Sophie then pours the remaining water onto her altar, and the new representation, an etymological *religio*, a fluid binding together of old and new, is completed.

With this true representation a new social order is established. Ginnistan is paired with the father, Arctur and Sophie are reunited, and Eros and Freya are joined together and instated as king and queen. Sophie then tells Freya to throw her armband into the air as a symbol of fluid bonding between the new regents and their subjects: "The armband dissolved into air, and soon shining rings were seen around each head, and a glistening band stretched over the town and the sea and the earth, which celebrated an eternal festival of spring" (314). Thus, the circle imagery introduced at the beginning of the fairy tale returns at the end, signaling completion, and the fairy tale ends happily with yet another spectacle, a drama in the realm of the Fates. Fable, in true Fichtean terms, hovers (*schwebt*) over the scene, singing a heavenly song and spinning the future with a thread that appears to come from her breast. With this organic combination of vision, word, and music reminiscent of both Arctur's constellation game and the imagery of the opening paragraphs of the fairy tale, Fable takes her place as the representer of the future.

A simple comparison of the two types of *Darstellung* embodied in the figures of the Writer and Fable would seem to indicate that Fable's dynamic, prophetic, visual representation stands in opposition to the static, verbal representation of the Writer, whose dictated writings chronicle what has already been. However, it would be rash to deduce from the fairy tale's story line—Fable defeats the Writer—that the theory of *Darstellung* developed here is a polemic against the written word in favor of visual representation. The functional equivalence of the two tests for true representation, Sophie's water and the nondistorting liquid mirror, is strong evidence of the reciprocal determination of visual and verbal representation being worked out in the fairy tale. Fable is also a writer, and her writing comes through Sophie's water test intact, whereas the Writer has a problem with his eyes: he tires of watching; Fable is a thorn in his eye; and she threatens his eyes with her nails. Thus, we might reasonably expect that Novalis would explicate this visual-verbal relationship in more detail, and *Klingsohr's Tale*, which carries "clear traces" of the poet's youth (286–287), contains several indications that Novalis had not finished working out the theory of representation built into the text.

The first is a seemingly innocent bit of surplus information: Fable's spiders, first identified as "tarantulas" (304–308), are later called *cross spinners* (*Kreuzspinner,* 308), and this terminological twist is clearly significant in a text where spinning is equated with representing. Perhaps Novalis intended to develop the reciprocal relationship between the Writer and Fable as a "cross spinning," a conjoining of extremes: "Remarkable, that an absolute, wonderful *synthesis* is often the axis of the fairy tale—or its goal" (III: 455, #989).

The second indication that Novalis was not done working out his theory of representation is a textual lacuna. The Writer's fate remains unknown: he is left caught up in the spiders' webs. This narrative suspension is made all the more interesting by the fact that he is the only major character who does not undergo some kind of transformation: Arctur and Sophie are reunited; Eros, who changes from baby to youth to cupid to king, marries Freya, who becomes queen; the father, reborn in the liquid mirror, marries Ginnistan, who has changed shapes with the mother; the mother is burned and the other characters literally incorporate her by drinking her ashes dissolved in Sophie's water; and Fable is awarded immortality and takes her place among the stars. Not surprisingly, Novalis had a theory about this figural metamorphosis: "People change against extremes and are what they can be only with respect to their environment and in opposition to objects and opposing people— hence mutability of character and relative character in general" (II: 281, #626). Hence we might expect that the Writer, Fable's "opposing character," would also undergo some kind of transformation; and Novalis's notes for the novel indicate that he did have further plans for the Writer: "Understanding is hostile—he will be changed" (I: 338).

Novalis, however, had not yet figured out what to do with his scribe: "The Writer becomes and the Fates—? the latter caryatids on the throne" (I: 339). The identification of the Writer with "numerals and geometric figures" (294) suggests that Novalis might have developed the character along these lines, because, like Kant, he considered mathematics, simultaneously "real science" and "art" (III: 473–474, #1126), to be the purest form of representation: "The concept of mathematics is the concept of science in general. All sciences should therefore become mathematics. . . . Internal cohesion, the sympathy of the universe, is its basis. Numerals, like signs and words, are appearances, quintessential representations (*Repraesentationen katexoxin*). . . . Pure mathematics is religion" (III: 593–594, #241). In opposition to Kant, however, Novalis believes that language is also capable of pure representation; and he argues that words, like mathematical formulas, express nothing but their own "wonderful nature" (*Monolog*, II: 672). In fact, what intrigues Novalis about mathematics is not that it circumvents human language, but rather that it provides a paradigm for written representation: "Wonder of mathematics. It's a *written instrument*—capable of infinite perfection—A major proof of the sympathy and identity of nature and spirit. Weavers' looms in signs. Painted instruments" (III: 684, #659).

The Writer's connection to this "written instrument" capable of infinite perfection is the third indication that Novalis was not done working out the theory of representation incorporated in the fairy tale. The phrase *weavers' looms in signs* suggests that he might have intended to "spin out" this mathematical dimension, because he did have plans to put the Writer at a loom (I: 339). The result of this weaving, an etymological *texere*, would be the creation of a poeticized mathematics, a text in the true sense of the word: "All sorts of sciences poeticized in the competition, also mathematics" (I: 343). Hence, in a poem that was to be incorporated into the second part of the novel and that might be read as a statement of his own poetic program,[15] Novalis concludes:

> When numerals and figures
> Are no longer the key to all creatures
> When they thus sing or kiss,
> More than the profoundly educated know,
> When the world makes its way into free life,
> And we go back into the free world,
> When light and shadows then
> Unite again in true clarity,
> When in fairy tales and poems
> One recognizes the old true world stories,
> Then the whole inverted essence
> Will fly away in the face of One secret word. (I: 344–345)

The last two lines of this poem present a noteworthy parallel to the true mirror created at the end of *Klingsohr's Tale*. The mirror contains an eternal "original image" that counteracts the necessary deception of *Darstellung* Novalis had identified in the *Fichte-Studies* ("The image is always the inverse of Being," II: 142, #63). Here "one secret word" vanquishes "the whole inverted essence." Novalis, a firm believer in the power of the word, was still in search of a true, verbal representation.

Astralis's song, the final section of the discourse on *Darstellung* built into *Heinrich von Ofterdingen*, supports my thesis that the theory of representation constructed in *Klingsohr's Tale* is not complete: "And what one believed had already happened / One can see just now coming from afar" (319). Hence, *Klingsohr's Tale* is a fitting ending to the first part of the novel, *Expectation*, while Astralis's song introduces the novel's fragmentary second part, *Fulfillment*, in which "each thing represents itself in everything" (*jedes in Allen dar sich stellt*, 319).

With this formula for an all-encompassing representation, Astralis's stellar song, a (re)presentation of Arctur's prophetic constellation game, augurs the overcoming of the limits of poetic representation that Klingsohr had identified in the introduction to his fairy tale. Accordingly, it occupies an important position in the formal development of *Heinrich von Ofterdingen*: in addition to picking up the story line from the first part of the novel, the song reiterates themes that were developed in *Klingsohr's Tale* and hence introduces the novel's gradual transition into fairy tale that Novalis had planned (I: 357). Given that Novalis considered the novel's second part to be a "commentary" on the first that was "already much more poetic" (I: 358), it is noteworthy that Astralis's song reproduces the same thematics of representation developed in *Klingsohr's Tale*, while at the same time presenting a new formal medium, the lyric verse.

In her song Astralis, an embodiment of the poesy that Novalis had intended to have speak at the beginning and end of each chapter of the second part of the novel (I: 643), describes her genealogy; that is, the birth of poesy. Her life begins on a summer morning with the stirrings of first love, "the longing for intimate, complete mixing," and she first takes form as a "yearning," an "inner welling" (317). Her development from this liquid welling is spurred on by Heinrich and Mathilde's first kiss, and when they "join themselves in a single image (*Bild*)" Astralis is "newborn" (318).

The liquid birth of Astralis, poesy, from this imagistic picture reiterates the genesis of the fluid, visual-verbal representation depicted in *Klingsohr's Tale*; and Astralis's song, like the fairy tale, emphasizes the development of sight or "fantasy" (319), a word derived from the Greek *phainein*, "to make visible." As she describes her birth, Astralis tells her audience, "You don't know me and saw me develop" (317), and in the process of maturation she herself undergoes a coming into sight: "I was still blind, but bright stars waved / Through the wonderful distance of my essence" (318). The visual semantics are then carried over to the same reversal of light and dark that was introduced in the fairy tale. Just as Fable rejoices in the realm of the Fates that she is in a "new world" in which "light and shadow appeared to have switched their places" (301), Astralis, too, announces the coming of an inverted luminosity that requires the construction of an "inner eye" (319): "The new world closes in / And darkens the brightest sunshine" (318). In a formulation reminiscent of the representational tensions built into the fairy tale, Astralis states that this new inner vision is augured by "powerful words" in which "each thing will represent itself in everything" (*jedes in Allen dar sich stellt*, 318–319):

> Sadness and desire, death and life
> Are in utmost sympathy here—
> He who has surrendered to highest love,
> Will never recover from its wound.
> Painfully the band must tear
> That stretches around the inner eye,
> Just abandon the truest heart,
> Before it escapes the dreary world.
> The body is dissolved in tears,
> The world becomes a wide grave
> Into which, consumed by anxious yearning,
> The heart, as ashes, falls. (319)

With its emphasis on light and dark, love and death, dream and world, binding and fluidity, and vision and word, Astralis's lyric song is unmistakably an intertext of the *Hymns to the Night*, the fulfillment of the prophetic representation of the fairy tale.

Hymns to the Night:
"Representing the Unrepresentable"

In addition to bringing the visual *poiesis* introduced in *Klingsohr's Tale* to completion, the *Hymns to the Night* introduce the question of form or genre into Novalis's theory of *Darstellung*. It is no accident that the transition between the prose of *Klingsohr's Tale* and the lyric of Astralis's song is repeated in the structure of the *Hymns*, because Novalis considered the lyric poem to be the intermediate step in the evolution of philosophy, which he equates with "prose" (III: 302, #342), to poesy: "It would be an interesting question whether the lyric poem is really a *poem*, plus-poesy, or prose, minus-poesy? Just as the novel has always been considered prose, the lyric poem has always been considered poesy—both incorrectly. The highest, most real prose is the lyric poem. What we call prose has been formed by limiting the absolute extremes—it is only here for the time being and plays a subaltern, temporal role. A time will come when it no longer will exist. Then limitation will have become penetration. *A true life has been formed*, and through it prose and poesy are conjoined most intimately, and put into flux" (II: 536, #51, emphasis mine; see III: 302, #342 for a similar formulation that ends with the phrase *poesy of the night and twilight*, a clear reference to the *Hymns*). Hence, the *Hymns*' alternations between prose and lyric are not only a demonstration of their internal rhythm, as the editors of the critical edition have suggested (I: 119), but also an expression of Novalis's highest philosophical convictions. With the phrase *a true life has been formed* Novalis indicates that the result of this mixing of prose and poesy is the "true" artistic construction of the pure subject, a subject whose unrepresentability has defined his poetic project from the *Fichte-Studies* onward. In this final section I will demonstrate that the ultimate form that Novalis's theory of *Darstellung* takes is the theory of the Romantic lyric incorporated in the *Hymns to the Night*.

With this reading of the *Hymns* as a Romantic theory of the lyric, I depart from most traditional Novalis scholarship, which has interpreted the text autobiographically. Correctly asserting that the piece was written in response to the mystical vision Novalis experienced at his fiancée Sophie's grave, most critics to date cite evidence from his philosophical fragments to bolster their analyses of the *Hymns* as a statement of the poet's most profound religious convictions.[16] Although this line of interpretation is certainly valid and has produced invaluable insights into the structure and import of the various verses, I approach the text from a different angle and will argue that the theory of the lyric expressed in the *Hymns* is an instantiation of self-reflexive Romantic criticism.

I offer this reading both in support of and against Lacoue-Labarthe and Nancy, who first exclude Novalis from Jena Romanticism in *The Literary Absolute* (p. 6) and then maintain that the missing component of early Romanticism was the lyric. According to their account, Friedrich Schlegel was aware of, yet never overcame, this lyrical lacuna, and the "subjective effusions" of Novalis did nothing but damage the Jena Romantic reputation. Moreover, they suggest, Hölderlin wrote the pure poetry that the Romantics sought in vain (pp. 99–100). Although Novalis is given short shrift in their analysis, Lacoue-Labarthe and Nancy correctly challenge traditional interpretations of Jena Romanticism as propounding a unilateral theory of the novel, and in this sense I take their lead in interpreting the *Hymns to the Night* as a theory of the Romantic lyric.

I will use a twofold notion of the term *theory* in my reading of the *Hymns*. We recall that for the Jena Romantics all discourse is self-representation or *Selbstdarstellung*: "Transcendental poetry must represent itself in each of its representations" (KA II: 204, #238). Perhaps the most obvious examples of this self-reflexive representation are the theory of the fragment presented in the fragments of the *Athenäum* and Friedrich Schlegel's famous definition of the novel, *der Roman*, as a "romantic book" (KA II: 335). Accompanying this definition is the statement that a theory of the novel would itself have to be a novel (KA II: 337). Similarly, I would suggest, a Romantic theory of the lyric would have to take the form of the lyric, and I will be concerned here with examining the immanent poetics of the *Hymns* to derive this lyric theory.

The second sense in which I understand the term *theory* is also Romantic. For the Romantics the word *theory* incorporates its original meaning, a spiritual act of seeing: Friedrich Schlegel explicitly invokes this etymological definition in his "theory of the novel" (KA II: 337), and sight and religion are essential to Novalis's theory of the lyric. Given that these are, after all, *hymns*, songs of worship, the religious component should come as no surprise to us, although it apparently disturbed Schlegel, who objected to the religious overtones in the title, preferring instead to call the piece simply *To the Night* (I: 115). The religion that is expressed in the *Hymns*, however, is not merely one of mystical Christianity: it is an etymological *religio*, a "binding together" of self and God in the lyric. For Novalis, I will argue, the lyric (re)presents a construction of self, an *auto-poiesis*, and sight is instrumental in this self-definition.

If we look at the development of images and metaphorical language in the first hymn, we begin to see how this process of self-definition takes place. The hymn opens with an adulation of light expressed in metaphors of water. The light is described in terms of its "rays and *waves*," and it "*swims* dancing in its blue *flood*" (131). The light is then characterized by its infinite powers of binding together and fusing: "Like a king of earthly nature it. . .*conjoins and dissolves infinite alliances*" (131). The fact that the light not only conjoins but also dissolves these bindings is an indication that empirical light and vision are problematic, and in the course of the *Hymns* Novalis will develop a notion of a new kind of binding, a poetic vision that defines the subject.

This process of poetic self-definition begins in the second section of the first hymn, where the metaphors of water and binding are united in a single image of subjectivity: "I want to sink down into the dewdrops and mix myself with ashes" (*In Thautropfen will ich hinuntersinken und mit der Asche mich vermischen*, 131). Homophony and alliteration emphasize the forcefulness of this yearning for a fluid mixing of subject. The narrator then turns away from the light to its polar opposite, the night. This notion of polar opposition is reinforced by the images with which day and night are described. Just as light is compared to the "*king* of *earthly nature*" (131), the night is associated with a "*queen* of the world, the exalted herald of *holy worlds*" (133). In the heavenly realm of this world-queen the narrator encounters the "serious face" of his dead lover. This experience fosters the construction of a new type of subjectivity. The narrator describes his lover as "the sun of the night" (133), and the oxymoronic fusion of light and dark is the source of the new subjectivity: "you have made me human" (133), the narrator reports. A destruction of the body is involved in this definition of the subject: "let the fire of spirits consume my body so that I can mix myself more intimately with you in the air" (*zehre mit Geisterglut mein Leib, dass ich luftig mit dir inniger mich mische*, 133), a phrase reminiscent of the previous "I want to sink down into the dewdrops and mix myself with ashes" (*In Thautropfen will ich hinuntersinken und mit der Asche mich vermischen*, 131). The juxtaposition of dewdrops and fire in these two images is further illustration of the principle that defines Novalis's subject: it is a fluid fusion of fire and water, day and night, earth and heaven, king and queen, male and female. Thus, Novalis's definition of the subject involves a binding together, a *religio* of polar opposites.

It is quite clear from the third hymn that fluidity is essential to the notion of *religio* under consideration. The third hymn is a redaction of the first hymn's story of the definition of the subject, and as in the first hymn, this definition is expressed in metaphors of fluidity and binding. The hymn begins with the narrator in a state of emotional destitution: he is spilling bitter tears, and his hope, dissolved in pain, melts. Then a *Dämmerungsschauer* (135), simultaneously a twilight shower and a fluid "shudder," pushes the narrator over the border from light into night, and the bond of birth is torn. With this birth a bad kind of binding is overcome: the light's "fetters" are broken, and the narrator's spirit is *entbunden*, a word that means both to be released from bonds and to be born: "my freed, newborn spirit hovered over the region" (*über der Gegend* **schwebte** *mein* **entbundner, neugeborner** *Geist*, 135). The invocation of the term *Schweben*, hovering or oscillating, indicates the philosophical provenance of this model of subjectivity, and the newborn Fichtean spirit then enters into a new, true type of bond. The narrator once again sees his dead beloved. He grasps her hands, and their tears become an "unbreakable bond" (135). Thus, a fluid binding characterizes this *religio.*

Sight is also central to the *religio.* The first and the third hymns recount the story of the birth of the subject, and the narratives are the same in each case: the narrator sees his dead beloved's face, and this vision results in a new subjectivity. The fifth hymn tells the same story, this time in Christian terms. The birth of the new world, of Jesus, is announced by a face: "Among the people the new world appeared with a face never seen before—In the poverty of a poetic hut—A son of the first Virgin and Mother" (145). The birth of this divine subject brings with it a new kind of vision: the world appears "with a face never seen before." In fact, each of the narratives in the first, third, and fifth hymns tells the story of an increased vision. In the first hymn the sight of the face opens up "infinite eyes" in the subject (133); in the third, the subject sees eternity resting in the eyes of his lover (135); and in the fifth, Jesus turns his prophetic eye to the future (147).

This notion of a higher vision is essential to the poetics of the *Hymns.* The *Hymns* revolve around a productive tension between image and word, where the ramifications of the visual imagery express something that the word cannot articulate. This tension is introduced in the opening sentences of the first hymn by the figure of "the glorious stranger with the *meaningful eyes*. . . and the *gently closed tone-rich lips*." The opposition between meaningful vision and muted verbal expression is then developed extensively in the first hymn. Light's "heavenly image" (131) is contrasted with the "holy, *unspeakable*. . . night" (131) that has an "*invisible* power" over the soul (131), and we are "*unspeakably* moved" by this experience (133). The narrator's personal encounter with this "*invisible* power" occurs when he sees a face, an *Antlitz* (133), etymologically, "that which returns the gaze." Following the encounter with this face of vision, the night opens up "infinite *eyes*" in humankind that can see further than their physical counterparts (133). They "*see through* the depths of a loving spirit," and this action fills the heavens with an "*unutterable* delight" (133).

The tension between vision and word takes on theoretical significance when its development is traced throughout the *Hymns*. The first hymn's "glorious stranger with the *meaningful eyes*, the hovering gait, and the *gently closed tone-rich lips*" (131) returns in the fifth as Jesus, who heralds the future with a "prophetic eye" in which vision and word are conjoined (*das weissagende Auge*: literally, the wisdom-speaking eye, 147). This fusion of language and sight is repeated in the description of Jesus's voice: "inexhaustible *words* fell like *sparks*. . . from his friendly lips" (147). Thus, the figure of Jesus, described here as hovering (*schwebend*), embodies a *religio* of vision and word, and this visual-verbal representation actually defines the lyric: the development of the meaningful eyes of the silent stranger into the eidetic speech of Jesus, announced by a singer in the fifth hymn, is a cipher for the transition into lyric that the *Hymns* (re)present.

Let me review the elements of the lyric theory I have uncovered so far. My basic thesis is that the *Hymns* are defined by a *religio*, a binding together of self and God in the lyric. I have argued that the development of metaphorical language within the *Hymns* gives us important indications about the nature of this *religio*: it is a fluid binding together of opposites, of vision and word. I have also suggested that the religio (re)presents the construction of a new kind of subjectivity, an *autopoiesis* of a subject that is created in and through the lyric. The *Hymns* themselves undergo a development from prose to lyric poetry, and if my thesis is correct, then the transition into lyric should reflect this new subjectivity. The shift from prose to lyric occurs in the course of the fourth and fifth hymns, and we turn now to these hymns in order to trace this genesis.

The prose section of the fourth hymn describes the passage from the earthly world to the heavenly realm. This heavenly realm is a realm of building, of *poiesis*, we might say: "up above he builds himself huts, huts of peace" (137). These "huts of peace" return in the fifth hymn, where they are explicitly identified with the poetic: Jesus is born "in the poverty of a poetic hut" (145). In the prose section of the fourth hymn the transition to this higher poetic realm is described with a metaphor of swimming: "the earthly floats upward" (137). This image of a fluid passage into the poetic is repeated in the first line of lyric verse, this time in terms of subjectivity: *hinüber wall ich* (139), where *wall* refers both to *wallfahren* (the pilgrimmage mentioned earlier in the hymn, 137), and to *wallen*, the welling up of liquids. Hence, the phrase *hinüber wall ich* means both "I travel over" and "I well over." This liquid *wallen* provides the narrator with eternal life: "Infinite life / Waves powerfully in me" (139). With this phrase the yearning for a fluidity of subject that was expressed in the first hymn's "I want to sink down into the dewdrops" (131) is realized. This fluid *religio* then initiates the coming of the self into the lyric, a coming of the self into word and into God.

This transition is concluded in the final strophe, the final turning, of the fifth hymn:

Die Lieb' ist frey gegeben,	Love is freely given,
Und keine Trennung mehr,	And no more separation,
Es wogt das volle Leben	The full life surges
Wie ein unendlich Meer.	Like an eternal sea.

Nur Eine Nacht der Wonne—	Just One Night of bliss—
Ein ewiges Gedicht—	An eternal poem—
Und unser aller Sonne	And the sun of us all
Ist Gottes Angesicht. (153)	Is God's face.

The union of self and God in an "eternal poem" is complete: there is "no more separation." A fluid subject is created in this *religio*: "The full life surges / Like an eternal sea." The fluid subject is bound together with God in the language of the lyric itself. The phrases *ewiges Gedicht* (eternal poem) and *Gottes Angesicht* (God's face) are conjoined by rhyme and by the phonic affinity of *g*'s (*ewiges Gedicht* and *Gottes Angesicht*). The rhyme differential of *Gesicht* and *Gedicht* contains the opposition of *sicht(en)*—sight—and *dicht(en)*—poetry. If we look even more closely at this juxtaposition of **sich**t and **dich**t we see the *Ich*, the subject, the *I*. Thus, the final lines of the stanza create the ultimate visual-verbal *religio*: the subject is inextricably bound together with God and lyric. With this the subject's transition into lyric is complete, and all that remains for the poet to do is to under-cut this empirical model of self-definition in a self-reflexive act of Romantic criticism, a feat Novalis accomplishes in the final hymn, "Yearning for Death": only in death do the empirical subject and the absolute subject truly become one.[17]

I would like to step back from the text now and discuss my reading of the *Hymns* in terms of the theory of *Darstellung* I have been reconstructing throughout this chapter. The groundwork for this theory was laid out in the *Fichte-Studies*, where Novalis argues that the mirror imaging (*Verkehrung*) of reflection introduces a necessary illusion into the subject's self-positing or self-representation. Therefore, the empirical subject cannot represent itself truly, and Novalis develops a paradoxical scheme for representing the unrepresentable, the pure Ego, via poesy. According to Novalis, this artistic construction of the subject should incorporate the Fichtean notions of the Ego as an activity, as a reciprocal determination of feeling and reflection, as a "hovering

(*Schweben*) between extremes, which must necessarily be united and necessarily separated" (II: 266, #55), as well as a visual dimension capable of circumventing the illusory mirror imaging of reflection. Thus, in *Klingsohr's Tale* a reciprocal determination of both feeling and reflection and visual and verbal representation is set up in the conflict between the Writer and Fable; Fable, established as the fairy tale's true represent, hovers; and the artistic construction of the subject, the father, takes place in a liquid mirror that reflects truly.

Novalis perfects this Fichtean theory of *Darstellung* in the *Hymns to the Night*. In comparison to *Klingsohr's Tale*, where the artistic construction of the subject is subsidiary to the genesis of the theory of *Darstellung* (re)presented in the fairy tale, in the *Hymns* the construction of the subject is actually identical to the visual-verbal *Darstellung* that the *Hymns* (re)present. The development of "the glorious stranger with the meaningful eyes, the hovering gait, and the gently closed, tone-rich lips" into the "prophetic eye" of Jesus is a cipher for the visual *poiesis* constructed in the *Hymns*, and the *religio* of the empirical Ego and the pure Ego, God, takes place in the conjoining of vision and word in the language of the lyric itself. In comparison with *Klingsohr's Tale*, a mirror no longer makes this true representation possible, but rather the notion of a higher sight, an infinite, prophetic vision. Interestingly, Novalis, who lays out the groundwork for his visual definition of the subject in the 1795 *Fichte-Studies*, clearly anticipates his philosophical mentor in working out this visual dimension of Fichtean ego philosophy: in 1798 Fichte defines self-consciousness as a "power in which an eye should be inserted"; in 1801, one year after the publication of the *Hymns*, Fichte defines *self-consciousness* as "an activity in which an eye is inserted"; and in 1805 he expresses this ocular theory in poetic form.[18]

In my reading of the *Hymns* I indicated other constitutive elements of Novalis's theory of *Darstellung*. For instance, the notion of fluidity plays an essential role in the definition of the subject in both *Klingsohr's Tale* (Sophie's water and the birth of the father in the liquid mirror) and in the *Hymns*, where I argued that the phrase "I well over" (*hinüber wall ich*) initiates a fluid transition of self into lyric. We recall that Novalis defines the subject as "a fluid" (III: 441, #900), and that the two tests for true representation in *Klingsohr's Tale*, Sophie's water and the liquid mirror, are both fluid. Novalis wanted to develop a "philosophy of fluidity" (III: 426, #802), and he defines *poesy* as "fluid in nature" (IV: 246), a definition I will return to shortly.

I have also emphasized the notion of polar opposition in the *Hymns*. In part, this polar opposition can be traced to Novalis's Fichtean notion of Being as a "hovering (*Schweben*) between extremes, which must necessarily be united and necessarily separated," but it is also related to Novalis's analysis of the illusory mirror imaging of reflection in the subject's self-positing: "All of our perceptive capabilities are like the eye. The objects have to pass through opposing media in order to appear correctly on the pupil" (II: 415, #9; cf. III: 342–343, #479). To be sure, this is not the only function of the reversed imagery in the *Hymns*. When Novalis ends the *Hymns* with a "yearning for death," he means it: his epistemological theory culminates in an apocalyptic coming into life via death. In *Klingsohr's Tale* the mother must die and her ashes must be incorporated into the other characters to effect the completion of the new, true *Darstellung*, and elsewhere Novalis concludes that the "true philosophical act is suicide" (II: 395, #54; cf. II: 417, #14). For Novalis an approximation of the Infinite is accomplished by a simultaneous movement of progress and regress (II: 457, #99)—here, of life and death—and it is precisely this movement of progress and regress around which he structures the *Hymns*.

The alternations in the *Hymns* between prose and lyric poetry are related to this progress-regress problematic. Novalis considered his present historical age to be "prosaic," and he saw himself at the beginning of a new, constructed, poetic period (III: 312-313, #392). The fact that this new poetic age is "constructed" is an indication of what Novalis thought he was doing with his own writing, and in a letter to August

Wilhelm Schlegel (IV: 245–247), he explicitly outlines his poetic program, a poetic program that finds its expression in the *Hymns*.

In this letter of 1798 Novalis defines *poesy* as a "fluid": "by nature fluid—completely malleable—and unlimited— [. . .]—an element of the *Geist*, an eternally still sea." While poesy expresses the infinite fluidity of the sea, prose is bounded: it is a "stream." Novalis goes on to say that the only way that poesy can expand is by limiting itself. Through this self-limitation poesy takes on the appearance of prose, yet its entire structure should reveal its fluid origin. This "expanded poesy" is the highest task of the practical poet, a task that can be solved only by an approximation embodied in a higher poesy, a poesy of the Infinite. We recall that the fluid transition of the *Hymns* into lyric culminates in images of the infinite sea and the eternal poem. Novalis's *Hymns* are this eternal poem, a poesy of the Infinite.

Novalis's assertion that poesy can expand only through a self-imposed self-limitation in which it appears as prose is reminiscent of the *negative Darstellung* of the Kantian sublime, which, as we saw in Chapter 1, is a rhetorical figure concerned with the establishment and transcendence of the limits between the beautiful and the sublime, the sensible subject and the moral subject, and philosophy and poetry. This connection to Kant is, perhaps, more than coincidental: Novalis quite possibly derives his notion of textual fluidity from §58 of the *Critique of Judgment*, where Kant argues in language remarkably similar to Novalis's that nature contains forms that are artistic in nature. Taking the crystallization of fluids as an example, Kant states that when a true fluidity, that is, one composed of a mass of oscillating parts (*ein Gemenge . . . schwebender Teile*), solidifies, the resultant figure takes on a specific webbed shape or texture (*Gewebe* or *Textur*, B 249). In other words, it forms a fluid "text" in the etymological sense of the word.

This terminological link to Kant may be fortuitous, but the intellectual affinity between Kant's and Novalis's theories of *Darstellung* is profound: the visual *poiesis* that structures the *Hymns* parallels the paradoxical configuration of the *negative Darstellung* of the Kantian sublime. The ultimate goal of Novalis's theory, we recall, is the representation of the unrepresentable, the pure Ego, via poesy. The paradoxical nature of Novalis's theory is evident in his conjoining of disjunct definitions in the phrase *Darstellung des Undarstellbaren* (representing the unrepresentable): *Darstellung* refers to both the a priori self-positing of the absolute subject, which cannot be represented empirically, and to the rhetorical representation of the poetic system in and through which the empirical subject becomes one with the absolute subject, which posits itself as *Darstellung*. Novalis's formula for "representing the unrepresentable" hence reiterates Kant's paradoxical notion of a *negative Darstellung* that is in fact a *Darstellung*: in Kant's "pure, negative representation" the critical and rhetorical definitions of *Darstellung* are merged and the borders between the sensible subject and the moral subject of reason and philosophy and literature are obliterated. Following Kant and Fichte, Novalis argues that the Absolute only can be recognized negatively (II: 270, #566)[19] and represented aesthetically as philosophical paradox: "The highest representation of the Ungraspable is synthesis—unifying the ununifiable, positing of contradiction as non-contradiction" (II: 111, #12). In effect, then, the *Hymns'* "representation of the unrepresentable" is an implicit instantiation of the *negative Darstellung* of the Kantian sublime, and Romantic poesy in its highest form is a sublime poesy, a poesy of the Infinite: "The poetic sense represents the unrepresentable (*stellt das Undarstellbare dar*); the poet is truly robbed of his senses—that's why everything represents (*vorstellen*) itself in him.[20] He represents (*vorstellen*) *subject object* in the true sense—*mind and world*. Thus the infiniteness of a good poem, the eternity. The poetic sense is closely related to the prophetic sense and the religious sense, to the seer's sense in general" (III: 685–686, #671). The poet, robbed of his senses, effects the Kantian subreption that transforms the sensible subject into an absolute subject, the sine qua non of Kant's, Novalis's, and Fichte's theories of *Darstellung*.

Finally, Novalis's statement that the poetic sense is closely related to the prophetic and the religious senses, to the "seer's sense" in general, supports my reading of the *Hymns* as a "spiritual act of seeing"; that is, a theory in the original sense of the word. I have emphasized the *Hymns'* status as self-reflexive discourse, as self-representation or *Selbstdarstellung*, grounding my analysis in the development of various images throughout the *Hymns*, and then arguing that the development of these images constitutes a theory whose goal is the artistic construction of the subject. In the same letter to August Wilhelm Schlegel cited previously, Novalis states that an essential component of the poetic *Geist* is the secret of beautiful development, of beautiful unfolding (*schöne Entfaltung*). This "beautiful unfolding" should play a major role in the lyric poem, "as a simultaneous reflective perception and description . . . a reciprocal completion of image (*Bild*) and concept . . . through which the object and the concept are completed in an instant" (IV: 245). This description of the reciprocal determination of visual image and verbal concept is a formula for the visual *poiesis* realized in the *Hymns*, where the object, the empirical subject, becomes one with the concept, the absolute subject or God, in the conjoining of image and word in the language of the lyric itself. As Novalis explains in the *Fichte-Studies*: "The completion of theory incorporates praxis into theory—and the I becomes a Not-I—something strange; namely, the practical in the theoretical, [the practical I becomes] a theoretical I" (II: 150, #97), a subject that posits itself as *Darstellung*. In other words, the *Hymns*—the piece that Novalis himself was most proud of[21]—are not only a theory of the Romantic lyric, but the quintessence of *Selbstdarstellung* (self-representation) in Romantic poesy.

This thesis is in accordance with the assessments of Novalis's contemporaries. In his *Philosophy of Art*, Schelling identifies the lyric poem as the epitome of art, the highest representation of the Infinite (5: 640); and in the conclusion to the second version of the *Conversation on Poesy* (1823), Friedrich Schlegel states that the lyric has "a far greater value and significance" than he had previously allotted it, and he goes on to identify the hymn as "the basic form of lyric poetry and precisely for that reason the beginning of all poesy" (KA II: 358).[22]

4

Kleist: Transcending the Transcendental

In Chapter One I argued that Kant's *negative Darstellung*
is a self-reflexive rhetorical figure, a control mechanism
whose function is to keep reason within its borders, thereby
preventing it from running amok, a state of affairs that
would precipitate "the death of all philosophy." In other
words, *negative Darstellung* safeguards the successful representation of Kant's rational, transcendental critique. Chapter 2 showed that Fichte employs an analogous strategy of
"negativity" in his definition of the subject as *Darstellung*.
Chapter 3 then demonstrated that the Jena Romantics
transform the poetic register repressed in Kant's and Fichte's
rhetoric into a productive transcendental poesy designed
to remedy the deficient *Darstellung* of philosophical
discourse. Kant's, Fichte's, and the Jena Romantics' theories
of representation are all situated within transcendental
investigations that by definition are concerned with determining the conditions and possibility of a priori knowledge,[1]
and underlying these various notions of *Darstellung* is a
belief that constructing a pure or true representation of this
a priori knowledge is practicable. In Kant's critical philosophy
this pure representation is expressed in the sublime's *negative Darstellung* of ideas, in Fichte's ego philosophy it is
incorporated into the model of the self-positing subject, and
the goal of Novalis's theory of *Darstellung* is to represent
the Fichtean pure Ego via a visual *poiesis*. These transcendental notions of representation presuppose two things: that
there is an original a priori knowledge, the Kantian idea or
the Fichtean pure Ego; and that this original knowledge can
be represented truly.

Philosophically speaking, these two points are open to debate. As Kleist puts it in his famous "Kant crisis" letter of 1801: "We cannot decide if that which we call truth really is true, or if it merely appears so to us" (*Wir können nicht entscheiden, ob das, was wir Wahrheit nennen, wahrhaft Wahrheit ist, oder ob es uns nur so scheint*, 634).[2] Kleist's critique of transcendentalism is three-pronged. First, we cannot decide whether a priori knowlege or truth really exists. Nor, if truth does exist, can we determine whether our representation of truth is itself true. Finally, it is possible that truth itself does not exist and that we mistakenly believe our representation of truth *is* truth. If this is the case, Kleist concludes despondently, then "the truth that we gather here ceases to exist after death—and all efforts to secure something that will follow us to the grave are in vain" (634). In other words, Kleist's "Kant crisis" is motivated by a representational quandary: the impossibility of knowing what kind of relationship, if any, exists between truth and appearance, *Wahrheit* and *Schein*. This concern for the relationship between knowledge and its representation runs throughout Kleist's oeuvre, and in this final chapter I will argue that, by calling into question the belief in *Darstellung* as productive (re)presentation, Kleist's writings effect a literary critique of Kant's, Fichte's, and the Jena Romantics' transcendental projects.

This transcendental caesura distinguishes Kleist from the Jena Romantics in two regards. Not only does he differ from Novalis and Schlegel in that his oeuvre can be seen as a critique, rather than a logical extension, of Kant's and Fichte's notions of *Darstellung*, his writings also present an opposing paradigm for the relationship between philosophy and literature. Like the Jena Romantics, Kleist is an author clearly influenced by Enlightenment and Idealist philosophers like Rousseau, Voltaire, Kant, and Fichte, yet this philosophical discourse has, at best, a vestigial status in Kleist's oeuvre. This shift from the Romantics' philosophical-literary expansion of Idealism to Kleist's literary-philosophical critique of Idealism is arguably of epochal significance, because the "Kant crisis" letter of late March

1801 corresponds chronologically to the demise of Jena Romanticism: the final issue of the short-lived Romantic journal *Athenäum* was published in August 1800, and Novalis died on March 25, 1801, three days after the "Kant crisis" letter was written.

The literary casting of Kleist's critique of transcendentalism is made all the more interesting by the close proximity of his notion of representation to the Jena Romantics'. In Chapter 3 I described Novalis's theory of *Darstellung* as a visual *poiesis* designed to circumvent the illusory mirror imaging of reflection in the Fichtean subject's self-positing. Furthermore, I suggested that my reading of Novalis was in line with Friedrich Schlegel's self-reflexive, self-representing transcendental poesy. By and large, the same parameters operative in Jena Romanticism—the critique of the subject, the specular dimension of reflection, illusion, visual representation, and self-representation—characterize Kleist's oeuvre, but his use of these motifs differs decisively from the Jena Romantics'. In particular, the visual dimension of Kleist's notion of representation calls into question the self-reflexive dimension of the Romantics' understanding of *Darstellung* as productive representation.

This thesis is supported by the fact that most of Kleist's texts are concerned with the relationship between visual representation and knowledge, and almost invariably this visual representation is linked with incorrect or incomplete knowledge: false identification, faulty inference, illusion, or logical lacunae. In *Amphitryon*, Alkmene, faced with the task of distinguishing Amphitryon from his doppelgänger, Jupiter, incorrectly identifies Jupiter as her husband; in *The Family Schroffenstein* disguise and veiling lead to mistaken identity and death; the invisible inexplicably wreaks havoc on the Marquis in *The Beggarwoman of Locarno*; the action of *Penthesilea* is not presented visually but reported teichoscopically; in *The Broken Jug* the shattering of the earthen jug actually masks the play's action; in *Robert Guiskard* the Normans falsely believe that seeing Guiskard is a sign of their salvation; Nicolo defines himself perhaps incorrectly via a painting in *The Foundling*; Kunigunde's presumably horrendous physical appearance remains hidden from the reader-viewer in *Kätchen von Heilbronn*; and in an epigram to the *Marquise von O* Kleist condemns the Marquise: "Shameless farce! She was, I know, only holding her eyes closed" (22). Thus, Kleist's use of vision in relationship to incomplete or incorrect knowledge forms a unique paradigm within what Michael Titzmann has identified as a visually coded notion of knowledge in philosophy and literature in the Age of Goethe, where sight is generally linked positively to cognition (Goethe, Fichte, Hoffmann, Tieck, Jean Paul, et al.).[3] The following analysis focuses on this relationship between knowledge and vision in order to demonstrate Kleist's overt criticism of Kant's, Fichte's, and the Jena Romantics' transcendental notions of representation.

The word *Darstellung* occurs rarely in Kleist's oeuvre. Thus, in contrast to my readings of Kant, Fichte, and Novalis, which traced the logical development of the term's function as a signifier within a textual corpus, I will consider Kleist's writings as implicit instantiations of the *Darstellung* problematic, taking examples from each of his major genres, the theoretical, the narrative, and the dramatic text. The first section interprets the essay *On the Marionette Theater* as a critique of philosophical reflection and transcendental representation. The second shows how this critique of reflection bears on the definition of the Fichtean subject in the novella *The Foundling*. The final section demonstrates that the synthesis of visual and verbal representation operative in the comedy *The Broken Jug* runs counter to the visual *poiesis* of Jena Romanticism. Although this selection of works is somewhat arbitrary, each text foregrounds visual representation in different ways, while sharing thematic affinities with the others: *On the Marionette Theater* and *The Broken Jug* are both "Fall" stories; and *The Broken Jug* and *The Foundling* are redactions of the Oedipus myth. Hence, all three texts are culturally precoded as stories of education, knowledge, illusion, insight, and blindness.

Before turning to the texts I must say a few words about my own methodology. In recent years there has been a trend in Kleist scholarship to devalue the importance of Kleist's

"Kant crisis" and to read *On the Marionette Theater* as fiction, irony, satire, or even dance, rather than as a philosophical statement.[4] Rushing, for example, correctly argues that the text is thoroughly informed by irony, but then concludes: "Recognition of this essential ironic structure makes 'straight' readings of the 'Marionettentheater' as philosophical argument appear naive, for the irony, once perceived, assures that the reader cannot be persuaded by Herr C.'s argument."[5] Irony, however, does not disqualify a discourse from being philosophical: both irony and paradox are cornerstones of Jena Romanticism, for example. Similarly, Ray argues that "the dialogued unfolding of the narrative's argument presents a serialized, discursive version of the specular paradigm" and then concludes that "the specular underpinnings of the dialogue clearly disqualify it as secure epistemological ground."[6] Although Ray does a remarkable job in analyzing the specular structure of the essay, he does not consider the implications of his findings with respect to Idealist and Romantic philosophies of reflection, and this, I am arguing, is Kleist's unique philosophical contribution. The following readings will indicate that I do believe that the "Kant crisis" letter provides a blueprint for Kleist's poetic program and that *On the Marionette Theater* is an intertextual critique of Kantian transcendental theory. Whether this critique is a conscious one or not, however, is ultimately of little consequence to my argument: Kleist's texts engage the Idealist and Romantic philosophical tradition, be it overtly or implicitly.

One final note. Kleist was a master craftsman in his use of language, syntax, and punctuation, and it is impossible to translate his writing without losing a good deal of its import. To preserve the sense of the original German as much as possible, I occasionally have found it necessary to sacrifice a certain amount of elegance in the translations.

On the Marionette Theater:
"Reflection Is Getting Darker and Weaker"

In the wake of Kant's *Critiques* reflection becomes a key issue in Idealist and Romantic theories of representation.[7] The impetus for this development is inherent in Kant's notion of the "transcendental." A transcendental investigation, by definition, entails subjective knowledge turning back upon itself to determine its own a priori conditions of possibility, and Kant defines reflection accordingly: "*Reflection (reflexio)* does not concern itself with objects themselves with a view to deriving concepts from them directly, but is that state of mind in which we first set ourselves to discover the subjective conditions under which [alone] we are able to arrive at concepts" (*CPR* B 316).[8] By extension, then, reflection is the condition of possibility, as it were, of *Darstellung*, "the making sensible of a concept." In fact, Kant goes on to explicitly link reflection and representation: reflection examines objective representations (*Vorstellungen*) to determine the relationship of these representations to our faculties of cognition, that is, to sensible intuition, pure understanding, and reason. By this process alone, Kant concludes, we can determine how these faculties of cognition are related to one another.

Despite this assertion, which would seem to accord reflection a central position in Kant's transcendental enterprise, his discussion of this pivotal notion is tacked on to the "Transcendental Analytic" as a mere "appendix," and it is Fichte who places reflection at the core of the critical philosophy. Fichte, expanding Kant's statement that the subject (*das Ich*) is the highest point of transcendental philosophy (*CPR* B 134, note), argues that the transcendental claim to examine the process by which subjective knowledge examines itself requires a theory of the self-reflecting subject. According to Fichte, a transcendental theory of the subject faces a fundamental problem. When the self-reflecting ego turns thought back upon itself to determine its own a priori conditions of possibility, it must presuppose what it sets out to prove; namely, the fact of its own self-consciousness. Hence, traditional formulations of this theory of reflection are inherently tautological, and Fichte attempts to break out of this vicious circle by introducing a model of the self-reflecting, self-positing, self-representing subject into critical philosophy.[9]

However, his critics, most notably Novalis and Hölderlin, argue that Fichte's theory of self-consciousness is also caught up in an ineluctable circularity.[10] According to Novalis, the reflexive act of self-positing necessarily results in a specular inversion in the Fichtean subject's self-representation or *Selbstdarstellung*. Thus, the prereflexive pure Ego cannot be represented, because, as Novalis puts it, "you're trying to represent nonreflection using reflection, and for precisely this reason you'll never get to nonreflection using these means" (II: 122, #125). Having exhibited considerable philosophical acumen in identifying the vicious circle of reflection in Fichte's theory of self-consciousness, Novalis then develops a remarkably uncritical solution to the problem: he creates a theory of representation in which the subject is constructed via a visual-verbal *poiesis* that circumvents, but does not escape, the illusory mirror imaging of reflection. The tenuousness of this theory becomes even more pronounced in literary form: in *Klingsohr's Tale* the construction of the subject takes place in a mirror that reflects truly; in Astralis's song one secret word rectifies "the whole inverted essence"; and in the *Hymns to the Night* the notion of a higher sight or an infinite prophetic vision defines the subject. Each of these solutions is introduced as a deus ex machina, and Novalis does not explain the mechanism by which the specular inversion of reflection is eluded.

Kleist takes this critique of reflection one step further. Whereas Fichte had theorized that self-consciousness is structured by self-reflexivity and Novalis had recognized that reflexivity introduces a specular inversion into the subject's self-representation, Kleist questions the transcendental notion of the self-reflecting subject. Kleist's critique of reflection can be divided into two distinct phases. In the first stage, which predates the "Kant crisis" by a few months, Kleist's critique is concordant with Novalis's. Kleist considers reflection suspect, because it introduces the possibility of false specularity and distortion into representation. In a pedagogical letter to his fiancée Wilhelmine dated November 29, 1800, Kleist writes of a "particularly splendid thought": "that with a person, as with a mirror, how foreign objects affect him depends on his own properties. . . .we must put the lesson to use, and diligently grind the mirror of our soul so that it becomes smooth and clear and reflects the image of beautiful nature truly. How many people would stop complaining about corrupt times and morals if it would just occur to them one single time that perhaps it's just that the picture of the world falls into a mirror that is distorted and dirty? How often did a person stand in front of a mirror that called out the instructive warning to him, if only he had understood it—*if only he had understood it!*" (605). Kleist warns of the importance of recognizing that human knowledge may be informed by bad mirroring and distorted representation. Like Novalis, he believes that this distorted representation can be rectified by "grinding the mirror of the soul" until it reflects truly. Kleist is obviously intrigued by this notion of false specularity. He repeats the preceding formulation verbatim a few months later in a letter to his sister Ulrike dated February 5, 1801 (628), and ten years later, in "Letter from One Poet to Another" he applies the same image to poetry: "the property of all true form is that *Geist* emerges from it instantaneously and immediately, while deficient form holds *Geist* captive like a bad mirror and reminds us of nothing but itself" (348). Like Novalis, Kleist seems to advocate the construction of a "true" poetic form that safeguards against distorted mirroring.

Kleist's critique of reflection is more trenchant in its second stage, the "Kant crisis" letter to his fiancée, Wilhelmine, of March 22, 1801. The problem that thought faces when it turns back on itself, Kleist maintains in what may well be a critique of Fichte's "newer so-called Kantian philosophy" (634),[11] is that it cannot know what it is seeing. Where he had previously argued that the self-reflecting subject is faced with a potentially false, but correctable, specularity, Kleist now states that it is impossible for the self-reflecting subject to ever *know* whether the representation it sees is true or distorted. Kleist provides two formulations of this problem. The first is the famous "green glasses" example: if our eyes were green glasses, we would always have to judge the objects we see to be green, without being able to determine whether "greenness" is inherent in the object or in our eyes. Kleist draws an analogy between this critique of visual reflection and the second example, the critique of the self-reflecting subject: "so it is with our understanding: we cannot decide if that which we take to be truth really is truth, or whether it merely appears to be truth" (634). In other words, Kleist argues that there is no intrinsic relationship between a priori knowledge and its representation. If this is the case, then representation can make no claims to (re)present an original state or object, and transcendental theories of *Darstellung* are null and void. Kleist's critique of reflection thus has a number of philosophical repercussions: a critique of the transcendental, a subversion of the epistemologically secure subject, and a drawing into question of the status of representation. It is no accident that Kleist broaches these issues in *On the Marionette Theater*: the essay, written in 1810, but set, like his "Kant crisis," in "Winter 1801" (338), (re)presents a critique of reflection.

The transcendental framework of *On the Marionette Theater* is set up in the opening sentences of the text. The narrator, on meeting Herr C. in a public garden in the winter of 1801, comments that he had been astonished to see C., a leading dancer at the local opera, at the marionette theater on several occasions. In the ensuing exchange between the narrator and C., the text establishes itself as a discourse on representation:

Ich sagte ihm, dass ich erstaunt gewesen wäre, ihn schon mehrere Mal in einem Marionettentheater zu finden, das auf dem Markte zusammengezimmert worden war, und den Pöbel, *durch kleine dramatische Burlesken*, mit Gesang und Tanz *durchwebt*, belustigte.

Er versicherte mir, dass ihm die *Pantomimik* dieser Puppen viel Vergnügen machte, und *liess nicht undeutlich merken*, dass ein Tänzer, der sich ausbilden wolle, mancherlei von ihnen lernen könne.

Da diese Äusserung mir, *durch die Art, wie er sie vorbrachte*, mehr, als ein blosser Einfall schien, so liess ich mich bei ihm nieder, um ihn über *die Gründe, auf die er eine so sonderbare Behauptung stützen könne, näher zu vernehmen.* (338–339, emphasis mine)

I told him that I had been astonished to find him on several occasions at a marionette theater that had been hammered together at the marketplace and that entertained the crowd with *short dramatic burlesques interwoven with song and dance.*

He assured me that he found the puppets' *pantomime* very pleasurable, and *let it be noticed not unclearly* that a dancer who wanted to educate himself could learn all sorts of things from them.

Since this utterance, *because of the manner in which he produced it*, seemed to me more than a passing fancy, I sat down next to him *to hear more about the grounds on which he could support such a strange assertion.*

The marionette theater, "*interwoven* with song and dance," is a cipher for the text (etymologically, *text* is derived from the Latin *texere*, "to weave"). It entertains its audience "with small dramatic burlesques," which, true to definition, "seek to ridicule by means of grotesque exaggeration or comic imitation."[12] What the text ridicules, and by extension criticizes, is imitation in its various forms: mimesis, representation, *Darstellung.* This critique of representation is enacted on two levels. First, the text unfolds in a series of "small dramatic burlesques," each of which presents a scene of representation: the marionettes, whose "pantomime" (literally, "copying everything") marks them as potentially perfect imitators, represent the epitome of grace in human dance; the narcissistic youth who sees himself representing the famous statue of the young man pulling a thorn out of his foot; and the fencing bear, who parries Herr C.'s blows by mirroring his true intentions. On closer examination, however, each of the scenes undermines its own claims to (re)present an original state, be it the perfect dance, the ideal statue, or the flawless fencer. This first facet of Kleist's critique of representation will be discussed in more detail later.

The second aspect of Kleist's critique is rhetorical. When Herr C. remarks in the exchange just quoted that dancers can learn from the puppets, "the manner in which he made this statement" (*die Art, wie er sie vorbrachte*), rather than the statement's content, catches the narrator's attention. The text provides a formula for Herr C.'s remarkable rhetorical *Darstellung*. Herr C. "let it be noticed not unclearly" (*liess nicht undeutlich merken*) that a dancer can learn from the puppets. Hence, by extension, one definition of *Darstellung*, "the manner of producing a statement," is "to let it be noticed not unclearly." Two things are noteworthy about this unwieldy formulation. The first is that the phrase *not unclearly* is tautological. The double negative *not unclearly* is logically equivalent to "clearly," yet on the semantic level it sets into play a dialectical relationship between the two words. In short, the phrase is an instantiation of a kind of Kantian *negative Darstellung*: it transcends the logical limits of language, while at the same time staying within its confines. The second distinctive feature of the formulation *to let it be noticed not unclearly* is that grammatically the passive construction places the responsibility of representation on the receiver. The foundation of Kleist's notion of *Darstellung* is a reader-response theory, designed, "not unclearly," to promote paradox and confusion.

This rhetorical representation is the transcendental condition of possibility, as it were, of the entire conversation between Herr C. and the narrator. The narrator, struck by the manner in which C. had stated that dancers can learn from the marionettes, is induced to sit down with him, "to hear (*vernehmen*) more about the grounds on which he could support such a strange assertion" (*um ihn über die Gründe, auf die er eine so sonderbare Behauptung stützen könne, näher zu **vernehmen***), a statement that clearly situates the essay within the tradition of Kant's transcendental *Critiques*. The appearance of the word *vernehmen* in this Kantian context is noteworthy. Not only does the term contain a double entendre in its simultaneous incorporation of sense perception (hearing) and intellectual activity (*Vernunft*, reason, is etymologically derived from *vernehmen*, "sensible perception"), it also refers to legal interrogation, to the Kantian tribunal of reason. Hence, the word presages on the rhetorical level what the text will present thematically; namely, a critique of a series of attempts to represent a mediation between sensible perception and reason. This, in a nutshell, is also the crux of Kant's *Darstellung* discussion, and Kleist's essay contains profound affinities to Kant's elaboration of the problem. It begins with a critical self-reflexive rhetorical gesture, is structured according to a principle analogous to Kant's definition of reflection, using discussions of the beautiful and the sublime as vehicles for a critique of representation; and concludes with an attack on reflection and the transcendental claim to discover and represent the a priori conditions of possibilty of pure cognition. In short, *On the Marionette Theater* couples a critique of reflection with a redaction and revision of the Kantian sublime.

If there is a thesis to Herr C.'s argument, it is this: human beings are not graceful because they are reflective. Thinking about what they do causes people to make mistakes, and Herr C. attributes this inability to be graceful to man's Fall: "Such mistakes (*Missgriffe*). . .are unavoidable since we have eaten from the Tree of Knowledge" (*Solche* **Missgriffe**. . . *sind unvermeidlich, seitdem wir von dem Baum der* **Erkenntnis** *gegessen haben*, 342, emphasis mine). Restated in philosophical terms, Herr C. claims that knowledge or *Erkenntnis* is not derived from **Be**griffe (concepts), as it is in Kant's epistemology, but from **Miss**griffe (mistakes). Hence, it is no accident that the semantic register *begreifen* (to understand) runs throughout the text: *Begriff* (concept, 340), *Missgriffe* (mistakes, 342), *greifen* (to reach, 343), *unbegreiflich* (incomprehensible, 344), *begreifen* (to understand, 345). The goal of the dialogue is to construct a mechanism by which cognition produces *Begriffe* (concepts) rather than *Missgriffe* (mistakes), to supply the reader with everything, as Herr C. puts it, "that is necessary in order to *understand* (*begreifen*) me" (*alles, was nötig ist, um* *mich zu **begreifen***, 345, emphasis mine). The dialogue, like Kant's definition of reflection, encourages the reader to examine the mechanism he or she uses to construct meaning, in Kant's words, to examine "that state of mind in which we first set ourselves to discover the subjective conditions under which we are able to arrive at concepts (*Begriffe*)" (*CPR* B 316). The text itself (re)presents this reflective gesture. The essay's anecdotes, internally contradictory and externally concatenated in a semblance of logical order, are designed to draw attention to the pitfalls of cognition.

The first of the "small dramatic burlesques" presented in the text concerns the marionettes themselves. The puppets' "pantomime" qualifies them as potentially perfect imitators, and Herr C. claims that they are capable of representing the epitome of grace—*Anmut* or *Grazie*—in human dance. *Anmut* or grace in late eighteenth-century critical disourse represents a mediation between beauty as an intellectual ideal and its sensible realization[13] and is hence analogous to the Kantian notion of *Darstellung*, "the making sensible of a concept." In Kant's theory this representation is expressed "indirectly" with respect to the beautiful. Similarly, in Kleist's text the marionettes indirectly incorporate the "concept of the beautiful in dance" through the puppetteer (340). Furthermore, just as the representational potential of the beautiful is dependent on that of the sublime in Kant's third *Critique*,[14] so, too, is the beauty of the puppets' dance derived from a Kantian *negative Darstellung*. The advantage that the puppets have over human dancers, Herr C. tells the narrator, is first and foremost "a negative one" (341): not only do they exhibit no affectations (341), they also counteract gravity with a negative movement (*antigrav*, 342), "since the force that *lifts* (*erhebt*) them to the heavens is greater than the one that chains them to the earth" (342, emphasis mine). This second attribute literally elevates the puppets to the sublime: *erheben*, to lift, is the etymological root of *das Erhabene*, the sublime. Their dance, like Kant's sublime (*CJ* B 98), comes about through a shaking up or *Erschütterung* (339). The puppets touch the ground only "to reanimate [their dance] through the momentary stoppage"

(*durch die augenblickliche Hemmung neu zu beleben*,
342), and it can hardly be coincidental that Kleist's phrase
is a direct quote of the ontological threat of the Kantian
sublime: "a momentary stoppage of the life forces" (*eine
augenblickliche Hemmung der Lebenskräfte, CJ* B 75).

The ontological threat of Kleist's sublime is not to the
puppets, of course, but to their observers, who follow the
formula for Kant's sublime in that they are both simultaneously attracted to and repelled by what they see (*CJ* B 98).
The audience is "amused" and Herr C. finds "much pleasure"
in the theater (339). Yet however alluring the puppets may
be, the narrator does not want to believe that something
mechanical can be more graceful than the human body
(342), and even Herr C. is hesitant to accept the narrator's
joking suggestion that the artist who produces artificial legs
for human beings might actually construct the perfect
puppet (341). Although, or perhaps because, this statement
is made in a joking manner, it provides the key to the nature
of the Kleistian sublime threat. These ersatz appendages
allow people who have lost their limbs to "dance," and this
spectacle dumbfounds the observer. The cripples' movements "are executed with a composure, lightness, and grace
that *astonishes* every thinking mind" (*die jedes denkende
Gemüt in* **Erstaunen** *setzen*, 341, emphasis mine). While
the Kantian sublime sets the mind in motion (*CJ* B 98),
Kleist's statement reduces the "thinking mind" to a marionette: *Erstaunen*, astonishment, literally means "to make
stiff or rigid."[15] Hence, it is not so much the fact that the
human being can be represented artificially that produces
the Kleistian sublime threat, but that the human mind can
become, like a puppet, *erstaunt*, stiff and rigid.[16]

In the second and third "dramatic burlesques," which
(re)present the sublime threat of the first, *Erstaunen* is a
function of reflection. In the second vignette, the narcissistic
youth, like the puppets, is the embodiment of *Anmut* or
grace (341). One day after bathing he looks in a large mirror
while lifting his foot to dry it off, and his reflection reminds
him of the famous statue of the young man pulling a thorn
from his foot. He is so taken by this image that he repeatedly

tries to re-create the representation: "Confused, he lifted his foot a third and a fourth time, he probably lifted it ten more times: in vain!" (*Er* **hob** *verwirrt den Fuss zum dritten und vierten, er* **hob** *ihn wohl noch zehnmal: umsonst!* 343, emphasis mine). The youth's attempted *Erhebung* or elevation to the sublime (*das Erhabene*) fails "in spite of all conceivable efforts" (*trotz aller ersinnlichen Bemühungen*, 341), and he becomes a captive of the mirror: "From this day, almost from this second, on, an incomprehensible change took place in this young man. He began to stand in front of the mirror for days on end; and one charm after another left him. An invisible and incomprehensible power seemed to drape itself like an iron net around the free play of his features, and after a year had gone by there was no trace of the delightfulness to be found in him that had captivated the eyes of the people who had surrounded him" (344). Unable to reproduce the reflection of that which he is not, namely, the statue, the youth loses his natural grace. An invisible and incomprehensible power descends, like an iron net, onto the free play of his features, in Kantian terms, onto the free play of his faculties (*CJ* B 28), and the youth, unable to cross the fine line between the beautiful and the sublime, is stultified, a victim of false specularity.

The tale of the youth functions as a proleptic complement to the third anecdote, Herr C.'s encounter with the fencing bear. Whereas the second story characterizes the beautiful at the brink of the sublime, the third story, "from which you will easily understand how it belongs here" (344), represents the epitome of the sublime. On a trip to Russia Herr C. engages in a fencing match with a Livonian nobleman's son who has just returned from the university (344), perhaps, given its proximity to Livonia, from the University of Königsberg. Despite the student's training, Herr C. recounts, "it so happened that I was superior to him" (*es traf sich, dass ich ihm überlegen war*, 344). Herr C.'s fighting advantage, however, quickly turns to philosophical defeat: the verbal *überlegen* (to be superior to) is textually transformed into a visual *Überlegung* or "reflection."[17] Having disarmed the student, Herr C. is led to the "master" (344), the fencing bear:

> Der Bär stand, als ich *erstaunt* vor ihn trat, auf den Hinterfüssen, mit dem Rücken an einem Pfahl gelehnt, an welchem er angeschlossen war, die rechte Tatze schlagfertig *erhoben*, und sah mir ins Auge: das war seine Fechterpositur. (344, emphasis mine)

> The bear stood, as I stepped, *astonished*, in front of him, on his back feet, his back leaned against a stake to which he was tethered, the right paw *lifted* ready to hit, and looked me in the eye: that was his fencing stance.

The bear, whose paw is "lifted ready to hit" (*schlagfertig* **erhoben**), exemplifies the sublime threat of *das Erhabene*, and Herr C., upon facing him, is astonished, *erstaunt*. While the bear assumes his fencing position by looking Herr C. in the eye, when Herr C. looks at the bear, he sees himself in a mirror: "I didn't know if I was dreaming, since I saw *myself* opposite such an opponent" (*Ich wusste nicht, ob ich träumte, da ich* **mich** *einem solchen Gegner gegenüber sah*, 344, emphasis mine). The self-reflecting subject C. then fights himself, rather than the bear. Having recovered slightly from his astonishment (345), C. begins to fence with the bear. The bear, predictably, mirrors C.'s moves selectively by parrying his blows and ignoring his feints: "eye to eye, as if he could read my soul, he stood there, his paw lifted ready to hit, and when my thrusts weren't meant seriously, he didn't budge" (345). Like Kant's sublime, the fencing match is not a game, but proves to be deadly serious.[18] Herr C. must make the first move in the fencing match, and when he engages the bear in fighting, he finds that the bear reflects his true moves, but ignores his feints, his paw elevated in a sublime threat (*die Tatze schlagfertig* **erhoben**). True to the sublime paradigm, the subject C. puts himself at stake in the fencing match. In opposition to the Kantian model, however, he loses: the bear's seriousness robs him of his composure (345), and he becomes like the puppets, *erstaunt*, stiff and rigid. The self-reflecting subject, be it Herr C. or the narcissistic youth, cannot escape his own reflection.

This, at least, is the claim on one level of the text. Yet the validity of both anecdotes is immediately drawn into question. Following his account of the narcissistic youth, the narrator asserts the authenticity of his story, thereby casting a shadow of doubt on its credibility: "Someone is still living who witnessed that strange and unfortunate event and can verify it word for word, *as I told it*" (344, emphasis mine). This statement renders the story suspect by drawing attention to the linguistic level of the narrative, in particular, to the possibility of rhetorical ruse. Similarly, Herr C. concludes his account of the fencing bear with a question: "Do you believe this story?" "Completely," answers the narrator, "from any stranger, it's so *probable*, so much the more so from you" (345, emphasis mine). Not only is Herr C.'s version of the story probable, *wahrscheinlich*, it also literally "appears to be true" (*wahr* = true, *Schein* = appearance). "And yet," Kleist comments elsewhere, "probability, as experience teaches, is not always on truth's side" (*Und doch ist die Wahrscheinlichkeit, wie die Erfahrung lehrt, nicht immer auf Seiten der Wahrheit*).[19] And indeed, each of the anecdotes presented in the text undermines its claims to (re)present.

To begin with, the puppets do not dance. Herr C. actually states only "that often, shaken in a merely chance manner, the whole thing came into a sort of rhythmic movement that was *similar* to dance" (339, emphasis mine). Moreover, he also does not say that the puppets are more graceful than human beings. He merely maintains that he believes that they have this potential: "He ventured to assert that if a mechanic could make him a marionette according to the specifications he supplied him, he could present (*darstellen*) a dance using the puppet that neither he nor any other talented dancer of his time. . .could achieve" (340–341). These custom-crafted marionettes do not exist, and Herr C.'s claim that he could create a superior *Darstellung* with them remains unproven. Similarly, the text never establishes the narcissistic youth as a representation of the famous statue. The narrator recounts the episode with the following words:

> Es traf sich, dass wir grade kurz zuvor in Paris den Jüngling gesehen hatten, der sich einen Splitter aus dem Fuss zieht; der Abguss der Statue ist bekannt und befindet sich in den meisten deutschen Sammlungen. Ein Blick, den er in dem Augenblick, da er den Fuss auf den Schemel setzte, um ihn abzutrocknen, in einen grossen Spiegel warf, erinnerte ihn daran; er lächelte und sagte mir, welch eine Entdeckung er gemacht habe. (343)

> It so happened that we had just seen the youth pulling a splinter from his foot in Paris; the cast of the statue is well-known and can be found in most German collections. A glance, which he, in that moment, as he placed his foot on the stool to dry it off, threw into a big mirror, reminded him of it; he smiled and told me what a discovery he had made.

The narrator states that he and his friend had been in Paris and seen "the youth" and that many copies of the statue exist. A glance in the mirror while drying his foot reminds the friend "of it" (*erinnerte ihn daran*). The *of it* has no clear antecedent: it could just as easily refer to the statue as to the trip to Paris. The narrator then reports that his friend "told me what a discovery he had made." The discovery remains unstated, and it is only by implication that the reader identifies the youth as a representation of the statue. The final anecdote would seem, as de Man has suggested, to offer a commentary on the reader's hermeneutic activity.[20] The bear parries Herr C.'s blows and ignores his feints by looking at him "eye to eye, *as if he could read* my soul" (345, emphasis mine). As if he were the perfect reader who can distinguish truth from appearance, the bear (re)presents Herr C's true intentions, a paragon of the specular paradigm.

Kleist's fencing bear, situated at the conclusion of the three anecdotes, is analogous to the mirror that Novalis uses to complete the genesis of the visual-verbal representation depicted in *Klingsohr's Tale*. To rectify the specular inversion in the Fichtean subject's self-positing, Sophie creates a mirror "that reflects everything in its true form, destroys all illusions, and holds the original image eternally" (I: 311–312). Kleist's bear, like Sophie's mirror, reflects only Herr C.'s true moves, but ignores his feints, thereby reflecting C. "in his true form."

In opposition to Novalis, however, Kleist immediately problematizes his "true mirror." Herr C.'s anecdote is dubbed *wahrscheinlich* or "probable" and followed by a critique of reflection, a critique that is initiated on the linguistic level by the word (*wahr*)(*schein*)(*lich*) itself. Its enclitic elements torn asunder, the word not only calls into question the reflective relationship between *Wahrheit* (truth) and *Schein* (appearance), it also incorporates *in nuce* Kleist's critique of the transcendental formulated in the "Kant crisis" letter: "We cannot decide if that which we call truth really is true, or if it just appears so to us" (*Wir können nicht entscheiden, ob das, was wir Wahrheit nennen, wahrhaft Wahrheit ist, oder ob es uns nur so scheint*, 634). In the face of this specular ambivalence, the self-reflecting subject, like the narcissistic youth or Herr C., becomes *erstaunt*; literally, stiff or rigid.

This, at least, is the upshot of the anecdotal exchange between Herr C. and the narrator, an exchange that is clearly marked as a prolegomenon to the conclusion of the text,[21] the critique of reflection and the transcendental: "Now, my splendid friend, said Herr C., you possess everything necessary to understand me. We see that as reflection becomes darker and weaker in the organic world, the grace therein becomes proportionately more radiant and dominant" (345). Herr C. explicates this statement with a qualifying *but* and two examples, one geometric, the other specular: just as the intersection of two lines, on the one side of a point, after it passes through infinity, suddenly reappears on the other side; or the image of a concave mirror, after it passes through infinity, suddenly reappears before us, so, too, does grace reappear after cognition has gone through an infinity, as it were. Thus, Herr C. concludes, grace simultaneously appears at its purest in that humanoid body which either has no consciousness whatsoever or which has an infinite consciousness; that is, in the marionette or in the god (345).

The overriding argument is clear enough: there is a reciprocal relationship between reflection and grace, and reflection is now on the decline. This statement is diametrically opposed to the thesis advanced in the anecdotes, where the subject, Herr C. or the narcissistic youth, is unable to escape his own reflection and cannot be graceful. In the anecdotes, the self-reflecting subject's stultification is an expression of the ontological threat of the sublime. Here an inversion of the sublime paradigm makes a weakening of reflection possible: grace will reappear after cognition (and not sensibility, as in Kant's model) has gone through an infinity. In opposition to Kant's sublime, which as the representation of ideas is the ultimate expression of the transcendental, here the claim is not to discover and represent the conditions of possibility of pure cognition, but of pure grace. Once reflection weakens, the transcendental claim to represent pure cognition is invalidated, and God (pure reason) and the marionette (the stultified quintessence of sensibility) are equally valid loci of pure representation.

If the goal of *Darstellung* is pure representation, as it is for Kant, Fichte, and the Jena Romantics, then the question is how to weaken reflection, a question that Kleist's text does little to answer. In fact, the point of the text is to illustrate the futility of such an attempt. Immediately following his statement that reflection is on the decline, Herr C. qualifies his contention with a specular example, the image of the concave mirror.[22] Similarly, the narrator's response to Herr C.'s argument is also predicated on recursion:

> So, I said, a bit confused, we'd have to eat from the Tree of Knowledge again, in order to fall back into a state of innocence?

> To be sure, he answered; that is the last chapter of the
> history of the world. (345)

Positioned as the last sentence of the text, Herr C.'s pat
answer would seem to be the conclusion of both the essay
and his argument, yet its linear logic is undercut by circularity. Previously C. had insisted that the key to everything
he says lies in the biblical account of the Fall and that one
must know this first chapter of human history to understand the last (343). He then explicates this linear claim with
a circular one: "But Paradise is locked and the cherub
behind us; we must make the trip around the world and see
if it is perhaps open again from the back somewhere" (342).
Herr C. repeats this circular argument when the narrator
insists that a marionette could not possibly be more graceful
than a human body: "He replied that it would be completely
impossible for a person to come close to the puppet. Only
a god could compete with matter in this field; and here was
the point where both ends of the ring-like world interlocked"
(343). The text itself is structured according to this circular
paradigm. The conversation between Herr C. and the narrator, which takes place "in an open garden" (338), (re)pre-
sents the circular path back to the closed Garden of Eden.
As if to underline this narrative circularity, the conclusion
of the final anecdote harks back to the opening sentences
of the essay: Herr C. meets the fencing bear in a "wooden
stall" (344) reminiscent of the "marionette theater, which
had been hammered together at the market" (338–339).
The text, which begins as a cipher, the marionette theater
"*interwoven* with song and dance," ends with a hermeneu-
tics of decoding, the bear who can read truth from feint.
Thus, the text presents itself as that which it is looking for:
it is an exercise in self-representation or *Selbstdarstellung*.[23]

Like the self-reflexive self-represention of the Jena
Romantics, Kleist's essay turns back on itself in an autocritical gesture and undercuts its own validity. Whereas the
Romantics' theories merely question the possibility of ever
achieving their stated goals,[24] Kleist's text actually nullifies
its own basic premises; and this is precisely the point of its

transcendental framework. The transcendental project almost
works, yet a slight linguistic perturbation separates "Para-
di*se*" from "parado*x*." *Paradox*, of course, does not merely
indicate self-contradiction, but also contention, *paradoxon*.
If Kleist's *On the Marionette Theater* is paradoxical, as the
text itself suggests (342), then perhaps the essay's title has
been misread, and "*Über* das Marionettentheater" ("[to rise]
above the marionette theater") indicates a transcendence
of the transcendental paradigm.

Hence the text's insistence on elevation or *Erhebung*.
It is no accident that Kleist chose to fictionalize the sublime,
das Erhabene, the mainstay of Kant's theory of *Darstellung*.[25] For Kant, we recall, the sublime has two functions.
First, it creates a *negative Darstellung* of the Kantian moral
subject of reason, "the idea of humanity in our subject" (*CJ*
B 97). Kleist's essay questions the feasibility of this artificial
representation of the epistemologically secure subject. The
Kleistian subject is faced with a profound dilemma: it either
strives to become God, the often unspoken and always un-
achievable goal of Idealism and Jena Romanticism; or it
becomes, like a puppet, *erstaunt* or stultified. The second
function of the Kantian sublime is rhetorical. *Negative
Darstellung* allows Kant to discuss issues that fall beyond
the confines of his transcendental *Critiques*. It is a control
mechanism designed to prevent reason "from running amok"
(*CJ* B 125). Kleist's essay, wrought with logical inconsis-
tences, circular argumentation, and a meandering structure,
is designed to promote it.

The Foundling:
The "Apparent Indifference" of the Subject

If *On the Marionette Theater* subverts the Kantian subject of reason, *The Foundling* undermines the self-positing
Fichtean Ego and hence the Romantic redaction of this
model of self-consciousness. Novalis, we recall, derives his
theory of *Darstellung* from the Fichtean first principle: "We
leave the Identical in order to represent it" (II: 104, #1). The
Kleistian subject in *The Foundling* inverts this process of

self-definition. Proceeding from a representation of what he presumes to be himself, the foundling Nicolo defines himself as identical to that which he is not, namely, the character Colino. In effect, Nicolo reverses the formula for the Fichtean subject's self-positing. For Fichte and Novalis the subject posits itself according to the equation: "$I = \text{Not-}I$." For Nicolo the equation reads: "$\text{Not-}I = I$." Ultimately, of course, the two equations are identical, and Kleist's innovation is to draw attention to the "equals" sign in the equation. It is impossible to conclude that Nicolo either is or is not, in some sense, Colino. This confusion of identity is a reiteration of the basic principle of Kleist's theory of representation, namely, the indistinguishability of truth and appearance, and here, as in *On the Marionette Theater*, the subject's self-definition is a function of reflection. The following analysis traces the narrative development of the subject Nicolo, focusing on the relationship between reflection and representation in his self-definition.

First a plot summary. Antonio Piachi, a merchant living in Rome, brings his son Paolo with him on a business trip to Ragusa. There he learns that a plaguelike illness has broken out in the area and a quarantine is about to be imposed. Concerned for his son's welfare, he decides to leave Ragusa, but is stopped by the plague-stricken Nicolo, who begs Piachi to take him with him. Piachi agrees to out of sympathy for the boy, but the police find out about the sick child, and the three are forced to stay in Ragusa until the quarantine is lifted. Piachi's son Paolo is infected by the plague and dies. Nicolo, however, recovers, and Piachi decides to bring the boy home with him to Rome. There he introduces Nicolo to his young wife Elvire, and after some time they adopt Nicolo and cede legal ownership of their estate to him. One night Nicolo comes home from the carnival wearing the costume of a Genoese nobleman and unexpectedly frightens Elvire. Unbeknownst to him, Elvire has apparently mistaken him for her true love, Colino, a Genoese nobleman's son, who years before had saved her from a fire and later died from injuries sustained in the rescue. Meanwhile Nicolo's wife Constanze dies in childbirth, and even before she has been buried Nicolo tries to arrange a tryst with Xaviera Tartini, a woman of ill repute. Piachi catches wind of this and publicly disgraces Nicolo, who incorrectly blames Elvire for blowing the whistle on him. Nicolo vows to avenge this public humiliation, and sets about finding a way to get even with Elvire. One day he hears her talking in her room with what he takes to be a lover, and Nicolo gleefully waits outside her door for the moment when he can confront her with her indiscretion. Much to his dismay, she emerges from the room alone, and when Nicolo goes into the chamber, he finds nothing but a life-size painting of a Genoese nobleman. The person depicted in the painting bears a striking similarity to Nicolo. Following a series of events that seem to Nicolo to confirm this identification, he comes to believe that Elvire is in love with him. Xaviera Tartini tries to dissuade him from this belief by disclosing that the person in the painting is in fact Colino, the young nobleman who had rescued Elvire from the fire. Consumed by jealousy and a desire for revenge, Nicolo dons the costume in which Elvire had mistaken him for Colino and attempts to rape her. He is caught in the act by Piachi, who orders him to leave the house. Nicolo, however, asserts his rights as legal owner of the estate and evicts his adoptive parents. Piachi tries to take legal action against Nicolo, but the authorities side with Nicolo and issue a decree declaring him owner of the property. Piachi, enraged by both this and the fact that Elvire has died from a fever brought on by these happenings, bashes in Nicolo's head. He then stuffs the decree down Nicolo's throat, surrenders to the authorities, and is hanged.

Not a pretty story by any standards, and the vehemence of character and plot development is extreme, even for Kleist.[26] Nonetheless, the novella is structured in a highly calculated manner. Piachi's reversal from a kindly father who takes in a sick child to an enraged man brutally intent on meting out revenge on his adopted son is symptomatic of one of the narrative principles of the text: specular inversion. At the beginning of the story Nicolo is taken in by Piachi and Elvire; at the end he evicts them. At the beginning Nicolo is identified as "God's son" (200); at the end he is described as "satanic" (212) and a "hellish rogue" (213). In Ragusa Piachi agrees to take the sick Nicolo with him, "although he had no idea in the world what he should do with him" (199); at the end Piachi demands to be hanged without absolution so that he can continue his revenge on Nicolo in Hell (213–214). In the opening paragraphs Nicolo takes a handful of nuts out of his pocket and eats them on the trip to Rome (200–201); Piachi inverts this wholesome gesture at the story's end when he takes the decree out of his pocket and stuffs it into the dead Nicolo's mouth (214). When the boy Nicolo is first introduced to Elvire he is described almost like a phallus, and Elvire willingly presses him to her breast, "as strangely and stiffly as he stood before her" (201); Nicolo later forces himself on Elvire in an attempted rape (212–213). The young Nicolo is identified as having two faults, "bigotry" and a "propensity for the female sex" (201); he turns both to his advantage in the final paragraphs by agreeing to marry Xaviera and take her off the Bishop's hands, thereby bribing the Church to side with him and declare him legal owner of the estate (214). Finally, at the start of the story the law prescribes that Piachi stay in Ragusa with the sick Nicolo, and his son Paolo dies as a result of the "gruesomeness of this measure" (200); at the story's end Piachi, "the unfortunate man protected by law" (215) is prevented from dying as he wishes. Hence, the text is structured by a series of reversals consistent with the specular inversion of reflection, and this mirroring principle proves to be instrumental in the subject Nicolo's self-definition.

Nicolo begins his new life with his adoptive parents as a replacement.[27] Piachi takes him "in his son's place" (200) to Rome, where he is given the dead Paolo's clothes and bed. Nicolo is then trained in his father's business, and when Piachi is unsatisfied with a clerk, he gives Nicolo, "instead of him" (201), his job. Piachi goes on to appoint Nicolo legal owner of his estate in his own stead. Nicolo later turns the tables on those who define him when he takes this replacement role to heart and tries to assume his adoptive father's position as sexual partner to Elvire.

Nicolo's attempt to define himself as Colino proceeds according to the same replacement logic. He is first put into Colino's role by Elvire and then defines himself accordingly. Nicolo is unaware of the identification when it first occurs. One night he comes home from the carnival disguised as a Genoese nobleman and frightens Elvire, who apparently mistakes him for her dead love Colino. It is also possible that Elvire sees him for what he is: her adoptive son who bears a striking resemblance to her dead lover. In fact, it is not entirely clear what happens, because Elvire, petrified, cannot speak: "the matter thus remained shrouded in an eternal secret" (204). Despite Elvire's silence, the reader, who has just been apprised of Elvire's rescue from the fire, draws a connection between Colino and Nicolo.

This is the first stage in the fusing together or confusion of the two characters, and it is noteworthy that the word *Vorspiegelung*, pretense or misrepresentation, is the operative term in the opening lines of the passage introducing the event:

> Einstmals war Nicolo, mit jener Xaviera Tartini, mit welcher er trotz des *Verbots* des *Vaters*, die *Verbindung* nie ganz aufgegeben hatte, heimlich, und ohne *Vorwissen* seiner Gemahlin, unter der *Vorspiegelung*, dass er bei einem Freund eingeladen sei, auf dem Karneval gewesen und kam, in der Maske eines genuesischen Ritters, die er zufällig gewählt hatte, spät in der Nacht, da schon alles schlief, in sein Haus zurück. (203–204, emphasis mine)

> Once Nicolo had gone, with Xaviera Tartini, with whom he had never completely broken off connections in spite of his father's forbidding, secretly, and without his wife's knowledge, under the pretense that he had been invited to a friend's, to the carnival, and came back home wearing the costume of a Genoese nobleman, which he had chosen by chance, late in the night, when everyone was already asleep.

The series of *V* words in the German passage (*Verbot, Vater, Verbindung, Vorwissen, Vorspiegelung*) culminates in the word *Vorspiegelung*. Graphically, the letter *V* is formed by a convergence of two lines in a single point. Thematically, two identities—Nicolo's and Colino's—converge at this point, this *Vorspiegelung*. The word *Vorspiegelung* refers first and foremost to pretense or misrepresentation, but on the literal level it also indicates a prereflexive state or act, a (*Vor*)(*Spiegelung*), and this detail proves significant in a text where literalization is taken literally. In fact, Nicolo's self-definition will involve a mirror, and it is unclear whether this mirror provides a misrepresentation or a reflection of the subject.

An interlude follows this prereflexive stage of Nicolo's definition. His wife Constanze dies in childbirth, and Nicolo finds himself once again free to pursue his two vices, his bigotry and his strong propensity for women. On the eve of Constanze's funeral Elvire discovers Xaviera Tartini's maid in Nicolo's room but does not say a word to anyone about what she has seen. Piachi, returning home, sees the maid and intercepts the note Nicolo has sent to his long-time lover requesting a meeting. Enraged at Nicolo's callousness, Piachi answers the note in Xaviera's name and arranges a tryst for the two lovers in the church where Constanze is to be buried. Nicolo shows up at the appointed time and is met by the funeral procession. When he asks Piachi to explain what this is supposed to mean and who is being carried in, Piachi only answers: "Xaviera Tartini," and the corpse is buried.

This scene might be called, to borrow terms used elsewhere in the text, a *Verstellung* (207) or a *Versetzung* (210), a displacement or disarrangement of elements. Two steps are involved in this process. First, Nicolo's wife Constanze is replaced by Xaviera. By labeling the corpse "Xaviera" Piachi in some sense puts Nicolo in the same position as Elvire: the object of his love is a "dead" person. The second step in the process is motivated by the fact that the events leading up to his public disgrace arouse in Nicolo an awareness of Elvire as a sexual object (206), and she now replaces Xaviera as the object of Nicolo's desire. Just as Elvire (perhaps) unconsciously shifts her love from the dead Colino to the living Nicolo, Nicolo now transfers his desire from the "dead" Xaviera to Elvire. To summarize, Nicolo's wife *Constanze*, constancy, is first replaced by Xaviera Tartini, whose name incorporates a crossing and a mirroring (the letter *X* and the repetition of sounds in the name Tartini). Replacing the *X* leads to the second substitution: *Xaviera* is displaced by *Elvire*. Hence, via the series of replacements: Constanze— Xaviera—Elvire, Nicolo transfers his love from his wife, Elvire's niece, to Elvire, his adoptive mother.

This displacement or *Verstellung* triggers Nicolo's self-definition. Determined to catch Elvire in a sexual transgression so that he might get even with her for disgracing him, Nicolo eavesdrops on her. Looking through the keyhole to her room, he sees Elvire lying at someone's feet. He then hears her speak "with an accent of love" (207) the whispered word: Colino. Nicolo, convinced that he now has ammunition to topple the "sanctimonious" Elvire (*die Scheinheilige;* literally: having the appearance of holiness, 207), waits outside the room so that he can confront her and her lover. Elvire, however, emerges alone and walks past him "with a glance that was completely *indifferent* (*gleichgültig*) and calm" (207, emphasis mine). This indifference or *Gleichgültigkeit* infuriates Nicolo, and he runs to find the keys to Elvire's chamber.

Keys and unlocking are recurring leitmotifs in the novella, and Nicolo's strong reaction to Elvire's behavior is obliquely identified as the "master key" (*Hauptschlüssel,* 207) to the series of replacements that runs throughout the text: "This *dissimulation,* this *apparent indifference,* seemed to him the epitome of insolence and cunning" (*Diese* **Verstellung***, diese* **scheinbare Gleichgültigkeit***, schien ihm der Gipfel der Frechheit und Arglist,* 207, emphasis mine). The equation of the phrases *Verstellung* and *scheinbare Gleichgültigkeit* is essential here. At first glance, it would appear that Nicolo is annoyed by Elvire's "dissimulation" and "apparent indifference," yet there is more to the words *Verstellung* and *Gleichgültigkeit* than first meets the eye. *Verstellung* refers not only to pretense or dissimulation, but also to a transposition, displacement, or misplacement of elements. *Gleich-*

gültigkeit means indifference, but on the literal level the word also indicates equal validity, (*Gleich*)(*gültig*)(*keit*). Hence, one way to read the sentence "Diese *Verstellung*, diese *scheinbare Gleichgültigkeit*, schien ihm der Gipfel der Frechheit und Arglist" is that presenting a displacement or misplacement of elements as apparently equal—that is, passing off displacement or deception as (re)presentation—is the epitome of insolence and cunning.

This formula, a cipher for the narrative technique that structures the novella, is of particular importance in the definition of the subject Nicolo. Nicolo is first put in the place of Colino by Elvire, and he then interprets this *Verstellung*, this displacement or misplacement, as valid. Nicolo's interpretation, however, is only part of the definition. The other characters, as well as the reader, must judge whether Nicolo is, in some sense, Colino, or whether the *Verstellung* or displacement involves dissimulation. According to the formula, both readings appear to be equally valid, and the text in fact provides evidence for both possibilities.

The narrative confusion of the two characters is heightened when the subject Nicolo finally takes on an identity for himself. Up until this point Nicolo has always been defined by others, but when he opens the door to Elvire's room convinced that he will find her lover secreted within, he begins to define himself: "But how astonished he was when he found everything empty, and discovered in all four corners that he peered into nothing that even remotely resembled a person: except for the life-size painting of a young nobleman that was displayed in a niche in the wall behind a red silk curtain, illuminated by a special light" (207). Nicolo's discovery of the painting behind the curtain is a redaction of a literary motif current at the time in the works of Kant, Schiller, Fichte, and Novalis, "the veiled image at Saïs." For Kant the injunction against lifting the goddess's veil is the epitome of the sublime (*CJ* B 197, note); in Schiller's poem "The Veiled Image at Saïs" a young man lifts the goddess's veil, is struck dumb by what he sees and dies young as punishment for his transgression;[28] whereas in Fichte's sonnet (*GA* I, 8: 32)[29] and Novalis's distich lifting the goddess's veil constitutes self-definition (II: 584,

#250). Similarly, for Kleist, lifting the curtain constitutes a definition of the subject, but in opposition to Novalis the Kleistian subject is not able to make the identification by himself: "Nicolo was startled, he himself didn't know why: and a multitude of thoughts went through his breast as he looked at the big eyes of the picture that gazed rigidly at him" (207). At this point Nicolo is unsure of what he sees.

Filled with a burning desire to find out "who might be meant by it" (207), he invites Xaviera Tartini to see the painting. She comes, bringing with her a small daughter who defines Nicolo when the curtain is lifted: "But how shocked Nicolo was when little Klara (that was the daughter's name), as soon as he had lifted the curtain, cried out: "God, my Father! Signor Nicolo, who is that, other than you?" (*Gott, mein Vater! Signor Nicolo, wer ist das anders, als Sie?* 208). Klara's identification is ambiguous. Her utterance can be divided into two distinct statements. One is the query: "Signor Nicolo, who is that, other than you?" The fact that this statement is expressed in the form of a question leaves open the possibility that the person in the painting is indeed someone other than Nicolo. The phrase appended to the question obliquely suggests who this other person might be. Klara first responds to the painting with the words: "God, my Father!" and this locution can be read as both an exclamation and an identification. The latter interpretation is of particular interest. It is quite possible that what Klara says is: "God = my father = Signor Nicolo = who is that, other than you?" This interpretation is plausible, because Nicolo is identified as "God's son" earlier in the text (200), and Klara's own parentage is questionable. She is described as *a* small daughter (therefore not necessarily *Xaviera's* small daughter) whom Xaviera had "von dem Kardinal" (208), which could mean either "by the Cardinal," implying that he is the father, or "from the Cardinal," indicating perhaps that he was merely an agent who somehow "delivered" Klara to Xaviera. Nicolo then responds to Klara's exclamation with a statement that draws her paternity into doubt: "*truly*, dearest Klara, the painting resembles me, as you do the person who believes himself your father!" (**wahrhaftig**, *liebste Klara, das Bild* *gleicht mir, wie du demjenigen, der sich deinen Vater glaubt*, 208, emphasis mine). The word *truly* or *wahrhaftig* (literally; truelike) triggers the same play between truth and appearance, *Wahrheit* and *Schein*, that is operative in the "Kant crisis" letter and *On the Marionette Theater*. In effect, Nicolo's statement sets up the following equation:

$$\frac{\text{painting}}{\text{Nicolo}} = \frac{\text{Klara}}{\text{"father"}}$$

For Klara's "father" to define himself as such, he must *believe* that he is the father. Similarly, Nicolo must *believe* he is the person in the painting to define himself as that person. Just as the Cardinal may err in thinking he is Klara's father, Nicolo may be mistaken in believing that he is the person depicted in the painting, and this is why the question of paternity is so crucial here. Because Nicolo and Xaviera have a long-standing relationship, it is not unthinkable that Nicolo *is* Klara's father. If this is the case, then the equation might be rewritten in the following way:

$$\frac{\text{Klara}}{\text{Nicolo}} = \frac{\text{painting}}{\text{"father"}}$$

In other words, as Frank Ryder has suggested, the person depicted in the painting may be Nicolo's father.[30] Xaviera will later claim that the painting is of Colino, Elvire's long-dead lover, and if Colino is indeed Nicolo's father, this would explain the "striking similarity" (208) between the two.

The text, however, remains inconclusive in this regard. At the end of the scene Xaviera is overcome by jealousy at the thought that Elvire may be in love with Nicolo, and she tries to discount the similarity she sees between Nicolo and the painting: "she said, *as she stepped in front of the mirror*, after all *it didn't matter* who the person was; excused herself rather coldly and left the room" (*sie sagte,* **indem sie vor den Spiegel trat**, *zuletzt sei es* **gleichgültig***, wer die*

Person sei; empfahl sich ihm ziemlich kalt und verliess das Zimmer, 208, emphasis mine). Once again the word *gleichgültig* ("indifferent" or "equally valid") appears at a decisive point in the text. On one level what Xaviera says is that it does not matter who the person is. On another, she implies that both identifications—Nicolo and Colino— are equally valid. It is extremely curious that Xaviera should step in front of a mirror when she makes this comment. This action suggests that self-definition is a function of reflection. In opposition to Idealist and Romantic definitions of the subject, here someone other than the subject reflects in the process of self-definition: Nicolo is being defined, Klara makes the identification, and Xaviera steps in front of the mirror. Hence, it should come as no surprise that the subject Nicolo has difficulty defining himself.

Nicolo emerges from the episode convinced that he is the person depicted in the painting. Somewhat disturbed by the fact that Elvire had uttered the name Colino rather than his own name in front of the picture, he nonetheless manages to explain away this nominal inconsistency by ignoring it. The name Colino for some reason "cradles his heart in sweet dreams" (209), and the newborn subject Nicolo, as yet blissfully unaware of the person Colino's existence, is convinced that Elvire is in love with him. He then justifies the appellation Colino in the second stage of his self-definition. One day Nicolo, dismayed by the indifference with which Elvire is treating him, toys with some ivory letters that spell his name. He rearranges the letters and finds out, quite by accident, the narrator reports, that the letters spell the name Colino. He leaves the letters on the table hoping Elvire will see them, and her strong reaction to the name confirms Nicolo's suspicions that she is in love with him: "Nicolo. . . no longer doubted that she hid his own name under this transposition or displacement (*Versetzung*) of letters" (210). His willingness to believe what he reads is related to the bigotry the narrator identifies as one of his two faults (etymologically, "bigotry" is derived from "a faith in letters"[31]), and Xaviera soon dissuades him from this conviction. She researches the issue and returns with the information that Colino, the Marquis von Montferrat, was the "original" of the picture (211). Xaviera's identification unpleasantly shakes the infant subject Nicolo from his cradle (211), and he must now use "deception" (*Betrug*, 212) to fight for his identity.

Donning the costume he had worn on the night when Elvire had mistaken him for Colino, Nicolo goes into Elvire's room, hangs a black cloth over the painting, and poses like the person in the picture. By covering the painting, Nicolo defines himself as the "original" and the picture as the representation. Elvire comes in, sees him, utters the words "Colino! My beloved," and sinks, unconscious, to the floor. Nicolo then rips the black cloth from the painting, and carries Elvire to the bed. In removing the cloth Nicolo relinquishes his status as an "original" and reestablishes himself as a representation of the picture. Piachi comes in, finds Nicolo assaulting his wife, is made speechless by a few words that Elvire utters, and attempts to evict Nicolo from the house. In other words, Piachi tries to strip Nicolo of the definition he has given him: his designation of Nicolo as adoptive son and legal owner of the estate. This, we recall, was the first stage in the subject Nicolo's development: his definition as a replacement for others. Nicolo now refuses to give up this definition, and this proves to be a fatal mistake. Piachi dashes his brains against a wall, thereby inflicting on Nicolo the same wound that had killed Colino (203), and crams down his throat the document granting Nicolo legal ownership of the estate. This is the final stage in Nicolo's definition: the subject incorporates the law.

Let us summarize the stages of Nicolo's definition. Following the incident in Ragusa, where the law dictates that Piachi and his son must stay in the plague-stricken area with the sick Nicolo, Nicolo is taken in by Piachi and defined by others as a replacement. Nicolo is thus *displaced* or even *misplaced* into the identity of an "other" (*Versetzung*). Elvire then sees him disguised as a Genoese nobleman and identifies him as Colino. Nicolo is hence defined via *dissimulation* (*Vorspiegelung*, also *prereflection*). Nicolo, unaware of this identification, finds the painting, and Klara supplies

Nicolo with his self-definition (reflection or *Spiegelung*). Nicolo confirms this definition with the ivory letters. Xaviera then identifies the picture as Colino (reflection interpreted as misplacement or dissimulation, *Verstellung*). Nicolo responds by covering the painting to deceive Elvire into thinking he is the picture's original (deception or *Vorspiegelung*). When he uncovers the painting he reestablishes himself as a representation (displacement or *Versetzung*). He then refuses to give up his definition as replacement, resulting in the final stage in his definition when Piachi shoves the legal document down his throat: the law is inscribed in the subject.

Hence, Nicolo's development unfolds symmetrically around an axis of reflection: law, displacement (*Versetzung*), dissimulation and prereflection (*Vorspiegelung*), reflection (*Spiegelung*), dissimulation (*Vorspiegelung*), displacement (*Versetzung*), law. This sequence would seem to confirm that the definition of the subject proceeds according to the same formula that Nicolo found so distasteful in Elvire's behavior: presenting a displacement or misplacement of elements as apparently equal—that is, passing off displacement or deception as (re)presentation—is the epitome of insolence and cunning (*Diese Verstellung, diese scheinbare Gleichgültigkeit, schien ihm der Gipfel der Frechheit und Arglist*, 207). In other words, Nicolo defines himself by interpreting his displacement onto the character Colino as an apparent equivalence of identity.

What is remarkable about Nicolo's self-definition, however, is that it is impossible to prove that the "*apparent* indifference" between the two characters, the "*apparently* equal validity" of either identification (*die* **scheinbare** *Gleichgültigkeit*) is not a de facto indifference or equivalence. To take the central mirror scene in front of the painting as a case in point, it is not clear that Nicolo does err in believing that he is a representation of the person depicted in the painting. The text itself motivates the definition. In the opening paragraphs of the novella the boy Nicolo, the only character to be described in any detail, is characterized as a picture: he has "a peculiar, rather rigid beauty," he is "untalkative," and his face never changes its mien (200). He also occupies the same physical position as the painting: he sits "in the corner" (200), while the painting stands "in a niche" (207). Moreover, he is identified as "God's son" (200), while Colino, who "suffers and dies" for Elvire (203), is clearly a Christ figure, and the two characters are killed by identical wounds to the head. The child Klara, whose name would seem to mark her with clear-sightedness, identifies the person in the painting as Nicolo; and Xaviera, who has a vested interest in disproving this identification, denies it. It is quite possible that Xaviera's identification of the person in the picture as Colino is deliberately false. When she makes the identification she is described as "strangely roguish" (211) and "arch" (212); and Frank Ryder has pointed out an overt inconsistency in her statement: she identifies the person depicted in the painting as a "Marquis," and Colino is not a marquis, but the *son* of a marquis.[32] Is it possible that Klara is correct in stating that Nicolo is, in some sense, Colino? The names are linked by more than an anagram. They are in fact virtually identical: Colino is a diminutive form of Nicolo.[33]

How, then, to interpret the "striking similarity" that exists between the two characters? Not surprisingly, the critics disagree. Frank Ryder has suggested that Nicolo may be Colino and Elvire's son.[34] J. Hillis Miller dismisses the possibility of any equivalence between the two characters, arguing that the text is structured by a process of substitution in which similarities are misread as identities.[35] Marjorie Gelus, in apparent agreement with Miller, claims that the narrator is intent on constructing an aura of mystery where none need exist; it is only because Nicolo believes that he is Colino that he sees the similarity.[36] Historically speaking, the text is indeed a "mystification," as Diethelm Brüggemann has shown. One of Kleist's sources for *The Foundling* was Cepari's chronicle of the historical figure Colino, Aloysius Gonzaga, Marquis of Montferrat. There is no character "Nicolo" in the chronicle. According to Brüggemann, Nicolo is a fictional construct of the historical Colino. At least two of his attributes, his bigotry and his propensity for women,

are derived from a reversal of the historical Colino's, who
had a sound relationship with the Carmelite monks and at
an early age declared he had no interest in women. In other
words, Nicolo is in some sense the "Not-I" of the historical
Colino.[37]

Nonetheless, Kleist did fictionalize, did mystify, did
create two characters who may or may not be one. To read
The Foundling as a study in the subject is to conclude that
Nicolo's identity is *scheinbar gleichgültig*, apparently
indifferent, that to define him as either Colino or not Colino
is "apparently equally valid." Given the repetition of the
word *gleichgültig* throughout the narrative, it is notewothy
that the law is identified as the only element in the text that
is *vollgültig*, fully valid (213). In fact, the law defines the
subject from the very beginning of the text. The novella
begins with Piachi protesting "the gruesomeness of the law"
(200) that forces him to stay in Ragusa with the sick Nicolo
and ends with Piachi cramming the legal document down
Nicolo's throat and cursing "the inhuman law" (215) that
will not allow him to die without absolution. This "inhuman
law" defines and kills the subject in *The Foundling*.
Representation, as Roland Barthes has suggested, is inherently legal,[38] and this is why Piachi will not accept absolution when he is condemned to die at the story's conclusion.
In refusing the Church sacrament, he refuses to be cut loose
(*ab-solvere*) from the legal and representational system that
forced this injustice on him, and in so doing he actually
circumvents the system: the Pope must break Church law
and order him hanged without his last rites. Piachi's death
is a kind of Kantian *negative Darstellung*. The Kleistian
subject, pushed to its limits, transcends the limits of representation, yet paradoxically stays within its confines.[39]

The definition of the subject lies at the root of the
Darstellung problematic. The reasons for this are clear: the
subject is the source of representation, the subject *stellt dar*.
In Kant's, Fichte's, and Novalis's theories of *Darstellung*,
what the subject represents is itself: the Kantian moral
subject of reason or the Fichtean absolute Ego. In other
words, the subject is both the origin and the goal of repre-

sentation, a state of affairs analogous to the vicious circle of reflection that Kleist criticizes in *On the Marionette Theater*. Unlike the Kantian, Fichtean, and Jena Romantic models of self-consciousness, the Kleistian subject does not posit itself but is posited by others in ways beyond its control. Without this epistemologically secure subject, representation becomes unstable. Kleist realized this early in his career. In February 1801, one month before his "Kant crisis," he writes: "Even language, the one thing that we do have, can't do it, it can't paint the soul, it gives us only tattered fragments" (626). Novalis, faced with a similar predicament, develops a visual *poiesis* designed to represent the subject, and Kleist's rhetoric here indicates a solution in kind, if not in spirit. In the final section I will argue that the "tattered fragments" of *The Broken Jug* actually "paint" an opposing paradigm of visual-verbal representation.

The Broken Jug:
"Deceived by Appearances"

At its Weimar premiere in 1808, a bored audience booed Goethe's production of *The Broken Jug* off the stage; and Kleist, chagrined, excised over sixteen pages from the play's conclusion.[40] Despite the fact that the original ending was printed in its entirety in the 1811 edition of Kleist's works, the shortened version of the text has entered the canon. As a result, the longer variant has received scanty attention in the scholarship, and the full text of the play remains curiously unread.[41]

The standard interpretation of the play is based on the following story line. Set in Huisum, a small Dutch town near Utrecht, the comedy presents the foiled attempt of the town judge, Adam, to coerce Eve, a young woman in the town, into granting him sexual favors in return for fabricating a document that would exempt Eve's fiancé Ruprecht from the draft. Late one evening around ten o'clock Adam appears in Eve's garden with the affidavit. Under the pretext that he needs light to complete the certificate, he convinces Eve to bring him to her room. Meanwhile, Ruprecht, who has stopped by to visit with his fiancée, sees Adam and Eve talking in the garden, and when the two disappear into Eve's chamber, Ruprecht follows in hot pursuit. He bursts into the room, surprising Adam, who jumps out the window. In the ensuing melee an earthen jug is broken, symbolizing, the other characters suppose, Eve's lost virginity. Eve's mother Marthe, hearing the noise, comes running. Finding Ruprecht in her daughter's room surrounded by pottery shards, she accuses him of the deed. Ruprecht denies the charge, and the next morning Marthe brings Eve and Ruprecht, together with the broken jug, to the town judge, Adam, whose own guilt in the matter becomes increasingly clear as the investigation proceeds. The trial, supervised by the justice Walter, whose name attests his Godlike authority, and recorded by the scribe Licht, whose name means "light," unfolds in a process of progressive enlightenment. As Adam's role in the previous night's happenings comes to light, the drama takes on the character of an inverted Fall story in which Adam's attempt to lead Eve astray fails. Hence, at the play's end Ruprecht is vindicated, Eve's reputation is restored, Adam is suspended from office, Licht is appointed judge in his stead, and the broken jug, incorrectly identified as a symbol of Eve's virginity, is to be replaced at the market in Utrecht.

But things are seldom so simple in the Kleistian world, and Frau Marthe is quite right to surmise that the play's story line is "split . . . from head to foot" (221). In fact, a much different story is told on another level of the text. To put it bluntly, Eve lies. The jug is in fact a symbol of her virginity, and Marthe's suspicion that "The destruction of the jug was not the only crime committed last night" (220) is well-founded. Adam breaks the earthen jug in his flight from Ruprecht, and although it is true that he is unsuccessful on the sexual level in breaking Eve's "jug," Ruprecht succeeds where Adam has failed. Although his actions are reprehensible, Adam is, as he himself claims, a scapegoat (229). Hence, the play begins with Licht describing Adam as "A sheep . . . hounded by dogs" (178) and ends with Adam running in the hills outside of town, whipped, like the traditional scapegoat figure, by his own wig (244). Walter is right to worry that he has been overhasty in believing Eve's testimony, "word for word" (57v). Eve, hardly the picture of innocence and naivité she purports to be,[42] twice admits to turning "cunning against cunning"(49v) to protect Ruprecht, who, true to his name, is a rogue: Knave Ruprecht, who accompanies St. Nikolaus, is traditionally associated with the Devil. Similarly, Licht and Walter are not the Enlightenment guarantors of law they would seem to be.[43] Their actions are as despicable as Adam's. Licht, guilty of embezzling tax money (182), states that he and Adam are "birds of a feather" (181); and Adam's characterization of Walter as "the worthy man who shears his own sheep" (179) is more than fitting: at the play's conclusion Walter mirrors Adam's exploitation of authority in return for sexual favors by giving Eve a kiss (58v). In other words, Kleist's *Lustspiel* (175) is not so much a "comedy" as a *Spiel der Lüste*, a play of passions.

There is, then, I am arguing, a subtext that subverts the traditional straightforward reading of the play just outlined. Kleist hinted as much when he wrote to Friedrich de la Motte Fouqué that only a very critical friend would be able to read the text as a blueprint of his soul (862). To be sure, this subtext is not readily apparent without close attention to the structure and language of the play. Perhaps Goethe realized this when he stated that the drama tended toward "the dialectical" and that it was unfortunate that Kleist had once again written a play that belonged to "the invisible theater."[44] Goethe's comment, written with an eye toward the stage, was clearly intended as censure, yet from a representational point of view, the notion of "invisible theater" is exceedingly interesting. *Theater*, by definition, involves an act of seeing (this, in fact, is the word's derivation, from the Greek *thea*), and *invisible theater* would seem to be a contradiction in terms. Paradoxically, however, vision can be heightened in "invisible theater." By having one's attention drawn to the visual, one sees what is not shown and is hence made aware of the limits of representation. Certainly this is the case in *The Broken Jug*: the play, grounded in a description of a copper engraving and liberally punc-

tuated with the imperative "See!" is thoroughly informed
by visual representation.

The play's Preface emphasizes the importance of visual
representation to the dialogue that follows.[45] Kleist had seen
Jean Jacques Le Veau's copper engraving "The Judge, or
The Broken Jug" in Bern in 1802, and this picture provided
the basis for his comedy:

> Diesem Lustspiel liegt *wahrscheinlich* ein historisches
> Faktum, worüber ich jedoch keine nähere Auskunft
> habe auffinden können, zum Grunde. Ich nahm die
> Veranlassung dazu aus einem Kupferstich, den ich vor
> mehreren Jahren in der Schweiz sah. Man bemerkte
> darauf—zuerst einen Richter, der gravitätisch auf dem
> Richterstuhl sass: vor ihm stand eine alte Frau, die
> einen zerbrochenen Krug hielt, sie *schien* das Unrecht,
> das ihm widerfahren war, zu demonstrieren: Beklagter,
> ein junger Bauerkerl, den, der Richter, als überwiesen,
> andonnerte, *verteidigte sich noch, aber schwach*: ein
> Mädchen, das *wahrscheinlich* in dieser Sache gezeugt
> hatte (denn *wer weiss*, bei welcher Gelegenheit das
> Deliktum geschehen war) spielte sich, in der Mitte zwi-
> schen Mutter und Bräutigam, an der Schürze; *wer ein
> falsches Zeugnis abgelegt hätte*, könnte nicht zer-
> knirschter dastehn: und der Gerichtsschreiber sah (er
> hatte *vielleicht* kurz vorher das Mädchen angesehen)
> jetzt den Richter misstrauisch zur Seite an, wie Kreon,
> bei einer ähnlichen Gelegenheit, den Ödip. Darunter
> stand: der zerbrochene Krug.—Das Original war, *wenn
> ich nicht irre*, von einem niederländischen Meister.
> (176, emphasis mine)

This comedy *probably* has as its basis a historical fact,
about which I have been unable to find further information. I took my inspiration for it from a copper engraving
that I saw several years ago in Switzerland. In it one
observed—first a judge, who sat gravely on the bench:
in front of him stood an old woman, who held a broken
jug, she *appeared* to be demonstrating the injustice

done to it: the accused, a young farmer, whom the judge thundered at as if already convicted, *still defended himself, but weakly*: a girl, who had *probably* testified in the case (for *who knows* what the circumstances of the crime were), stood between mother and bridegroom, and played with her apron; *one who had given false testimony* couldn't have stood there more contritely: and the court scribe (who had *perhaps* looked at the girl shortly before), now glanced sideways at the judge suspiciously, like Creon, under similar circumstances, had looked at Oedipus. Underneath stood: The Broken Jug.—The original was, *if I don't err*, by a Dutch master.

Kleist does in fact err in his description: in the original picture the jug is held by the girl, not the old woman; the judge does not thunder at the accused youth, but sits complacently; the scribe glances sideways at the old woman, not the judge; and Le Veau's engraving is not a reproduction of a Dutch master, but of the French painter Louis Philibert Debucourt.[46]

Literary invention aside, Kleist's description of the engraving raises the question of its own veracity. The passage begins with the assertion that the comedy is "probably" rooted in historical fact, yet this fact does not lend itself to further investigation (*Diesem Lustspiel liegt **wahrscheinlich** ein historisches Faktum, worüber ich jedoch keine nähere Auskunft habe auffinden können, zum Grunde*). By inverting his sentence structure, Kleist shifts the emphasis from the "historical fact" to the word *wahrscheinlich*, "probably." In qualifying the asserted historical facticity with this word *wahrscheinlich*, Kleist sets into motion the same tension between *Wahrheit* and *Schein*, truth and appearance, that is at play in the "Kant crisis" letter, *On the Marionette Theater*, and *The Foundling*. The notion of "probability" is then carried over to the description of the picture: the old woman "seemed" to be demonstrating the injustice done to the jug; the girl had "probably" testified in the matter, but "who knows" under what circumstances the crime was committed; and the scribe had "perhaps" looked at the girl shortly before. However, the notion of "probability" proves to be just as suspect here as in *On the Marionette Theater* and *The Foundling*, and it is therefore significant to the understanding of the text that Kleist concludes his Preface by introducing a potential "error," the ascription of the "original" to a Dutch master.

Drawing into question the status of the "original" perforce draws into question the status of (re)presentations of the original, and precisely this representational credibility is at stake in *The Broken Jug*. The play's title suggests as much: at issue here is whether or not the broken jug represents Eve's *innocence perdue*. The play's characters come to believe that it does not, yet the Preface indicates that it might. In his description of the picture Kleist characterizes the girl as perhaps lying: "one who had given false testimony couldn't have stood there more contritely" (*wer ein falsches Zeugnis abgelegt hätte, könnte nicht zerknirschter dastehn*). In typically Kleistian fashion, this is the only sentence in the Preface written in the subjunctive, a fact that calls into question the truth value of this pivotal statement. Similarly, the passage also suggests that the youth, too, may be lying: he is described as "still defending himself, but weakly." If the Preface represents the action of the play, and perhaps it is a hermeneutic faux pas to assume that it does, then it would seem that Eve and Ruprecht may be guilty.

In addition to setting into play the tension between *Wahrheit* (truth) and *Schein* (appearance) that runs throughout the drama, the Preface also contains a further indication of the representational principle used to structure the text; namely, the identification of the judge as an Oedipus figure. Like Sophocles' *Oedipus Rex, The Broken Jug* unfolds in a series of progressive revelations about previous actions. Unlike Oedipus, Adam, of course, is well aware of his transgression from the very beginning of the play. Nonetheless, Adam's similarity to Oedipus is profound: he not only has a club foot, his eye is also wounded during his nocturnal visit to Eve's garden (178).

This sight motif is especially important to *The Broken Jug*. Since the Greeks, ideation has been represented using visual metaphors, and one of the central oppositions in Sophocles' play is between the blind prophet Teiresias, who "sees," and Oedipus, who blinds himself because he does not. Similarly, Kleist uses a visual semantics to play out the representational tension between truth and appearance in *The Broken Jug*. As the characters realize, the ability to see through appearances is critical to discovering what really happened in Eve's chamber. Eve claims her mother was "deceived by appearances" (*vom Schein getäuscht*, 54v) when she accuses Ruprecht, and Adam protests that he has been "damned by appearances" (*vom Anschein verdammt*, 239). Hence, the characters are constantly exhorting each other to "see," to distinguish truth from appearance.

The tension between sight and appearance is set up in the opening lines of the dialogue. The first scene begins with the apposition of the words *Aussehen* and *sehen*, appearance and sight:

LICHT: Ei, was zum Henker, sagt, Gevatter Adam!
         Was ist mit Euch geschehn? Wie *seht* Ihr *aus*?
ADAM: Ja, *seht*.   (177, emphasis mine)

LICHT: Well, what the devil! Tell me, Father Adam!
         What happened to you? What do you *look like*
         (*aussehen*)?
ADAM: Yes, *see* (*sehen*).

Having reduced *Aussehen* (appearance) to its visual root, *sehen* (sight), Adam proceeds to apply the same logic to the word *unbildlich*, "unmetaphorical" or "literal":

ADAM: Hier bin ich hingefallen, sag ich Euch.
LICHT: Unbildlich hingeschlagen?
ADAM: Ja, unbildlich.
         Es mag ein schlechtes Bild gewesen sein. (177)
LICHT: Bei meiner Treu! und keiner malts Euch nach.[47]

ADAM: I fell down here, I tell you.
LICHT: You literally (*unbildlich*) were stuck down?

ADAM: Yes, unmetaphorically (*unbildlich*).
         It must have been a bad picture (*Bild*).
LICHT: On my honor! and no one will be able to repaint
         it for you.

This description of Adam's "Fall" incorporates *in nuce* the
representational issues at stake in the text. First, it illustrates
the literalization of metaphor, and the point of the entire
play is to determine whether the "broken jug" is in fact a
metaphor for Eve's virginity. Second, reducing the metaphor
unbildlich (unmetaphorical) to its root, *Bild* (picture), not
only points out the essential figurativeness of language (à
la Nietzsche), it also raises the question of the relationship
between visual and verbal representation. This, of course,
is one of the central issues of the eighteenth century's debate
on aesthetic imitation (*Nachahmungsdebatte*), and Kleist
changes the terms of the debate. The problem is no longer
to examine the representational limits of a given medium
(Winckelmann, Lessing, et al.) or to determine how the two
media might complement each other (Novalis's visual-verbal
poiesis), but to draw attention to the fact that representation
may be predicated on false assumptions or error. Hence, in
the preceding passage Adam states that the picture may be
"bad," and this suggestion in turn raises the question of
the status of the play's other two images: the copper engraving described in the Preface and the picture painted on
the jug. Intuitively one would expect that these images are
somehow related to the play's action, yet Adam's warning
about "bad" pictures suggests that the play's verbal representations of these images also may be spurious. Finally,
Licht's response, "and no one will be able to repaint it for
you," implies that at least one of these pictures may be
irreproducible. "Repainting the picture" of the previous
night's action is, of course, what the play's characters, as
well as its viewers or readers, purport to do. Thus, Adam's
Fall, marked by its name as a representational event in a
long biblical tradition, calls into question the status of
(re)presentation.[48]

The play's second "Fall," that of the jug, reiterates the representational issues at stake in the first. Just as Adam introduces his Fall with a play on sight and appearance, Frau Marthe, presenting the broken jug to the other characters, urges them to consider what it is that they see:

FRAU MARTHE: Seht ihr den Krug, ihr wertgeschätzten Herren?
Seht ihr den Krug?
ADAM: O ja, wir sehen ihn.
FRAU MARTHE: Nichts seht ihr, mit Verlaub, die Scherben seht ihr;
Der Krüge schönster ist entzwei geschlagen. (200)

FRAU MARTHE: Do you see the jug, you worthy gentlemen,
Do you see the jug?
ADAM: Oh, yes, we see it.
FRAU MARTHE: You see nothing, begging your pardon, you see shards;
The most beautiful of jugs has been broken in two (*entzwei geschlagen*).

According to Marthe, the characters see two different, yet syntactically equivalent, things when they look at the jug: they see "nothing" and they see "shards." The jug, Marthe reports, has been "*entzwei geschlagen*," a phrase that on the metaphorical level means "smashed to pieces" and on the literal level means "broken in two." Indeed, in the previous night's escapade, the jug has literally been broken in two: as a result of its fall, it not only is broken into pieces, it also becomes a signifier of Eve's virginity. Before according it this new representational status, however, Marthe considers it necessary to establish what the jug, "this earthen jug, the jug of clay" (201), represented before its fall. Her lengthy description is divided into two parts. First, she describes the shattered image depicted on the jug, the ceding of the Netherlands to the Spanish and the passing on of legal authority. This image has now been replaced by a "hole" (200), a crude sexual allusion to the jug's new definition as Eve's "jug." Adam then rejoins her to forget about this "shattered pact" (201), a phrase reminiscent of both the "historical fact" of the play's Preface (176) and the shattering of the jug, and Marthe then recounts how the jug's seamless history is "broken" by its fall.

It is noteworthy that these two representational aspects of the jug, the jug as a guarantor of both legal authority and historical genealogy, are related to the major tenets of the German legal scholar and historian Pufendorf, a propounder of natural law and historical methodology,[49] whose writings, Adam indicates, have yet to take hold in Huisum (188). Indeed, both legal authority (that of Adam, Licht, and Walter) and the historical reconstruction of past events (the breaking of the jug) are under scrutiny in the text, and the integrity of both is mooted, like the question of whether the jug symbolizes Eve's virginity, by linguistic confusion: Adam reports that "The legal files . . . lie toppled like the Tower of Babel" in Huisum (182). With this linguistic caveat in mind, consider the characters' testimonies regarding the breaking of the jug.

The previous night around eleven o'clock, Marthe reports, she heard a commotion in her daughter's room, and when she went to investigate, she found the door to the chamber forced open. Inside she saw the broken jug, Eve wringing her hands, and Ruprecht raging in the middle of the room; and she then accused Ruprecht of the crime: "I demand to know what he's looking for here in the middle of the night, breaking the house *jugs* in a rage . . ." (203, emphasis mine). Marthe's use of the plural *jugs* here indicates that she has now attached symbolic significance to the jug and is accusing Ruprecht of breaking two jugs: the earthen jug and Eve's "jug." It is therefore noteworthy that Ruprecht denies breaking only the *earthen* jug: "He says, someone else knocked the jug off the sill" (203–204). Marthe then turned to Eve and asked her if Ruprecht broke the jug. Eve, Marthe reports, swore that Ruprecht did indeed do so. Eve, however, now adamantly denies that she had *sworn* this (204), yet she does admit that she *said* that Ruprecht broke the jug (205). One way to interpret this is that Eve now claims she was lying when she said Ruprecht was guilty. Another is to wonder whether she in fact was admitting that Ruprecht broke her "jug" when asked about it the previous evening and has now cleverly shifted the signifier back to its material referent to cover up his actions and salvage her reputation.

Ruprecht's version of the story supports the latter interpretation. Around ten o'clock that night, he reports, he decided to go visit Eve. He had to take a detour because the river is swollen and did not arrive at Eve's until close to eleven. (One has to wonder how big the village is and what really happened during the missing hour).[50] Upon arriving, Ruprecht heard Eve in the garden with someone else. Unable to believe what he was witnessing, he "sends his eyes" three times to the scene to confirm his suspicions (208). He was both enraged and aroused by what he saw: "By my soul, I think desire will make me—" (209). (Eve interrupts his testimony at this point, and Ruprecht does not complete his statement.) When Eve disappeared into the house with the person, Ruprecht continues, he fell into a jealous rage. He followed the two into the house, and in what is unmistakably a thinly veiled description of sexual arousal and rape, he recounts breaking down Eve's door:

Jetzt hebt, Herr Richter Adam,
Jetzt hebt sichs, wie ein Blutsturz, mir. Luft!
Da mir der Knopf am Brustlatz springt: Luft jetzt!
Und reisse mir den Latz auf: Luft jetzt sag ich!
Und geh, und drück, und tret und donnere,
Da ich der Dirne Tür, verriegelt finde,
Gestemmt, mit Macht, auf einen Tritt, sie ein. (209–210)

Now it rises, Judge Adam,
Now it rises, like a rush of blood, in me. Air!
The button on my jacket pops off: Air now!
And I rip it open: Air I say!
And then I go, and push, and kick, and thunder,
Since I find the slut's door locked,

And levered up, using force, with one thrust, I break
it down.

Upon hearing this account, Adam, whose own sexual advances have been unsuccessful, replies, "Like greased light-
ning, you!" (210). (In the original manuscript, Adam's recognition of Ruprecht's sexual feat is even more apparent: he
responds to Ruprecht's account with an admiring "that's
what I call agile!").[51] Ruprecht then describes hitting the
intruder over the head with the door handle, which is shaped,
appropriately, like a phallus.[52] The intruder responded by
throwing sand in his eyes, and Ruprecht retreated. Marthe
came in with a lamp, and Ruprecht, seeing Eve trembling,
was once again aroused: "So I say to myself, being blind
isn't so bad. I'd have given my eyes. . . to play with that"
(212). He then comments:

> It was a *spectacle*, and Frau Marthe asked
> The maiden there who broke her jug,
> And she, she said, as you know, that I did it.
> Upon my soul, she's not so wrong, gentlemen.
> *I broke the jug she took for water.* . . . (212, emphasis
>   mine)

Ruprecht describes the scene as a "spectacle," a sight to
be seen. However, his next comment indicates that what
should be seen is invisible. The statement "I broke the jug
she took for water" ("Den *Krug*, den sie zu Wasser *trug*,
zerschlug ich"), emphatically stressed by internal rhyme,
raises the question of what "jug" it is that Ruprecht says
he broke. Clearly he is not referring to the earthen jug,
because he has adamantly denied this charge. More probably, referring to the German adage "the jug goes to water
only until it breaks" (meaning "you'll do that once too
often"), Ruprecht implies that he has put an end to Eve's
flirtatious activities. And yet there is a third possibility:
Ruprecht admits to having had sexual intercourse with Eve.
    This would explain why he tries to stop Eve from telling
her version of the story: "Keep it to yourself, what do we

need to know it for" (44v). Indeed, Eve's testimony, whose special status is marked by being recorded on a separate sheet of paper in the trial proceedings (214), also indicates that a sexual transgression may have occurred. Eve, like Ruprecht, merely denies that he broke the *earthen* jug: "Ruprecht did not break the *earthen* jug" (217, emphasis mine); "I'll swear upon the holy altar that Ruprecht didn't touch *that* jug" (219, emphasis mine). Whether he has broken the other "jug" remains unstated. Eve, however, does reprimand him for not *saying* that he has, ostensibly because he should trust her in her lie: "Supposing I had my reasons for hiding it, why, Ruprecht, why shouldn't I count on your trust, and say it was you? Why shouldn't I? Why shouldn't I?" (216–217). Perhaps, however, what Eve is really asking Ruprecht is why she shouldn't say that he has broken her "jug," because Ruprecht responds by accusing Eve of infidelity. Eve retorts: "Oh, you despicable, ungrateful man! . . .Worthy, that I should save my honor with a single word and condemn you to eternal ruin" (217). Eve's language would be remarkably strong if she were merely asking Ruprecht why he did not trust her in her lie and say that he broke the earthen jug. To call Ruprecht "despicable" and "ungrateful" would make perfect sense, however, if he had indeed broken Eve's "jug" and now denies it. The latter part of the passage supports this reading. Eve threatens Ruprecht with a single word that would both damn him and clear her name. If she were to say that Ruprecht had broken only the earthen jug, this certainly would not condemn him to "eternal ruin." If she were to say that he had broken her "jug" with her consent, no word could now "bring her to honor." Hence, the unspoken word is *rape*.

Eve, however, does not utter the word. She concludes her tirade against Ruprecht with the simple statement that he did not break "the *earthen* jug" (217, emphasis mine). At the same time, she admits that there is more to the story than meets the eye:

That Ruprecht didn't touch *that* jug, I'll
Swear by oath, if you demand,

Upon the holy altar.
But what happened yesterday,
With every other detail, is my own,
And my mother can't demand the whole knitted piece
Just because a single thread belonging to it
Runs through the *fabric* (*Gewebe*). (219, emphasis
mine)

Eve clearly identifies the jug as a "textual" element with
many different features. Contrary to her assertion, however,
the "knitted piece" does unravel in the course of her testimony, because she implicates both herself and Ruprecht
in her account of what happened when Ruprecht burst into
her room. Ruprecht, she recalls, shoved her away from him,
and she staggered senseless over to the bed, grabbed onto
it, and tried to embrace Ruprecht, who had returned from
the window blinded by the sand thrown in his eyes. Ruprecht, however, "rages," and, Eve reports, "I avoid him with
horror" (54v). Marthe then came with the light and, finding
Ruprecht surrounded by pottery shards, accused him of
breaking the jug. Ruprecht, Eve recounts, protested, "That
not he, that another broke the pottery that just shattered"
(54v). Marthe then turned to Eve and asked her if Ruprecht
had done it. Eve recounts:

EVE: And I—I was silent, gentlemen; I lied, I
                   know,
                   But I didn't lie, I swear, except by being
                   silent.
RUPRECHT: On my soul, she didn't say a word, I have
                   to say.
FRAU MARTHE: She didn't say anything, no, she just
                   nodded her head
                   When she was asked if it was Ruprecht.
RUPRECHT: Sure, nodding, good.
EVE: I nodded? Mother!
RUPRECHT: No?
                   Also good.

EVE:	When did I—?
FRAU MARTHE:	So? You didn't, When Muhme Suhse stood in front of you, and asked: No, Eve, it was Ruprecht? nod yes?
EVE:	What? Mother? Really? I nodded? See—
RUPRECHT:	When you blew your nose, When you blew your nose, Eve! Leave it at that. You held the cloth, and honked mightily into it; My soul, it seemed as if you nodded a little.
EVE (*confused*):	It must not have been noticeable.
FRAU MARTHE:	It was just enough to notice. (55v)

Eve purports to have lied only by being silent. According to Marthe, however, Eve clearly nodded when asked if Ruprecht broke the jug. The movement of Eve's head— denied by Eve, interpreted as a nod by her mother, and explained away as a blowing of the nose by Ruprecht—draws into question on the corporeal level the acts of signification and interpretation that are under scrutiny on the textual level. Although Marthe may err in interpreting the movement as a nod, she is right to say that an act of signification occurred the previous night. In her own testimony Marthe swears that Eve *said* that Ruprecht broke the jug (205), and at this point in the testimony Eve admits to *saying* that Ruprecht broke the jug: "Who denies that I *said* it" (205, emphasis mine). Ruprecht, too, testifies that Eve *said* he broke the jug: "she *said*, as you know, that I did it" (212, emphasis mine). Eve now denies that she had *said* anything. Hence, the credibility of Eve's testimony is undermined by her statement here that she had lied only by being silent, and Ruprecht's "Sure, nodding, good . . . No? also good" indicates that he is more than happy to support Eve's fabrications.

If Ruprecht did indeed break Eve's "jug," it would not be the first time a sexual encounter has gone unreported in a Kleistian text. *The Marquise von O* is a case in point; and there, as in *The Broken Jug*, there is a fine line between rape and consensual intercourse. In an epigram to the novella Kleist condemns the Marquise: "Shameless farce! She was, I know, only holding her eyes closed" (22). What distinguishes *The Broken Jug* from *The Marquise von O*, however, is that the reader of the novella is well aware that a sexual act has occurred, and this is not the case in *The Broken Jug*, where the linguistic confusion of *jug* and "*jug*" obscures the events of the previous evening. This signifier-referent problematic clearly situates *The Broken Jug* in the tradition of the eighteenth-century aesthetic theories of *Darstellung* surveyed in Chapter 1, where one of the central issues is to determine whether representation implies that something "stands for" something else in an even exchange (*Tausch*) or whether *Darstellung* relies on deception (*Täuschung*).[53] It is therefore significant that this relationship between *Tausch* and *Täuschung*, exchange and deception, is thematized in the play's other story line, the breaking of the earthen jug.

The events of the previous evening were set into motion, Eve recounts, when Adam offered to give her a document exempting Ruprecht from the draft in exchange for certain unstated favors: "It's a transaction, like buying a breakfast roll" (47v). Eve first refused this exchange (*Tausch*), but when Adam told Eve that Ruprecht would be sent to Asia, and that the authorities were supposed to deceive the recruits into thinking that they would stay in the Netherlands, Eve exclaims: "That's no open, honest conscription, that's deception" (49v). She then decided to combat this deception (*Täuschung*) with an exchange (*Tausch*): she would turn "cunning against cunning" to protect Ruprecht (49v). That night Adam brought the certificate—called, appropriately, a *Schein*, both a document and an "appearance"—to Eve's garden. Eve brought him to her room so that he could fill in the form. Adam placed his wig on the earthen jug, sat down, took Eve's hands, and stared at her for two minutes.

Then Ruprecht burst into the room, and Adam grabbed his wig and jumped out the window, breaking the jug as he went (53v).

Walter, hearing Eve's story, tells her she has been misled by a "common, base deception" (56v): the draftees are to stay in the Netherlands and will not be shipped out to Batavia, as Adam had told her. Eve, however, does not believe Walter and says to Ruprecht, "You hear it, everything, everything, even this, that they're supposed to deceive us" (56v). Walter gives them his word that he is telling the truth, but Ruprecht remarks it would not be the first time that the authorities had been guilty of this deception. Walter then tries to disprove this suspected deception (*Täuschung*) by offering them an exchange (*Tausch*). He will give Eve enough money to buy Ruprecht's freedom from the draft, but if it turns out that Ruprecht is to stay in Holland, as Walter has said, then Eve must return the money with interest. She may keep the money if Ruprecht is shipped off to Asia as she fears. As Eve tries to work through the convoluted logic of this deal, Walter shows her a freshly minted coin imprinted with a picture of the Spanish king, and asks, "Do you think the King would deceive you?" (58v). Ironically, the Spanish king he shows her is a false guarantor of his words, because the Netherlands had been independent since 1648.[54] Nonetheless, Eve is convinced by Walter's reasoning and returns the money, sure now that Ruprecht will stay in the Netherlands. Walter, pleased by her decision, kisses her, an extremely curious action in light of Adam's attempt to abuse authority in return for sexual favors. Although Ruprecht attempts to justify Walter's action as "honest" and "good" (58v), Walter is clearly just as guilty as Adam is of sexual exploitation.

Hence, what first appears as textual economy or *Tausch*, the exchange of Adam's heinous behavior for Walter's rectitude, is really *Täuschung*, deception. Despite the fact that Licht is guilty of embezzling tax money, Walter goes on to appoint him town judge in Adam's stead.[55] Similarly, although Adam is clearly guilty of abusing his authority, Walter does not dismiss him from public service: "I'm sure we'll find a place for him somewhere" (60v). Walter then completes this textual economy in the final scene of the play, where Marthe asks him where to take the jug so that it may "receive its justice," and he sends her to the market in Utrecht (60v). With this statement, Walter strips the jug of its symbolic significance, thereby ensuring that the play's events will be reconstructed accordingly. But the attentive reader, told time and again to "see," will reject this ruse. "Those with sharp eyes" (*Wer scharfe Augen hätte*, 59v) will see that much more than an earthen jug has been broken in the course of the play. When the jug—symbol of Eve's virginity, the law, and the historical reconstruction of past events—shatters, so does representation.

In comparison to Novalis's visual *poiesis*, where visual imagery is designed to complement and complete verbal expression, the visual representation of *The Broken Jug* reinforces its linguistic fragmentation. As Frau Marthe succinctly puts it, one sees "nothing" when one looks at the jug. Goethe's description of the play as "invisible theater" is surprisingly fitting as a general formula for Kleist's theory of *Darstellung. Theater*, etymologically akin to the word *theory*, involves an act of seeing. By drawing attention to what is not shown, Kleist delimits the limits of representation, be it in the linguistic confusion of *jug* and "*jug*" in his drama, the indeterminacy of the Fichtean subject Nicolo / Colino in *The Foundling*, or the subversion of the Kantian subject of reason in *On the Marionette Theater.*

By systematically undermining the epistemological presuppositions that structure Kant's, Fichte's, and Novalis's theories of *Darstellung* from within their own critical framework, Kleist calls into question the transcendental belief in the possibility of constructing a perfect or true representation, arguing from his "Kant crisis" onward that representation itself is predicated on the indistinguishability between *Wahrheit* and *Schein*, truth and appearance. Whereas the ultimate goal of Kant's, Fichte's, and Novalis's transcendental theories of *Darstellung* is to represent the sensible subject as the rational, moral, free being that they would like to believe it to be, and all three theoreticians ultimately resort to a Kantian *negative Darstellung* to effect this transformation, Kleist's carefully crafted critique of representation reveals this paradoxical figure for what it really is: a figure of negativity, an admission of the failure of transcendental theories of *Darstellung.*

Kant knew this when he first introduced *negative Darstellung* into critical discourse, ostensibly for precisely the same reason that Kleist does: to delimit the transcendental limits of representation. In comparison to Kleist, however, who time and again invites his reader to see through the interstices in his rhetorical representation, Kant supresses the visual at this crucial juncture in his *Darstellung* discussion in the third *Critique*:

> This pure, soul-uplifting, merely negative presentation of morality brings with it, on the other hand, no danger of fanaticism, which is *an illusional belief in our capacity to see something beyond all bounds of sensibility*, i.e. of dreaming in accordance with fundamental propositions (or of going mad with reason); and this is so just because this presentation is merely negative. For the uninvestigatability of the idea of freedom completely cuts it off from any positive presentation, but the moral law is in itself sufficiently and originally determinant in us, *so that it does not permit us to look around* at any ground of determination external to itself. (*CJ* B 125, p. 116, emphasis mine)

The Kleistian subject looks over the border, looks around, and sees nothing. This "nothing" is the death knoll not merely of representation, but of *Darstellung* as a transcendental construct.

Epilogue:
Romanticism Represented

But Nothing, as Heidegger astutely observes in *The Age of the World Picture*, is the keenest opposite of negating when it pertains to the having-of-being, as Kleist's critique of representation clearly does: "Nothing is never nothing; it is just as little something, in the sense of an object [*Gegenstand*]; it is Being itself, whose truth will be given over to man when he has overcome himself as subject, and that means when he no longer represents that which is as object [*Objekt*]."[1] I began this study by suggesting that Kleist's oeuvre anticipates Heidegger's critique of the metaphysical basis that structures the modern age, and we are now in a position to substantiate this assertion. According to Heidegger's analysis, the Cartesian *cogito* is predicated on an objectifying representation (*Vorstellung*) in human perceptions of truth and of Being, whereby the human being defines itself as a subject and the world as a picture, a structured visual image that it itself creates. Heidegger considers this Cartesian conception of the subject to be problematic because it does not allow the human being to define itself according to its true being, and he argues that the modern subject can escape this representational paradigm through reflection or *Besinnung*, a turning of sensible thought back on itself. Heidegger suggests that this reflexive critique can be accomplished either philosophically or poetically: by means of creative questioning one will overcome oneself as subject and will eventually join with true Being, which first unveils itself as "Nothing," in a space withdrawn from representation.

Heidegger's critique of representation is concordant with Kleist's. To recast Kleist's oeuvre in Heideggerian terms: Kleist's "Kant crisis"—succinctly summed up in the sen-

175

tence "We cannot decide if that which we call truth really is true, or if it merely appears so to us"—calls into question the Cartesian premise that truth is the certainty of representation; the autocritical discourse of *On the Marionette Theater*, which turns back on itself and undercuts its own basic premises, is comparable to Heidegger's concept of *Besinnung* or sensible reflection; the bifurcation of the signifier that ultimately signifies "nothing" in *The Broken Jug* shatters the visual objectification of representation, and *The Foundling* and *On the Marionette Theater* effectively undermine the human being's self-definition as subject. Perhaps the one decisive difference between the two critiques is that the redemptive dimension of Heidegger's analysis is absent in Kleist's: the Kleistian subject is driven to the banks of the Wannsee in Berlin, to despair, insanity, or suicide; whereas Heidegger's modern man is to join with Being in a space withdrawn from representation. In this respect Heidegger is closer to the Jena Romantics than he is to Kleist.

I am not arguing that Kleist is a proto-Heideggerian; nor am I suggesting a Heideggerian reading of Kleist. The point of my comparison is rather this: Heidegger's critique of representation is profoundly Romantic in its inception, parameters, and goals, thereby substantiating Lacoue-Labarthe and Nancy's thesis that modernity is inscribed in the German Romantic paradigm. Azade Seyhan has detailed the Romantic provenance of modern critiques of representation from the Romantics through Nietzsche and Heidegger to poststructuralism and deconstruction in her excellent study, *Representation and Its Discontents: The Critical Legacy of German Romanticism*, focusing on the relation of representation to the concepts of time and alterity, rather than on the question of representation itself in her analysis.[2] Although I will not attempt a complete overview of the complex genealogy of the *Darstellung* problematic in the course of the nineteenth and twentieth centuries, I would delineate its contours according to the framework that we have established in this investigation.

Since its inception in Kant's *Critiques*, the notion of *Darstellung* has been inextricably linked to the question of the relationship between philosophy and literature. We have traced the increasing poetization of transcendental idealism in Kant's realization that language prevents philosophical discourse from achieving the "pure" representation of mathematics and his unwilling admission of the poetic into the rhetorical exposition of his *Critiques*, in the Idealist attempt to resolve Kant's crisis in representation that culminates in poetic discourse in Fichte's later philosophy and sonnets, in the transcendental poesy of the Jena Romantics, and in the literary critique of transcendental idealism that is incorporated in Kleist's writings. In short, where Kant had attacked linguistic ambiguity as the bane of philosophical discourse, his successors capitalize on its productive or *poietic* potential.

The complex interplay of philosophy and literature that is established around 1800 is repeated in the history of the development of nineteenth- and twentieth-century theories of *Darstellung*. At the same time that Kleist was demonstrating the pitfalls of transcendental theories of representation from a literary vantage, Hegel was developing a new Idealist philosophy of reflection grounded in the Kantian notion of *Darstellung* that forms the basis of the great system philosophies of the nineteenth century. Like Kant, Hegel propounds a separation of philosophical and literary discourse, arguing in philosophical, rather than poetic, terms that the goal of the *Phenomenology* is the *Darstellung* of developing knowledge,[3] whereas the goal of art is the sensible *Darstellung* of the Absolute.[4] In opposition to Kant, however, Hegel lays out a linguistic foundation for his system in the Preface and Introduction to the *Phenomenology of Spirit* (1807), thereby legitimizing language as the medium of philosophical discourse, rather than lamenting its inherent ambiguities, as Kant had done.

In the course of the late nineteenth and early twentieth centuries new forms of philosophical discourse begin to challenge the Hegelian insistence on logical systematicity, focusing, as the Romantics had, on the *poietic* dimension of language. Kleist's "Kant crisis" and his literary critique of representation are echoed in Nietzsche's famous description of truth as "a mobile army of metaphors, metonyms, and anthropomorphisms—in short, a sum of human relations, which have been enhanced, transposed, and embellished poetically and rhetorically, and which after long use seem firm, canonical, and obligatory to a people: truths are illusions about which one has forgotten that this is what they are."[5] Like Nietzsche, Heidegger effects a linguistic critique of representation in his philosophy, arguing in *The Age of the World Picture* that we must "track out and expose the original naming power of the worn-out word and concept 'to represent'"[6] in order to overcome its objectifying confines. Nietzsche's and Heidegger's critiques of representation both aim to analyze the poetic and productive dimensions of language and its impact on philosophical discourse, thereby paving the way for poststructuralism and deconstruction.

The early twentieth century sees an explicit revival of the Kantian notion of *Darstellung* in the works of Walter Benjamin. Although Benjamin broaches the issue of *Darstellung* in his dissertation, *The Concept of Criticism in German Romanticism*, he first lays out his own theory of *Darstellung* in the enigmatic Preface to his *Habilitationsschrift*, *The Origin of German Tragic Drama* (1925). Like Nietzsche and Heidegger, Benjamin valorizes the linguistic dimension of philosophy: he obliquely chastizes Kant for trying to eliminate the *Darstellung* problematic from philosophy by modeling his *Critiques* on a mathematical paradigm, arguing that mathematics may lead to pure cognition but never to the truth that is contained in language.[7] Like the Romantics, Benjamin considers Kant's *Critiques* to be the threshhold of great prosaic art,[8] and he also adopts the Romantic stance that all science (*Wissenschaft*) should be art.[9] In opposition to the Jena Romantic notion of *Darstellung*, however, in which philosophy is transformed into poesy, in Benjamin's theory philosophy retains its basic scientific form, yet takes on artistic features. The genre for this new artistic philosophy is the essay or tractate, which has a latent theological nature and cannot dispense with scientific proof, yet is characterized by lack of intention: "*Darstellung* is the essence of its method. Method is detour. *Darstellung* as detour—that's the methodological character of the tractate."[10] The goal of this meandering *Darstellung* is the representation of ideas. Where Kant had tried to achieve this goal via the paradoxical notion of *negative Darstellung*, Benjamin constructs "constellations" of ideas by assembling fragments of phenomena and attempting to restore their lost ideality negatively, utilizing the primacy of the symbolic nature of language in his analysis. In this respect Benjamin's messianic criticism can be seen as a direct response to aporiae in Kant's critical and rhetorical definitions of *Darstellung*.

Obviously this brief overview of Hegel's, Nietzsche's, Heidegger's, and Benjamin's critiques of philosophical representation cannot do justice to the complex aftermath of the Kantian notion of *Darstellung* in modern critical discourse. In my readings of Kant, Fichte, Novalis, and Kleist, I have attempted to illustrate the constitutive force of Kant's notion of *Darstellung* in early German Romanticism, which structures our own critical consciousness in ever-changing permutations today. Benjamin recognized this when he wrote that the trademark of philosophical writing is that at every turn it must confront the question of *Darstellung* anew.[11]

Notes

Introduction

1. Page references are to Martin Heidegger, *The Age of the World Picture. The Question Concerning Technology and Other Essays*, trans. William Lovitt (New York: Harper & Row, 1977), pp. 116–154.

2. Philippe Lacoue-Labarthe and Jean-Luc Nancy, *The Literary Absolute*, trans. Philip Barnard and Cheryl Lester (Albany: State University of New York Press, 1988), p. 15.

3. Ibid., p. 31.

4. See Christiaan Hart Nibbrig, "Zum Drum und Dran einer Fragestellung. Ein Vorgeschmack," *Was heisst ≫Darstellen≪?* ed. Hart Nibbrig (Frankfurt am Main: Suhrkamp, 1994) p. 10; and in the same volume, Vilém Flusser, "Abbild-Vorbild," p. 34.

Chapter 1. Kant and the Genealogy of the Romantic Notion of *Darstellung*

1. *Über den Begriff der Wissenschaftslehre (1794)* (Stuttgart: Reclam, 1972), p. 47.

2. *Phänomenologie des Geistes, Hegel, Werke in 20 Bänden, Band 3* (Frankfurt am Main: Suhrkamp, 1970), p. 31; cf. "Die Darstellung des erscheinenden Wissens," p. 72.

3. *Vorlesungen über die Ästhetik I, Hegel, Werke in 20 Bänden, Band 13* (Frankfurt am Main: Suhrkamp, 1970), p. 100.

4. Schelling, *Philosophie der Kunst, Texte zur Philosophie der Kunst* (Stuttgart: Reclam, 1982), p. 191.

5. Ibid., p. 152.

6. Bernhardi, *Sprachlehre* (Hildesheim and New York: Olms, 1961), p. 14.

7. *Kritische Friedrich-Schlegel-Ausgabe, Band II*, ed. E. Behler (Munich: Ferdinand Schöningh, 1963), p. 204, #238. Hereafter cited as KA.

8. Novalis, *Schriften, Band II*, ed. Richard Samuel (Darmstadt: Wissenschaftliche Buchgesellschaft, ²1965), p. 217, #305.

9. My discussion of Kant throughout this chapter is strongly influenced by Jean-Luc Nancy, "Logodaedalus: Kant écrivain," *Poétique* 21 (1975): 24–52; Nancy, "L'offrande sublime," *Po&SIE* 30 (1984): 76–103; and Hans Graubner, "Kant," *Klassiker der Literaturtheorie*, ed. Host Turk (Munich: Beck, 1979), pp. 35–61.

10. All references to the *Critique of Pure Reason*, the *Critique of Practical Reason*, and the *Critique of Judgment* are to the *Immanuel Kant Werkausgabe*, ed. W. Weischedel (Frankfurt am Main: Suhrkamp, 1974): *Kritik der reinen Vernunft (Band 3 und Band 4); Kritik der praktischen Vernunft (Band 7)*, and *Kritik der Urteilskraft (Band 10)*. I have used the following translations, modifying them on occasion to reflect the literal meaning of the German: Kant, *Critique of Pure Reason*, trans. Norman Kemp Smith (New York: St. Martin's Press, 1965), hereafter cited as *CPR*; and Kant, *Critique of Judgment*, trans. J. H. Bernard, (New York: Hafner, 1951), hereafter cited as *CJ*. Page references are to the standard "A" and "B" *Akademie-Ausgabe* pagination indicated in the *Kant Werkausgabe*. Kemp Smith follows this pagination in his translation. Bernard does not, and I have also included page references to his translation in the text.

11. See for example, Novalis: "The sensible must be represented spiritually; the spiritual, sensibly" (II: p. 283, #633); and Friedrich Schlegel's celebration of mythology for its ability to capture the sensible spiritually (KA II: 194).

12. KA XVIII.1: p. 62 #428.

13. Novalis, III: p. 442, #906.

14. Nancy, "Logodaedalus," pp. 33–34.

15. *Deutsches Wörterbuch von Jacob Grimm und Wilhelm Grimm, Neubearbeitung*, ed. Deutsche Akademie der Wissenschaften zu Berlin, vol. 6.3 (Leipzig: Hirzel, 1972), pp. 328–336.

16. "Herstellen / sive Darstellen / offere, repraesentare, ante oculos ponere, statuere, quod etiam dicitur für die Augen stellen."

Der Teutschen Sprache Stammbaum und Fortwachs / oder Teutscher Sprachschatz (2147). Cited in Heuer, *Darstellung der Freiheit* (Cologne and Vienna: Böhlau, 1970), p. 14.

17. Heuer, ibid., p. 15.

18. Moses Mendelssohn, "Über die Hauptgrundsätze der schönen Künste und Wissenschaften." Cited in Heuer, ibid., p. 21.

19. Grimm documents an exponential growth in the frequency of the term's usage at the end of the eighteenth century (333).

20. My discussion of the history of the term *Darstellung* in aesthetic theory draws on J. Nieerad's and U. Theissmann's articles under the entry *Darstellung* in *Historisches Wörterbuch der Philosophie*, ed. Joachim Ritter (Basel: Schwabe, 1972), pp. 11–14, and on Bruno Markwardt's *Geschichte der deutschen Poetik, Band 2* (Berlin: de Gruyter, 1956).

21. Schiller, *Kallias oder Über die Schönheit. Briefe an Gottfried Körner, Friedrich Schiller, Sämtliche Werke, Band 5*, ed. Gerhart Fricke and Herbert G. Göpfert (Munich: Hanser, 1959). See especially his letter of 28 February 1793. For extensive analyses of Schiller's theory of *Darstellung*, see Heuer, *Darstellung der Freiheit*, and Azade Seyhan, *Representation and Its Discontents* (Berkeley, Los Angeles, and Oxford: University of California Press, 1992).

22. Hölderlin equates *Darstellung* with *Ausdruck*, the mediation between the "sinnlichem Stoffe und dem Geiste, der idealischen Behandlung." "Über die Verfahrensweise des poetischen Geistes," *Sämmtliche Werke, Band 4*, ed. F. Beissner (Stuttgart: Kohlhammer, 1959), p. 244. Manfred Frank and Gerhard Kurz briefly discuss the Kantian basis of Hölderlin's notion of *Darstellung* in "Ordo Inversus," *Geist und Zeichen, Festschrift für Arthur Henkel*, ed. H. Anton (Heidelberg: Carl Winter, 1977), pp. 75–97, see especially p. 85.

23. Cited in Theissman, "Darstellung," p. 13.

24. August Buchner, *Anleitung zur deutschen Poeterey/ Poet*, ed. Manian Szyrock (Tübingen: Niemeyer, 1966), p. 32.

25. *Klopstock, Ausgewählte Werke*, ed. K. A. Schleiden (Munich: Hanser, [4]1981), p. 1033.

26. Lessing, *Laokoon* (Stuttgart: Reclam, 1964), p. 28.

27. See Section XI of *Laokoon*.

28. Kirchenstein's argument that *Darstellung* applies only to *Malerei* in Lessing seems to me to be somewhat overstated. One of the examples that he cites from Lessing speaks against such a one-dimensional delineation of the term: "Es gibt malbare und unmalbare Fakta, und der Geschichtsschreiber kann die malbarsten ebenso unmalerisch erzählen, als der Dichter die unmalbarsten Fakta darzustellen vermögend ist." Max Kirchenstein, *Klopstocks Deutsche Gelehrtenrepublik* (Berlin: de Gruyter, 1928), pp. 172ff.

29. Winfried Menninghaus, "Klopstocks Poetik der schnellen ≫Bewegung≪," *Klopstock, Gedanken über die Natur der Poesie*, ed. Menninghaus (Frankfurt am Main: Insel, 1989), pp. 259–351, here p. 341. Menninghaus, following Kirchenstein, finds evidence in Klopstock for a new eighteenth-century notion of *Darstellung* that is based on a sharp separation of *vorstellen* and *darstellen*. Menninghaus goes on to argue that Klopstock's poetic theory anticipates both Kant's and the early Romantics' notions of *Darstellung* and hence constitutes a caesura in the eighteenth-century discourse on *Darstellung* that is absolutely essential to the development of "modern" poetics (332–334). For an expanded treatment of this argument, see Menninghaus, " ≫Darstellung≪. Friedrich Gottlieb Klopstocks Eröffnung eines neuen Paradigmas," *Was heisst ≫Darstellen≪?* ed. Christiaan Hart Nibbrig (Frankfurt am Main: Suhrkamp, 1994), pp. 205–226.

30. *Deutsche Gelehrtenrepublik, Klopstock, Ausgewählte Werke*, p. 880.

31. For an in-depth analysis of Lessing's "aesthetics of representation," see David E. Wellbery, "Das Gesetz der Schönheit: Lessings Ästhetik der Repräsentation," *Was heisst ≫Darstellen≪?* ed. Christiaan Hart Nibbrig (Frankfurt am Main: Suhrkamp, 1994), pp. 175–204.

32. Fr. L. Stolberg, "Vom Dichten und Darstellen," *Gesammelte Werke der Brüder Christian und Friedrich Leopold Grafen zu Stolberg, Band 10* (Hamburg: Perthes and Besser, 1822), p. 379.

33. G. A. Bürger, "Von der Popularität der Poesie," *Sämtliche Werke*, ed. G. Häntzschel and H. Häntzschel (Munich and Vienna: Hanser, 1987). The date of the article's composition is unknown. First published in 1824, the essay shares similarities with the 1778 Preface to Bürger's *Gedichte*, as well as to his Preface to the second edition of the *Gedichte* (1789). On the dating of the essay, see the editors' comments on p. 1314.

34. Bürger, ibid., p. 727.

35. Lenz, "Anmerkungen übers Theater." *Jakob Michael Reinhold Lenz. Werke und Briefe in 3 Bänden*, vol. 2, ed. S. Damm (Munich and Vienna: Hanser, 1987), p. 653.

36. Goethe, *Maximen und Reflexionen* #1028, *Werke. Hamburger Ausgabe in 14 Bänden. Band 12. Schriften zur Kunst* (Munich: Beck, 1988), pp. 510–511.

37. Herder, *Kalligone, Herders Sämmtliche Werke, Band 22*, ed. B. Suphan (Berlin: Weidmann, 1880), p. 147.

38. See Heuer, *Darstellung der Freiheit*, pp. 16–18.

39. Herder, *Kalligone*, p. 5.

40. See Beiser, *The Fate of Reason: German Philosophy from Kant to Fichte* (Cambridge, Mass., and London: Harvard University Press, 1987), pp. 149–157.

41. Graubner, "Kant," p. 35.

42. Rodolphe Gasché, "Some Reflections on the Notion of Hypotyposis in Kant," *Argumentation* 4 (1990): 85–100, here pp. 89–90.

43. "Proposita quaedam forma rerum ita expressa verbis, ut cerni potius videantur quam audiri." Cited in G. Buck, "Hypotypose," *Historisches Wörterbuch der Philosophie, Band 3*, ed. Joachim Ritter (Basel: Schwabe, 1974), pp. 1266–1267.

44. Gasché, "Some Reflections on the Notion of Hypotyposis," p. 90.

45. In his *Lexicon Philosophicum Terminorum Philosophis Usitatorum* of 1662, Johannes Micraelius defines *hypotyposis* as "narrationis evidentia, qua rem oculis in sermone ita subjicimos, ut non narrari, sed geri videatur." Johannes Micraelius, *Lexicon Philosophicum Terminorum Philosophis Usitatorum* (photo-

mechanischer Nachdruck der 2. Auflage [Stettin 1662] Düsseldorf: Stern, 1966), p. 582.

46. Gasché, "Ideality in Fragmentation," Foreword to
Friedrich Schlegel, *Philosophical Fragments*, trans. Peter
Firchow (Minneapolis and Oxford: University of Minnesota Press,
1991), pp. vii–xxxii, here p. xix.

47. Graubner, "Kant," pp. 36–41.

48. The following discussion is based on Gasché, "Ideality
in Fragmentation," pp. xv–xxvii.

49. See Jean Beaufret, "Kant et la Notion de *Darstellung*,"
Dialogue avec Heidegger, vol. 2 (Paris: Éditions de Minuit, 1973),
pp. 77–109, here p. 81.

50. Nancy, "Logodaedalus," p. 31.

51. Ibid., p. 34. Novalis, in comparison, embraces the notion
of a rhapsodic philosophy: "Wissenschaftler—Rapsodiker oder
Freygeister" (*Schriften*, vol. 2, p. 233, #394).

52. See Manfred Frank, "Intellektuale Anschauung," *Die
Aktualität der Frühromantik*, ed. E. Behler and J. Hörisch
(Paderborn: Schöningh, 1987), pp. 96–126.

53. See Gasché, "Some Reflections on the Notion of Hypotyposis," *Argumentation* 4 (1990): 85–100.

54. Graubner, "Kant," pp. 40–41.

55. Gasché, "Ideality in Fragmentation," p. xxvii.

56. Graubner, "Kant," pp. 40–41.

57. Bernard inexplicably omits this *also* in his translation.

58. This same dialectic between infinity and an infinity that
has a totality ascribed to it will be incorporated into the Romantic
theory of the fragment. See Gasché, "Ideality in Fragmentation,"
pp. xxviii–xxxi.

59. Nancy, "Kant a *évité* d'ecrire la *Critique* en vers."
("Logodaedalus," p. 50.)

60. This emphasis on deception and illusion works its way
into Idealist and Romantic theories of *Darstellung*. In the 1794
Doctrine of Knowledge, Fichte will comment on the productive
nature of deception for philosophy, and Novalis will accord deception
a central role in his theory of *Darstellung* in the *Fichte-Studies*.

61. The fourth section of Lambert's *Neues Organon* of 1764, *Phänomenologie: oder die Lehre von dem Schein*, is perhaps the precursor to this Kantian visual presentation. Lambert defines phenomenology as a "transcendent optic," and Kant was such a great fan of Lambert's that he considered dedicating the first *Critique* to him. Johann Heinrich Lambert, *Neues Organon, oder Gedanken über die Erforschung und Bezeichnung des Wahren und dessen Unterscheidung vom Irrtum und Schein* (Berlin: Akademie-Verlag, 1990).

62. "Von einem neuerdings erhobenen vornehmen Ton in der Philosophie" (1796). *Immanuel Kant. Werke in Sechs Bänden, Band 3*, ed. Wilhelm Weischedel (Darmstadt: Wissenschaftliche Buchgesellschaft, 1966), pp. 375–397, see A 423–424.

63. Jean Paul, *Vorschule der Ästhetik* ed. N. Miller (Munich: Hanser, 1963), p. 278, §77, emphasis mine.

64. Clemens Brentano, *Sämtliche Werke und Briefe*, vol. 16 (Stuttgart: Kohlhammer, 1978), p. 314.

65. KA II: 182, #116.

Chapter 2. The Idealist Response: From Reinhold to the Romantics

1. My discussion of Reinhold is based on the analysis of Breazeale, "Between Kant and Fichte: Karl Leonhard Reinhold's 'Elementary Philosophy,'" *Review of Metaphysics* 35 (1982): 785–821; and, especially, on Beiser, *The Fate of Reason: German Philosophy from Kant to Fichte* (Cambridge, Mass. and London: Harvard University Press, 1987), who provides a thoroughgoing explication and critique of the Elementary Philosophy (pp. 226–265).

2. Cited in Beiser, ibid., p. 165.

3. Breazeale, "Between Kant and Fichte," p. 791.

4. Beiser, *The Fate of Reason*, pp. 232–233.

5. Reinhold's main works on the Elementary Philosophy are *Versuch einer neuen Theorie des menschlichen Vorstellungsvermögens* (1789), *Beyträge zur Berichtigung des bisherigen Missverständnisse der Philosophen* (2 vol., 1790 and 1794), *Über*

das Fundament des philosophischen Wissens (1791), and a second volume of the *Briefe* (1792).

6. Beiser, *The Fate of Reason*, pp. 226–227.

7. Breazeale, "Between Kant and Fichte," p. 793.

8. Beiser, *The Fate of Reason*, p. 244.

9. Ibid., p. 238.

10. Cited in Breazeale, "Between Kant and Fichte," p. 797.

11. Ibid., p. 797.

12. Beiser, *The Fate of Reason*, pp. 254–255.

13. Cited in Breazeale, "Between Kant and Fichte," p. 799.

14. Breazeale, "Fichte's *Aenesidemus* Review and the Transformation of German Idealism," *Review of Metaphysics* 34 (1981): 545–568, here pp. 557–558.

15. Beiser, *The Fate of Reason*, pp. 255 and 178.

16. Ibid., p. 263.

17. Ibid., pp. 263–265.

18. Reinhold and Fichte had a falling-out over the atheism controversy surrounding Fichte at Jena, and Reinhold soon became interested in the "rational realism" of C. G. Bardili. Breazeale, "Between Kant and Fichte," pp. 817–818.

19. Beiser, *The Fate of Reason*, p. 265.

20. Ibid., p. 227.

21. Ibid., pp. 266–270. For a full discussion of Schulze's skepticism, see ibid., pp. 266–284 and Breazeale, "Fichte's *Aenesidemus* Review."

22. Beiser, ibid., p. 269.

23. Cited in Breazeale, "Fichte's *Aenesidemus* Review," p. 552.

24. Cited in Beiser, *The Fate of Reason*, pp. 269–270.

25. "Ein Kunstwerk des philosophischen Geistes," cited in Breazeale, "Fichte's *Aenesidemus* Review," p. 554.

26. Fichte, *Gesamtausgabe der Bayrischen Akademie der Wissenschaften*, ed. Reinhard Lauth and Hans Jacob (Stuttgart-Bad Canstatt: Fromann, 1962–), vol. II, 3, p. 7. Hereafter cited as GA.

27. Cited in Breazeale, "Fichte's *Aenesidemus* Review, " p. 551.

28. The texts of the *Own Meditations on Elementary Philosophy* and the *Practical Philosophy* are published in GA II, 3: 3–266; the prepublication drafts of the *Aenesidemus* review in GA II, 2: 287–314, and the published review in GA I, 2: 33–67.

29. GA II, 3: 23–24.

30. Cited in Jürgen Stolzenberg, *Fichtes Begriff der Intellektuellen Anschauung* (Stuttgart: Klett-Cotta, 1986), p. 36.

31. See ibid., pp. 13–60. For a different interpretation of the Kantian notion of construction in Fichte's ouevre, see Reinhard F. Koch, *Fichtes Theorie des Selbstbewusstseins* (Würzburg: Königshausen and Neumann, 1989).

32. GA II, 3: 10.

33. Stolzenberg (*Fichtes Begriff*, p. 35) argues that Fichte's mention of Maimon is erroneous in his discussion of mathematical construction.

34. Beiser, *The Fate of Reason*, p. 285.

35. See Fichte, *Early Philosophical Writings*, ed. and trans. D. Breazeale (Ithaca, N.Y., and London: Cornell University Press, 1988), p. 94.

36. Beiser, *The Fate of Reason*, p. 286.

37. Ibid., p. 286.

38. GA I, 2: 46; Fichte, *Early Philosophical Writings*, p. 63.

39. Cited in Fichte, *Early Philosophical Writings*, p. xiv.

40. Adding to the linguistic confusion, however, Fichte at one point equates *Darstellung* with *Repräsentation* (GA II, 3: 88).

41. GA II, 3: 89.

42. GA II, 3: 153–154.

43. GA II, 3: 89–90.

44. GA II, 2: 295.

45. GA II, 2: 292.

46. GA II, 2: 292–298.

47. Page references are to GA II, 3.

48. Published in GA I, 6: 312–360.

49. KA II: 284.

50. GA II, 3: 89.

51. Fichte did actually make a concerted effort to come to terms with the linguistic limitations of philosophical rhetoric. In his essay *On Linguistic Competence and the Origin of Language* (*Von der Sprachfähigkeit und dem Ursprung der Sprache*, 1795), Fichte had attempted to redefine terminology from linguistic theory and philosophy from a transcendental perspective (on Fichte's relationship to Romantic linguistic theory, see Kurt Mueller-Vollmer, "Fichte und die frühromantische Sprachtheorie," *Der transzendentale Gedanke*, ed. K. Hammacher [Hamburg: Meiner, 1981], pp. 442–459.) In later years he pursued this interest in language in collaboration with August Ferdinand Bernhardi, whose *Doctrine of Language* (*Sprachlehre*, 1801–1803) is modeled after Fichte's *Doctrine of Science*. In this and a later work, *Elements of Linguistics* (*Anfangsgründe der Sprachwissenschaft*, 1806) Bernhardi develops a linguistic theory of *Darstellung*, and in his "applied linguistics" he attempts to delineate a strict separation of philosophical and poetic discourse based on their different representational properties, though the model he proposes is far from convincing (see Wild-Schedlbauer, "Einleitung." *Anfangsgründe der Sprachwissenschaft* [Stuttgart-Bad Canstatt: Fromann-Holzboog, 1990] pp. vii–lvi, and "Reflexionen über A. F. Bernhardis Leben und sprachwissenschaftliches Werk," *Neuere Forschungen zur Wortbildung und Historiographie der Linguistik*, ed. B. Asbach-Schnitker and J. Roggenhofer (Tübingen: Günter Narr, 1987) pp. 367–385, for a discussion of Bernhardi's linguistic theory and Klin, *August Ferdinand Bernhardi als Kritiker und Literaturtheoretiker* [Bonn: Bouvier, 1966], for an analysis of Bernhardi's literary criticism). Interestingly, Reinhold, too, eventually decided that the shortcomings of transcendental philosophy stem from a failure to analyze the medium in which

it is presented, namely, language, and in his later philosophy he attempts a linguistic critique of philosophy (see Hermann-Josef Cloeren, "Philosophie als Sprachkritik bei K. L. Reinhold," *Kant-Studien* 63 [1972]: 225–236).

52. The first two sonnets were published anonymously in the *Musenalmanach* of 1805, and the third was not published for unknown reasons (GA II, 9: 450). The three sonnets appear in GA I, 8: 25–35 (along with two hymns that Fichte translated from the Latin) and in GA II, 9: 451–454.

53. This according to Chamisso and Schelling. GA I, 8: 25–28.

54. Henrich, "Fichtes ursprüngliche Einsicht," *Subjektivität und Metaphysik*, ed. D. Henrich and H. Wagner (Frankfurt am Main: Klostermann, 1966), pp. 188–232, here p. 216 (in Lachterman's English translation, "Fichte's Original Insight," *Contemporary German Philosophy*, vol. 1, ed. D. E. Christensen et al. [University Park and London: Pennsylvania State University Press, 1982], pp. 15–53, here p. 39).

Chapter 3. Novalis:
The Jena Romantic Poetization of *Darstellung*

1. All references are to the third edition of Novalis, *Schriften*, ed. Paul Kluckhohn and Richard Samuel, 5 vols. (Stuttgart: Kohlhammer, 1975–1988). The translations are my own. For a reading of the ethical dimension of Novalis's philosophy, see Géza von Molnár, *Romantic Vision, Ethical Context* (Minneapolis: University of Minnesota Press, 1987).

2. See Jochen Hörisch, *Die fröhliche Wissenschaft der Poesie* (Frankfurt am Main: Suhrkamp, 1976), p. 77, note 34. Novalis, however, did consider Kant's discussion of the schematism, albeit cursorily (III: 303, #305).

3. Menninghaus, "≫Darstellung≪. Friedrich Gottlieb Klopstocks Eröffnung eines neuen Paradigmas," *Was heisst ≫Darstellen≪?* ed. Christiaan Hart Nibbrig (Frankfurt am Main: Suhrkamp, 1994), p. 217.

4. In his introduction to the *Fichte-Studies* in the critical Novalis edition (II: 31), Hans-Joachim Mähl suggests that at the time of writing of the *Fichte-Studies* Novalis was acquainted with

Über den Begriff der Wissenschaftslehre oder der sogenannten Philosophie (1794), *Grundlage der gesammten Wissenschaftslehre* (Parts 1 and 2, 1794; Part 3, 1795), *Einige Vorlesungen über die Bestimmung des Gelehrten* (1794), *Grundriss des Eigenthümlichen der Wissenschaftslehre, in Rücksicht auf das theoretische Vermögen* (1795), *Von der Sprachfähigkeit und dem Ursprung der Sprache* (1795), and, for the later fragments, *Grundlage des Naturrechts nach Principien der Wissenschaftslehre* (Part 1, 1796).

5. The editor's introduction to the *Fichte-Studies* (II: 31). Hölderlin formulated his criticism of Fichte's theory of self-consciousness in *Urteil und Sein* at the same time that Novalis wrote the *Fichte-Studies*, and Hölderlin later incorporated the notion of *Darstellung* into his philosophy. Manfred Frank and Gerhard Kurz, who point to the parallels between Novalis's and Hölderlin's critiques of Fichte in "Ordo inversus," suggest that Hölderlin's notion of *Darstellung* is derived from Kant (85).

6. Mähl, who glosses the critical edition with references to Fichte, makes no mention of Fichte's notion of *Darstellung*. Haering (*Novalis als Philosoph*) and von Molnár (*The Fichte-Studies*) both have extensive sections devoted to Novalis's notion of *Darstellung* yet do not discuss its origins; nor does Frank ("Ordo inversus" and *Einführung in die frühromantische Philosophie*), who analyzes Novalis's notion of *Darstellung* as a critique of Fichte's theory of self-consciousness and also comments on Hölderlin's Kantian use of the word. Even Hörisch (*Die fröhliche Wissenschaft der Poesie*), who cites the Fichte quotation under consideration, does not analyze Novalis's *Fichte-Studies* in this context (131).

7. Manfred Frank, *Einführung in die frühromantische Ästhetik. Vorlesungen* (Frankfurt am Main: Suhrkamp, 1989), p. 248, Lecture 15. Frank argues that, although Hölderlin's *Urteil und Sein*, written at the same time as the *Fichte-Studies*, comes to similar conclusions about the self-positing of the Fichtean Ego, Novalis's analysis, which introduces the poetic, is more subtle and far-reaching than Hölderlin's. Furthermore, Frank claims, Novalis's *Fichte-Studies* anticipate the development of Fichte's later philosophy.

8. For a differing interpretation of the status of prereflexive being in Novalis's oeuvre, see Alice Kuzniar, "Reassessing Romantic Reflexivity: The Case of Novalis," *Germanic Review* 63 (Spring 1988): 77–86, especially note 25, p. 85.

9. Novalis probably derives this term *hieroglyphic* from Fichte's essay "On Linguistic Competence and the Origin of Language" of 1795 (GA I, 3: 95–127).

10. On the notion of *Schweben* (hovering or oscillating) in Fichte and Novalis, see Menninghaus, "Die frühromantische Theorie von Zeichen und Metapher," *German Quarterly* 62 (Winter 1989): 48–58.

11. All page references to *Heinrich von Ofterdingen* and the *Hymns to the Night* are to vol. 1 of the critical edition.

12. I will take *Klingsohr's Tale* to be paradigmatic of Novalis's notion of the fairy tale, because his only other complete fairy tale, "Hyacinth and Rosenblüthchen" from his first fragmentary novel, *The Apprentices at Saïs*, also (re)presents the genesis of the visual *poiesis* that is developed in *Klingsohr's Tale*. In *The Apprentices at Saïs*, the fairy tale functions as a meta-critique of one of the central themes of the main text: the search for nature's holy writing. The apprentices' task is to learn to reconstruct—though not necessarily to read—this ciphered writing. One day a child with large, dark eyes appears in their midst and augurs the end of the apprenticeship. In the fairy tale Hyacinth, who has suddenly become blind, acts as a counter to this messianic figure. Hyacinth receives from an old man a small book that no one can read—a cipher for the holy writing of nature in the main text of the *Apprentices*—and he loses his peace of mind. He then meets an old woman, who heals him by burning the book and sending him off on a quest, which culminates in his lifting the veil of the Saïs virgin. When he lifts the veil, his love Rosenblütchen falls into his arms. In an alternate ending from the fragments—which commentators uniformly consider more interesting than the original text—when Hyacinth lifts the veil, he sees himself (II: 584, #250). In either case, lifting the veil is a visual metaphor, a coming into sight. In the fairy tale this new sight cures Hyacinth's metaphorical blindness. More interesting, in the distich lifting the veil constitutes a visual definition of self, a theme that not only harks back to the reflection problematics of the *Fichte-Studies*, but also anticipates the cave scene in *Heinrich von Ofterdingen*, where Heinrich sees his own future depicted in a curious pictorial language he cannot read. With its emphasis on vision and writing, "Hyacinth and Rosenblüthchen" thus can be read as a prelude to the critique of writing embodied in the character of the Writer in *Klingsohr's Tale*.

13. This tradition of equating the Writer with "petrified understanding" seems to begin with the editors' comments in the critical edition (I: 639). Novalis, however, does not refer to him per se when he talks of this petrification (I: 358).

14. For an excellent psychoanalytic reading of *Klingsohr's Tale*, see Friedrich Kittler, "Die Irrwege des Eros und die 'absolute Familie.' Psychoanalytischer und diskursanalytischer Kommentar zu Klingsohrs Märchen in Novalis' *Heinrich von Ofterdingen*," *Psychoanalytische und psychopathologische Literaturinterpretationen*, ed. B. Urban and W. Kudszus (Darmstadt: Wissenschaftliche Buchgesellschaft, 1981), pp. 421–473.

15. This according to Tieck, who describes the poem as expressing *in nuce* the "inner spirit" of Novalis's "books" (I: 360).

16. See, for example, the editors' introduction to the critical edition (I: 115–128); Haywood, *Novalis: The Veil of Imagery* (Cambridge, Mass.: Harvard University Press, 1959), pp. 52–77; Ritter, *Novalis' Hymnen an die Nacht* (Heidelberg: Carl Winter Universitätsverlag, [2]1974); Friedrichsmeyer, *The Androgyne in Early German Romanticism* (Bern, Frankfurt am Main, and New York: Lang, 1983) pp. 91–107; and O'Brien, *Novalis: Signs of Revolution* (Durham, N.C., and London: Duke University Press, 1995) pp. 256–271. Pfefferkorn, whose study *Novalis* (New Haven, Conn., and London: Yale University Press, 1988) is subtitled *A Romantic's Theory of Language and Poetry*, defers treatment of Novalis's poems to a later date (p. 6).

17. See Kuzniar, *Delayed Endings* (Athens: University of Georgia Press, 1987), pp. 93–94, for a similar discussion of the conclusion of the *Hymns*.

18. See Chapter 2.

19. See von Molnár, *Novalis' "Fichte Studies"* (The Hague: Mouton, 1970), pp. 38–39.

20. Novalis uses the term *Vorstellung* (representation) here to refer to the thought perception (as opposed to the sense perception or *Anschauung*) of the empirical subject. For a discussion of the function of these terms in Novalis's epistemology, see ibid.

21. This according to Tieck. See Heinz Ritter, *Novalis' Hymnen and die Nacht*, p. 2.

22. There are important parallels between the elements of the lyric theory I have outlined here and many statements Schlegel makes about transcendental poesy in the 1800 version of the *Conversation on Poesy*. For example, Schlegel shares Novalis's notion of the fluid subject (KA XII: 408), and in the opening section he describes poesy as a fluid binding together of subjects. For a reading of this section of Schlegel's theory, see David E. Wellbery, "Rhetorik und Literatur. Anmerkungen zur poetologischen Begriffsbildung bei Friedrich Schlegel," *Die Aktualität der Frühromantik*, ed. E. Behler and J. Hörisch (Paderborn and Munich: Schöningh, 1988), pp. 161–173.

Chapter 4. Kleist:
Transcending the Transcendental

1. R. Eisler, *Wörterbuch der philosophischen Begriffe*, *Band 3* (Berlin: Mittler, ³1930), p. 258.

2. Page references are to Heinrich von Kleist, *Sämtliche Werke und Briefe in Vier Bänden*, ed. Helmut Sembdner (Munich and Vienna: Hanser, 1982). The translations are my own.

3. Michael Titzmann, "Bemerkungen zu Wissen und Sprache in der Goethezeit (1770–1830), Mit dem Beispiel der optischen Kodierung von Erkenntnisprozessen," *Bewegung und Stillstand in Metaphern und Mythen*, ed. J. Link and W. Wülfling (Stuttgart: Klett-Cotta, 1984), pp. 100–120.

4. See, for example, Beda Allemann, "Sinn und Unsinn von Kleists Gespräch 'Über das Marionettentheater,' " *Kleist-Jahrbuch* (Berlin: Schmidt, 1981/82): 50–65; Helene Cixous, "Les marionettes," *Prénoms de personne* (Paris: Éditions du Seuil, 1974), pp. 127–152; Richard Daunicht, "Heinrich von Kleists Aufsatz 'Über das Marionettentheater' als Satire betrachtet," *Euphorion* 67 (1973): 307–322; William Ray, "Suspended in the Mirror: Language and Self in Kleist's 'Über das Marionettentheater," *Studies in Romanticism* 18 (Winter 1979): 521–546; and James Rushing, "The Limitations of the Fencing Bear: Kleist's 'Über das Marionettentheater' as Ironic Fiction," *German Quarterly* 61 (Fall 1988): 528–539.

5. Rushing, ibid., p. 536.

6. Ray, "Suspended in the Mirror," pp. 536–538.

7. On the importance of reflection in Idealism and Romanticism, see Dieter Henrich, "Fichtes ursprüngliche Einsicht," *Subjektivität und Metaphysik: Festschrift für Wolfgang Cramer*, pp. 188–232; Rodolphe Gasché, *The Tain of the Mirror* (Cambridge, Mass., and London: Harvard University Press, 1986); Walter Benjamin, *Der Begriff der Kunstkritik in der deutschen Romantik* (Frankfurt am Main: Suhrkamp, 1973); Winfried Menninghaus, *Unendliche Verdopplung: Die frühromantische Grundlegung der Kunsttheorie im Begriff absoluter Selbstreflexion* (Frankfurt am Main: Suhrkamp, 1987); and Alice Kuzniar, "Reassessing Romantic Reflexivity," pp. 77–86.

8. I have paraphrased Rodolphe Gasché's translation of Kant's definition here (Gasché, *The Tain of the Mirror*, p. 18).

9. See Henrich, "Fichtes ursprüngliche Einsicht," p. 193.

10. Hölderlin makes this argument in "Urteil und Sein," *Stuttgarter Hölderlin-Ausgabe, Band 4*, ed. Friedrich Beissner (Stuttgart: Kohlhammer, 1962), pp. 226–227.

11. Ernst Cassirer has argued convincingly that Kleist's "Kant crisis" was in fact a "Fichte crisis." Cassirer, *Heinrich von Kleist und die Kantische Philosophie* (Berlin: Reuther und Reichard, 1919).

12. *Webster's New Collegiate Dictionary*. Adelung, to quote a contemporaneous reference, lists the word only in its adjectival and adverbial forms, "welches ohne Noth aus dem Französischen *burlesque* entlehnet ist, geschickt, durch das unnatürliche oder ungereimte Lachen zu erregen, possierlich." Johann Christoph Adelung, *Grammatisch-Kritisches Wörterbuch der Hochdeutschen Mundart* (Leipzig: Breitkopf, 1793), p. 1268. Grimm, interestingly, does not list the word at all.

13. See Benno von Wiese, "Das verlorene und wieder zu findende Paradies. Eine Studie über den Begriff der Anmut bei Goethe, Kleist und Schiller," *Kleists Aufsatz über das Marionettentheater*, ed. H. Sembdner (Berlin: Erich Schmidt, 1967), pp. 196–220, here p. 203. Goethe, for instance, discusses the importance of the "ideal" in art and then comments, "The object, and the manner of representing (*vorstellen*) it are subject to the

sensible laws of art . . . through them it [the object] becomes beautiful, i.e., graceful (*anmutig*) to the eye" ("Über Laokoon," HA III: 57).

14. See Chapter 1.

15. According to Grimm, *erstaunen* is equivalent to *staunen*, which is derived from the Germanic root *stu*, "steif, starr sein" (to be stiff or rigid). *Deutsches Wörterbuch von Jacob Grimm und Wilhelm Grimm* (Leipzig: Hirzel, 1862), vol. 3, p. 998, and vol. 10, pp. 1176–1177. In Adelung's definition of *erstaunen* the astonished subject is, as it were, "set outside himself or herself": "mit dem Hülfsworte seyn, vor Verwunderung über einen unerwarteten Gegenstand, von welchem man noch nicht weiss, ob er gut oder böse ist, *gleichsam betäubt, ausser sich selbst gesetzt werden*" (p. 1942).

16. Fichte also discusses the Kantian sublime in terms of *Staunen* (GA II, 3: 229–232).

17. Kleist explicitly pairs *überlegen* with *Überlegung* in "Von der Überlegung, eine Paradoxe" (337–338).

18. In comparison with the "playing imagination" of the beautiful, Kant states, that of the sublime is "no game, but seriousness" (*CJ* B 75).

19. Kleist makes this statement in *Unwahrscheinliche Wahrhaftigkeiten* (*Improbable Truths*), which can be read as the converse of the representational argument presented here. In opposition to the three anecdotes presented in the *Marionette Theater* essay that appear to be true, but are not, the three stories presented in *Improbable Truths* appear not to be true but are in fact, it is claimed, true.

20. Paul de Man, "Aesthetic Formalization: Kleist's *Über das Marionettentheater*," *The Rhetoric of Romanticism* (New York: Columbia University Press, 1984), pp. 263–290, here p. 271.

21. Ray ("Suspended in the Mirror"), whose analysis focuses on the specular structure of the essay, surprisingly offers no interpretation of the concluding comment on reflection, apparently preferring instead to leave the subject "suspended in the mirror" (p. 521), and de Man ("Aesthetic Formalization") cursorily dismisses the text's conclusion, thereby neatly, but unjustifiably, skirting the issue: "It has been very easy to forget how little this pseudo-

conclusion has to do with the rest of the text and how derisively ungermane it is to the implications of what comes before" (p. 268).

22. Kleist's other example—the geometric description of the intersection of two lines, on the one side of a point, after it passes through infinity, suddenly reappearing on the other side—is further evidence of his critique of transcendental representation: for Kant and Novalis, mathematics is the locus of pure representation; for Kleist mathematics can only (re)present approximately, "like numbers to their logarithms or the asymptotes to the hyperbola (*Hyperbel*)" (340). The German word *Hyperbel* designates both the geometric figure (hyperbola) and the rhetorical figure (hyperbole).

23. Kleist's essay *Empfindungen vor Friedrichs Seelandschaft* (*Perceptions in Front of Friedrich's Seascape*), which also contains a redaction of the Kantian sublime, comes to similar conclusions about *Selbstdarstellung* (327–328).

24. See Kuzniar, "Reassessing Romantic Reflexivity" and Menninghaus, *Unendliche Verdopplung*.

25. Werner Hamacher has argued that it is possible to read Kleist's *Das Erdbeben in Chili* in the same vein. However, as I suggest here, there is a decisive difference in import between Kant's *negative Darstellung* and Kleist's. See Werner Hamacher, "Das Beben der Darstellung," *Positionen der Literaturwissenschaft. Acht Modellanalysen am Beispiel von Kleists "Das Erdbeben in Chili,"* ed. David E. Wellbery (Munich: Beck, [2]1985) pp. 149–173, especially pp. 157–162.

26. See Werner Hoffmeister, "Heinrich von Kleists *Findling*," *Monatshefte* 58 (1966): 49–63, here pp. 49–50.

27. J. Hillis Miller makes a similar argument in "Just Reading: Kleist's *Der Findling*," *Versions of Pygmalion* (Cambridge, Mass., and London: Harvard University Press, 1990), pp. 82–140, here pp. 120–121.

28. Schiller, "Das verschleierte Bild zu Saïs," *Sämmtliche Werke, Band 1*, pp. 224–226.

29. See Chapter 2 for a reading of the sonnet as an instantiation of the Kantian sublime.

30. Frank G. Ryder, "Kleist's *Findling*: Oedipus Manqué?," *MLN* 92 (1977): 509–524.

31. Wahrig lists the derivation from the French *bigot*, "abergläubisch, fromm, *buchstabengläubig*." Wahrig, *Deutsches Wörterbuch* (Munich: Bertelsman, 1991), p. 271. Ryder also links Nicolo's rearrangement of the ivory letters to Elvire's name, *parquet*, which means a "jeu d'addresse, qui consiste à arranger plusiers petits morceaux de bois peint les uns à côté des autres, de manière à former des dessins et des figures" (p. 523).

32. Ryder, "Kleist's *Findling*," p. 513.

33. Ibid., p. 515.

34. Ibid., p. 523.

35. Miller, "Just Reading," p. 120. Surprisingly, Miller makes no reference to Ryder's argument.

36. Marjorie Gelus, "Displacement of Meaning: Kleist's *Der Findling*," *German Quarterly* 55 (November 1982): 541–553.

37. Diethelm Brüggemann, "Aloysius, Marquis von Montferrat: der 'genuesische Ritter' in Kleists Erzählung *Der Findling*," *Drei Mystifikationen Heinrich von Kleists* (New York, Berne, and Frankfurt am Main: Peter Lang, 1985), pp. 175–211. Brüggemann points out other motifs that Kleist adapted from the chronicle; for instance, the fire in Elvire's childhood story, the sheets, and the whip. Brüggemann also suggests that the painting described in the story actually exists and that Kleist had seen it during his travels.

38. "In theater, in cinema, in traditional literature, things are always seen *from somewhere*; this is the geometric basis of representation: there must be a fetishistic subject in order to project this tableau. This point of origin is always the Law: law of society, law of struggle, law of meaning. Every militant art, therefore, must be representative, legal. For representation to be really deprived of origin and for it to transcend its geometrical nature without ceasing to be a representation, the price to pay is enormous: it is nothing less than death." Roland Barthes, "Diderot, Brecht, Eisenstein," *The Responsibility of Forms*, trans. Richard Howard (Berkeley and Los Angeles: University of California Press, 1985), pp. 89–97, here p. 96.

39. Kleist's own suicide, interpreted sheerly as the artistic event that he intended it to be, can be read in the same vein. After months of careful scripting and exquisite orchestration, Kleist

went to the shores of the Wannsee in Berlin to carry out the ultimate expression of *negative Darstellung* the human subject is
capable of creating: the aestheticization of his own death.

40. H. Sembdner, ed., *Erläuterungen und Dokumente:
Heinrich von Kleist: Der zerbrochne Krug* (Stuttgart: Reclam,
1973), pp. 84ff. Kleist blamed the play's failure on Goethe's production, and was so enraged by the play's negative reception that
he threatened to challenge Goethe to a shooting match (*Erläuterungen* p. 91).

41. A number of commentators do discuss various aspects
of the variant ending, yet fail to recognize how profoundly it draws
Eve's character into question. See, for example, Ilse Graham, "The
Broken Jug—Hero of Kleist's Comedy," *Modern Language
Quarterly* 16 (1955): 99–113; Peter Michelson, "Die Lügen Adams
und Evas Fall. Heinrich von Kleists *Der zerbrochne Krug*," *Geist
und Zeichen: Festschrift für Arthur Henkel,* ed. H. Anton, B.
Gajek, and P. Pfaff (Heidelberg: Carl Winter, 1977), pp. 268–304;
and Bernhard Greiner, "Die Wende in der Kunst—Kleist mit
Kant," *Deutsche Vierteljahrsschrift für Literaturwissenschaft
und Geistesgeschichte* 64 (1990): 96–116. The fact that the
standard Hanser edition of Kleist's *Sämtliche Werke* that I am
using here does not include the "variant" ending is symptomatic
of the general lack of attention the text is usually accorded. In
the following section I will refer to the "variant" ending printed
in the *Erläuterungen und Dokumente,* pp. 42–60. Page references
to the "variant" will be followed by a *v.*

42. The secondary literature overwhelmingly interprets Eve
as the embodiment of goodness and virtue. Helbling's succinct
assessment of the character is representative of this tradition:
"the naïve Eve has such depth of pure feeling that she could never
become an agent of conscious deception, though she must engage
in temporary dissimulation to protect Ruprecht" (pp. 123–124).
Robert E. Helbling, "The Comedy of Deception: *The Broken Jug,*"
The Major Works of Heinrich von Kleist (New York: New
Directions, 1975), pp. 119–130.

43. Wolfgang Wittkowski has argued that *Der zerbrochne
Krug* is a satire on authority and on uncritical obedience to
authority. Wolfgang Wittkowsi, "*Der zerbrochne Krug:* Juggling
of Authorities," *Heinrich von Kleist Studien,* ed. Alexej Ugrinsky
(Berlin: Erich Schmidt, 1980), pp. 69–79.

44. Sembdner, *Erläuterungen*, p. 87.

45. The Preface was not included in the 1811 edition of Kleist's works. Ibid., p. 3.

46. Ibid., p. 3. A copy of the original picture is printed on p. 5 of the *Erläuterungen*.

47. The last line I have quoted here is included only in the *Phöbus* version of the play. Ibid., p. 64.

48. Both the biblical Fall and the Oedipus motif introduced in the play's Preface involve a transgression committed in a state of innocence, and in both stories these transgressions result in a loss of innocence. Like the Fall depicted in *On the Marionette Theater*, Adam's Fall inverts this paradigm: he knowingly tries to mislead Eve and is not expelled from public service.

49. See Hinrich C. Seeba, *"Overdragt der Nederlanden in 't Jaar 1555*: Das Historische Faktum und das Loch im Bild der Geschichte bei Kleist," *Barocker Lust-Spiegel. Studien zur Literatur des Barock. Festschrift für Blake Lee Spahr*, ed. M. Bircher, J. Fechner, and G. Hillen (Amsterdam: Rodopi, 1984), pp. 409–433, here pp. 416–419.

50. Oskar Seidlin has pointed out a number of discrepancies in the times various characters report actions to have occurred. Ruprecht first sees Adam and Eve in the garden at eleven o'clock, which is the same time that Marthe reports discovering the devastation in Eve's room. According to his maid, Adam also returns home at eleven, yet Frau Briggy reports seeing him running from the garden "around midnight." Oskar Seidlin, "What the Bell Tolls in Kleist's *Der zerbrochne Krug*," *Deutsche Vierteljahrsschrift für Literaturwissenschaft und Geistesgeschichte* 51 (1977): 78–97.

51. Sembdner, *Erlaüterungen*, p. 28.

52. Ruprecht describes the door handle with the following words: "On the handle there was a lump of lead, like a sword handle" (210). The lump of lead (*Klumpen Blei*) also refers to Adam's *Klumpfuss* (club foot, 178).

53. Herder in particular draws an explicit connection between the words *Tausch* and *Täuschung* in his discussion of *Darstellung* in *Kalligone*. See Chapter 1, "Eighteenth-Century Aesthetic Theories of *Darstellung*."

54. Sembdner, *Erläuterungen*, p. 58.

55. This textual economy between Adam and Licht is set up at the beginning of the text when both are identified as "out of place" or *verlegen* (184, 185, 190).

Epilogue

1. Heidegger, *The Age of the World Picture*, p. 154.

2. Seyhan, *Representation and Its Discontents: The Critical Legacy of German Romanticism* (Berkeley and Los Angeles: University of California Press, 1992), p. 9.

3. Hegel, *Phänomenologie des Geistes, Werke in 20 Bänden, Band 13* (Frankfurt am Main: Suhrkamp, 1970), p. 31.

4. Hegel, *Vorlesungen über die* Ästhetik I, *Werke in 20 Bänden, Band 13* (Frankfurt am Main: Suhrkamp, 1970), p. 100.

5. Nietzsche, "On Truth and Lie in an Extra-Moral Sense," *The Portable Nietzsche*, trans. and ed. Walter Kaufmann (New York: Viking, 1968), pp. 42–47, here pp. 46–47.

6. Heidegger, *The Age of the World Picture*, p. 132.

7. Benjamin, *Ursprung des deutschen Trauerspiels* (Frankfurt am Main: Suhrkamp: 1974), p. 9

8. Benjamin, *Briefe*, ed. Gerschom Scholem and Theodor Adorno, 2 vols. (Frankfurt am Main: Suhrkamp, 1978), vol. 1, p. 150.

9. Benjamin, *Ursprung des deutschen Trauerspiels*, p. 9.

10. Ibid., p. 10.

11. Ibid., p. 9.

Bibliography

Adelung, Johann Christoph. *Grammatisch-Kritisches Wörterbuch der Hochdeutschen Mundart*. Leipzig: Breitkopf, 1793.

Allemann, Beda. "Sinn und Unsinn von Kleists Gespräch 'Über das Marionettentheater.'" *Kleist-Jahrbuch*. Berlin: Schmidt, 1981–82: 50–65.

Barnard, Philip and Cheryl Lester. "Translators' Introduction: The Presentation of Romantic Literature." Philippe Lacoue-Labarthe and Jean-Luc Nancy, *The Literary Absolute*, trans. Barnard and Lester, pp. vii–xx. Albany: State University of New York Press, 1988.

Barthes, Roland. "Diderot, Brecht, Eisenstein." *The Responsibility of Forms*, trans. Richard Howard, pp. 89–97. Berkeley and Los Angeles: University of California Press, 1985.

Beaufret, Jean. "Kant et la Notion de *Darstellung*." *Dialogue avec Heidegger*, vol. 2, pp. 77–109. Paris: Éditions de Minuit, 1973.

Beiser, Frederick C. *The Fate of Reason: German Philosophy from Kant to Fichte*. Cambridge, Mass. and London: Harvard University Press, 1987.

Benjamin, Walter. *Der Begriff der Kunstkritik in der deutschen Romantik*. Frankfurt am Main: Suhrkamp, 1973.

———. *Briefe*, ed. Gerschom Scholem and Theodor Adorno, 2 vols. Frankfurt am Main: Suhrkamp, 1978.

———. *Ursprung des deutschen Trauerspiels*. Frankfurt am Main: Suhrkamp, 1974.

Bernhardi, August Ferdinand. *Anfangsgründe der Sprachwissenschaft. Faksimile-Neudruck der Ausgabe Berlin 1805*. Stuttgart - Bad Cannstatt: Frommann-Holzboog, 1990.

———. *Sprachlehre. Nachdruck der 2. erweiterten umarbeiteten Ausgabe Berlin 1801/1803*. Hildesheim and New York: Olms, 1973.

Breazeale, Daniel. "Between Kant and Fichte: Karl Leonhard Reinhold's 'Elementary Philosophy.'" *Review of Metaphysics* 35 (1982): 785–821.

———. "Fichte's *Aenesidemus* Review and the Transformation of German Idealism." *Review of Metaphysics* 34 (1981): 545–568.

Brentano, Clemens. *Godwi: oder Das versteinerte Bild der Mutter. Brentano. Sämtliche Werke und Briefe, Band 16.* Stuttgart: Kohlhammer, 1978.

Brüggemann, Diethelm. "Aloysius, Marquis von Montferrat: der 'genuesische Ritter' in Kleists Erzählung *Der Findling.*" *Drei Mystifikationen Heinrich von Kleists*, pp. 175–211. New York, Berne, and Frankfurt am Main: Peter Lang, 1985.

Buchner, August. *Anleitung zur deutschen Poeterey/Poet*, ed. Manian Szyrock. Tübingen: Niemeyer, 1966.

Buck, G. "Hypotypose." *Historisches Wörterbuch der Philosophie, Band 3*, ed. Joachim Ritter, pp. 1266–1267. Basel: Schwabe, 1974.

Bürger, Gottfried August. "Von der Popularität der Poesie." *Sämtliche Werke*, ed. Günter Häntzschel and Hiltrud Häntzschel, pp. 725–730. Munich and Vienna: Hanser, 1987.

Cassirer, Ernst. *Heinrich von Kleist und die Kantische Philosophie.* Berlin: Reuther und Reichard, 1919.

Cixous, Helene. "Les marionettes." *Prénoms de personne*, pp. 127–152. Paris: Éditions du Seuil, 1974.

Cloeren, Hermann-Josef. "Philosophie als Sprachkritik bei K. L. Reinhold. Interpretative Bemerkungen zu seiner Spätphilosophie." *Kant-Studien* 63 (1972): 225–236.

Daunicht, Richard. "Heinrich von Kleists Aufsatz 'Über das Marionettentheater' als Satire betrachtet." *Euphorion* 67 (1973): 307–322.

de Man, Paul. "Aesthetic Formalization: Kleist's *Über das Marionettentheater.*" *The Rhetoric of Romanticism*, pp. 263–290. New York: Columbia University Press, 1984.

Derrida, Jacques. *The Truth in Painting*, trans. Geoff Bennington and Ian McLeod. Chicago and London: University of Chicago Press, 1987.

Deutsches Wörterbuch von Jacob Grimm und Wilhelm Grimm. Leipzig: Hirzel, 1862.

Deutsches Wörterbuch von Jacob Grimm und Wilhelm Grimm, Neubearbeitung, ed. Deutsche Akademie der Wissenschaften zu Berlin in Zusammenhang mit der Akademie der Wissenschaften zu Göttingen. Leipzig: Hirzel, 1972.

Eisler, R. *Wörterbuch der philosophischen Begriffe.* Berlin: Mittler, ³1930.

Fichte, Johann Gottlieb. *Early Philosophical Writings,* ed. and trans. Daniel Breazeale. Ithaca, N.Y., and London: Cornell University Press, 1988.

―――. *Gesamtausgabe der Bayrischen Akademie der Wissenschaften,* ed. Reinhard Lauth and Hans Jacob. Stuttgart-Bad Canstatt: Fromann, 1962–. Cited as GA.

―――. *Über den Begriff der Wissenschaftslehre oder der sogennanten Philosophie.* Stuttgart: Reclam, 1972.

Flusser, Vilém. "Abbild-Vorbild." *Was heisst ≫ Darstellen ≪?* ed. Christiaan Hart Nibbrig, pp. 34–48. Frankfurt am Main: Suhrkamp, 1994.

Frank, Manfred. *Einführung in die frühromantische Ästhetik. Vorlesungen.* Frankfurt am Main: Suhrkamp, 1989.

―――. "Intellektuale Anschauung." *Die Aktualität der Frühromantik,* ed. Ernst Behler and Jochen Hörisch. pp. 96–126. Paderborn: Schöningh, 1987.

――― and Gerhard Kurz. "Ordo Inversus." *Geist und Zeichen. Festschrift für Arthur Henkel,* ed. H. Anton, pp. 75–97. Heidelberg: Carl Winter, 1977.

Friedrichsmeyer, Sara. *The Androgyne in Early German Romanticism.* Bern, Frankfurt am Main, and New York: Lang, 1983.

Gasché, Rodolphe. "Ideality in Fragmentation." Foreword to Friedrich Schlegel, *Philosophical Fragments,* trans. Peter Firchow, pp. vii–xxxi. Minneapolis and Oxford: University of Minnesota Press, 1991.

―――. "Some Reflections on the Notion of Hypotyposis in Kant." *Argumentation* 4 (1990): 85–100. A German translation of the essay, "Überlegungen zum Begriff der Hypotypose bei Kant," is reprinted in C. Hart Nibbrig, *Was heisst ≫Darstellen≪*? pp. 152–174.

————. *The Tain of the Mirror.* Cambridge, Mass., and London: Harvard University Press, 1986.

Gelus, Marjorie. "Displacement of Meaning: Kleist's *Der Findling.*" *German Quarterly* 55, no. 4 (November 1982): 541–553.

Goethe, Johann Wolfgang von. *Werke. Hamburger Ausgabe in 14 Bänden.* Munich: Beck, 1988. Cited as HA.

Graham, Ilse. "The Broken Jug—Hero of Kleist's Comedy." *Modern Language Quarterly* 16 (1955): 99–113.

Graubner, Hans. "Kant." *Klassiker der Literaturtheorie,* ed. Horst Turk, pp. 35–61. Munich: Beck, 1979.

Greiner, Bernhard. "Die Wende in der Kunst—Kleist mit Kant." *Deutsche Vierteljahrsschrift für Literaturwissenschaft und Geistesgeschichte* 64, no. 1 (1990): 96–116.

Haering, Theodor Lorenz. *Novalis als Philosoph.* Stuttgart: Kohlhammer, 1954.

Hamacher, Werner. "Das Beben der Darstellung." *Positionen der Literaturwissenschaft. Acht Modellanalysen am Beispiel von Kleists "Das Erdbeben in Chili,"* ed. David Wellbery, pp. 149–173. Munich: Beck, ²1985.

Hart Nibbrig, Christiaan L., ed. *Was heisst ≫Darstellen≪*? Frankfurt am Main: Suhrkamp, 1994.

————. "Zum Drum und Dran einer Fragestellung. Ein Vorgeschmack." *Was heisst ≫Darstellen≪*? ed. Hart Nibbrig, pp. 7–13. Frankfurt am Main: Suhrkamp, 1994.

Haywood, Bruce. *Novalis: The Veil of Imagery.* Cambridge, Mass.: Harvard University Press, 1959.

Hegel, G. W. F. *Phänomenologie des Geistes. Hegel, Werke in 20 Bänden, Band 3.* Frankfurt am Main: Suhrkamp, 1970.

————. *Vorlesungen über die Ästhetik I. Hegel, Werke in 20 Bänden, Band 13.* Frankfurt am Main: Suhrkamp, 1970.

Heidegger, Martin. *The Age of the World Picture. The Question Concerning Technology and Other Essays,* trans. William Lovitt, pp. 116–154. New York: Harper and Row, 1977.

————. *Die Zeit des Weltbildes. Gesamtausgabe, Band 5: Holzwege*, pp. 75–113. Frankfurt am Main: Klostermann, 1977.

Helbling, Robert E. *The Major Works of Heinrich von Kleist.* New York: New Directions, 1975.

Henrich, Dieter. "Fichtes ursprüngliche Einsicht." *Subjektivität und Metaphysik: Festschrift für Wolfgang Cramer*, ed. Henrich and H. Wagner, pp. 188–232. Frankfurt am Main: Klostermann, 1966.

————. "Fichte's Original Insight," trans. David Lachterman. *Contemporary German Philosophy*, vol. 1, ed. D. E. Christensen et al., pp. 15–53. University Park and London: Pennsylvania State University Press, 1982.

Herder, Johann Gottfried. *Kalligone. Herders Sämtliche Werke, Band 22*, ed. B. Suphan. Berlin: Weidmann, 1880.

Heuer, Fritz. *Darstellung der Freiheit. Schillers transzendentale Frage nach der Kunst.* Cologne and Vienna: Böhlau, 1970.

Hoffmann, E. T. A. *Werke*, 4 vols. Frankfurt am Main: Insel, 1967.

Hoffmeister, Werner. "Heinrich von Kleists *Findling.*" *Monatshefte* 58 (1966): 49–63.

Hölderlin, Friedrich. "Urteil und Sein." *Stuttgarter Hölderlin-Ausgabe, Band 4*, ed. Friedrich Beissner, pp. 226–227. Stuttgart: Kohlhammer, 1962.

————. "Über die Verfahrensweise des poetischen Geistes." *Stuttgarter Hölderlin-Ausgabe, Band 4*, ed. Friedrich Beissner, pp. 251–276. Stuttgart: Kohlhammer, 1962.

Hörisch, Jochen. *Die fröhliche Wissenschaft der Poesie.* Frankfurt am Main: Suhrkamp, 1976.

Kant, Immanuel. *Beobachtungen über das Gefühl des Schönen und Erhabenen. Immanuel Kants Werke, Band 2*, ed. A. Buchenau. Berlin: Cassirer, 1912.

————. *Critique of Judgment*, trans. J. H. Bernard. New York: Hafner, 1951. Cited as *CJ.*

————. *Critique of Pure Reason*, trans. Norman Kemp Smith. New York: St. Martin's Press, 1965. Cited as *CPR.*

————. *Kritik der reinen Vernunft. Immanuel Kant Werkausgabe, Bde. 3 und 4*, ed. Wilhelm Weischedel. Frankfurt am Main: Suhrkamp, 1974.

————. *Kritik der praktischen Vernunft. Immanuel Kant Werkausgabe, Band 7,* ed. Wilhelm Weischedel. Frankfurt am Main: Suhrkamp, 1974.

————. *Kritik der Urteilskraft. Immanuel Kant Werkausgabe, Band 10,* ed. Wilhelm Weischedel. Frankfurt am Main: Suhrkamp, 1974.

————. "Von einem neuerdings erhobenen vornehmen Ton in der Philosophie." *Immanuel Kant. Werke in Sechs Bänden, Band 3,* ed. Wilhelm Weischedel, pp. 375–397. Darmstadt: Wissenschaftliche Buchgesellschaft, 1966.

Kirchenstein, Max. *Klopstocks Deutsche Gelehrtenrepublik.* Berlin: de Gruyter, 1928.

Kittler, Friedrich. "Die Irrwege des Eros und die 'absolute Familie.' Psychoanalytischer und diskursanalytischer Kommentar zu Klingsohrs Märchen in Novalis' *Heinrich von Ofterdingen.*" *Psychoanalytische und psychopathologische Literaturinterpretationen,* ed. B. Urban and W. Kudszus, pp. 421–473. Darmstadt: Wissenschaftliche Buchgesellschaft, 1981.

Kleist, Heinrich von. *Sämtliche Werke und Briefe in Vier Bänden,* ed. Helmut Sembdner. Munich and Vienna: Hanser, 1982.

Klin, Eugen. *August Ferdinand Bernhardi als Kritiker und Literaturtheoretiker.* Bonn: Bouvier, 1966.

Klopstock, Friedrich Gottlieb. *Deutsche Gelehrtenrepublik. Klopstock. Ausgewählte Werke,* ed. K. A. Schleiden, pp. 875–929. Munich: Hanser, ⁴1981.

————. "Von der Darstellung." *Klopstock, Ausgewählte Werke,* ed. K. A. Schleiden, pp. 1031–1038. Munich: Hanser, ⁴1981.

Koch, Reinhard F. *Fichtes Theorie des Selbstbewusstseins. Ihre Entwicklung von den "Eignen Meditationen" über Elementar-Philosophie" 1793 bis zur "Neuen Bearbeitung der W.L."* 1800. Würzburg: Königshausen and Neumann, 1989.

Kuzniar, Alice A. *Delayed Endings: Nonclosure in Novalis and Hölderlin.* Athens: University of Georgia Press, 1987.

————. "Reassessing Romantic Reflexivity: The Case of Novalis." *Germanic Review* 63 (Spring 1988): 77–86.

Lacoue-Labarthe, Philippe, and Jean-Luc Nancy. *The Literary Absolute,* trans. Philip Barnard and Cheryl Lester. Albany: State University of New York Press, 1988.

Lambert, Johann Heinrich. *Neues Organon, oder Gedanken über die Erforschung und Bezeichnung des Wahren und dessen Unterscheidung vom Irrtum und Schein.* Berlin: Akademie-Verlag, 1990.

Lenz, Jakob Michael Reinhold. "Anmerkungen übers Theater." *Jakob Michael Reinhold Lenz, Werke und Briefe in 3 Bänden,* vol. 2, ed. S. Damm, pp. 641–671. Munich and Vienna: Hanser, 1987.

Lessing, Gottfried Ephraim. *Laokoon.* Stuttgart: Reclam, 1964.

Markwardt, Bruno. *Geschichte der deutschen Poetik.* Berlin: de Gruyter, 1956.

Menninghaus, Winfried. " ≫ Darstellung ≪. Friedrich Gottlieb Klopstocks Eröffnung eines neuen Paradigmas." *Was heisst ≫ Darstellen ≪?* ed. Christiaan Hart Nibbrig, pp. 205–226. Frankfurt am Main: Suhrkamp, 1994.

———. "Die frühromantische Theorie von Zeichen und Metapher." *German Quarterly* 62 (Winter 1989): 48–58.

———. "Klopstocks Poetik der schnellen ≫ Bewegung ≪." *Klopstock, Gedanken über die Natur der Poesie,* ed. Menninghaus, pp. 259–351. Frankfurt am Main: Insel, 1989.

———. *Unendliche Verdopplung: Die frühromantische Grundlegung der Kunsttheorie im Begriff absoluter Selbstreflexion.* Frankfurt am Main: Suhrkamp, 1987.

Michelson, Peter. "Die Lügen Adams und Evas Fall. Heinrich von Kleists *Der zerbrochne Krug.*" *Geist und Zeichen: Festschrift für Arthur Henkel,* ed. H. Anton, B. Gajek, and P. Pfaff, pp. 268–304. Heidelberg: Carl Winter, 1977.

Micraelius, Johannes. *Lexicon Philosophicum Terminorum Philosophis Usitatorum. Photomechanischer Nachdruck der 2. Auflage, Stettin 1662.* Düsseldorf: Stern, 1966.

Miller, J. Hillis. "Just Reading: Kleist's *Der Findling.*" *Versions of Pygmalian,* pp. 82–140. Cambridge, Mass., and London: Harvard University Press, 1990.

Mueller-Vollmer, Kurt. "Fichte und die frühromatische Sprachtheorie." *Der transzendentale Gedanke. Die gegenwärtige Darstellung der Philosophie Fichtes,* ed. Klaus Hammacher, pp. 442–459. Hamburg: Meiner, 1981.

Nancy, Jean-Luc. "Logodaedalus: Kant écrivain." *Poétique* 21 (1975): 24–52.

———. "L'offrande sublime." *PO&SIE* 30 (1984): 76–103.

Naumann, Barbara. >*Die Sprache ist ein musicalisches Ideen Instrument<. Studien zur Funktion des Musikalischen in der frühromantischen Poetik.* Stuttgart: Metzler, 1990.

Nieerad, J. "Darstellung." *Historisches Wörterbuch der Philosophie, Band 2*, ed. Joachim Ritter, pp. 11–12. Basel: Schwabe, 1972.

Nietzsche, Friedrich. "On Truth and Lie in an Extra-Moral Sense." *The Portable Nietzsche.* trans. and ed. Walter Kaufmann, pp. 42–47. New York: Viking, 1968.

Novalis. *Schriften*, ed. Paul Kluckhohn and Richard Samuel, 5 vols. Stuttgart: Kohlhammer, ³1977–1988.

O'Brien, W. Arctander. *Novalis: Signs of Revolution.* Durham, N.C. and London: Duke University Press, 1995.

Pfefferkorn, Kristin. *Novalis: A Romantic's Theory of Language and Poetry.* New Haven, Conn., and London: Yale University Press, 1988.

Ray, William. "Suspended in the Mirror: Language and Self in Kleist's 'Über das Marionettentheater.'" *Studies in Romanticism* 18 (Winter 1979): 521–546.

Richter, Jean Paul Friedrich. *Vorschule der Ästhetik*, ed. N. Miller. Munich: Hanser: 1963.

Ritter, Heinz. *Novalis' Hymnen an die Nacht.* Heidelberg: Carl Winter Universitätsverlag, ²1974.

Rushing, James. "The Limitations of the Fencing Bear: Kleist's 'Über das Marionettentheater' as Ironic Fiction." *German Quarterly* 61 (Fall 1988): 528–539.

Ryder, Frank G. "Kleist's *Findling*: Oedipus Manqué?" *MLN* 92 (1977): 509–524.

Schelling, F. W. J. *Texte zur Philosophie der Kunst.* Stuttgart: Reclam, 1982.

Schiller, Friedrich von. *Sämtliche Werke*, ed. Gerhart Fricke and Herbert G. Göpfert, 5 vols. Munich: Hanser, 1959.

Schlegel, Friedrich. *Kritische Friedrich-Schlegel-Ausgabe*, 24 vols. to date, ed. Ernst Behler and Hans Eichner. Munich, Paderborn, and Vienna: Schöningh, 1958–. Cited as KA.

Seeba, Hinrich. "*Overdragt der Nederlanden in 't Jaar 1555*: Das Historische Faktum und das Loch in der Bild der Geschichte bei Kleist." *Barocker Lust-Spiegel. Studien zur Literatur des Barock. Festschrift für Blake Lee Spahr*, ed. M. Bircher, J. Fechner, and G. Hillen, pp. 409–433. Amsterdam: Rodopi, 1984.

Seidlin, Oskar. "What the Bell Tolls in Kleist's *Der zerbrochne Krug*." *Deutsche Vierteljahrsschrift für Literaturwissenschaft und Geistesgeschichte* 51 (1977): 78–97.

Sembdner, Helmut, ed. *Erläuterungen und Dokumente: Heinrich von Kleist: Der zerbrochne Krug*. Stuttgart: Reclam, 1973.

Seyhan, Azade. *Representation and Its Discontents. The Critical Legacy of German Romanticism*. Berkeley, Los Angeles, and Oxford: University of California Press, 1992.

Stolberg, Friedrich Leopold. "Vom Dichten und Darstellen." *Gesammelte Werke der Brüder Christian und Friedrich Leopold Grafen zu Stolberg, Band 10*, pp. 375–381. Hamburg: Perthes and Besser, 1822.

Stolzenberg, Jürgen. *Fichtes Begriff der intellektuellen Anschauung. Die Entwicklung in den Wissenschaftslehren von 1793/94 bis 1801/02*. Stuttgart: Klett-Cotta, 1986.

Theissmann, U. "Darstellung." *Historisches Wörterbuch der Philosophie, Band 2*, ed. Joachim Ritter, pp. 12–14. Basel: Schwabe, 1972.

Titzmann, Michael. "Bemerkungen zu Wissen und Sprache in der Goethezeit (1770–1830), Mit dem Beispiel der optischen Kodierung von Erkenntnisprozessen." *Bewegung und Stillstand in Metaphern und Mythen*, ed. J. Link and W. Wülfling, pp. 100–120. Stuttgart: Klett-Cotta, 1984.

Trübners Deutsches Wörterbuch, ed. A. Götze. Berlin: de Gruyter, 1940.

von Molnár, Géza. *Novalis' "Fichte-Studies."* The Hague: Mouton, 1970.

————. *Romantic Vision, Ethical Context.* Minneapolis: University of Minnesota Press, 1987.

von Wiese, Benno. "Das verlorene und wieder zu findende Paradies. Eine Studie über den Begriff der Anmut bei Goethe, Kleist und Schiller." *Kleists Aufsatz über das Marionettentheater,* ed. H. Sembdner, pp. 196–220. Berlin: Erich Schmidt, 1967.

Wahrig, Gerhard. *Deutsches Wörterbuch.* Munich: Bertelsman. 1991.

Wellbery, David E. "Das Gesetz der Schönheit: Lessings Ästhetik der Repräsentation." *Was heisst* ≫*Darstellen*≪? ed. Christiaan Hart Nibbrig, pp. 175–204. Frankfurt am Main: Suhrkamp, 1994.

————. "Rhetorik und Literatur. Anmerkungen zur poetologischen Begriffsbildung bei Friedrich Schlegel." *Die Aktualität der Frühromantik,* ed. Ernst Behler and Jochen Hörisch, pp. 161–173. Paderborn and Munich: Schöningh, 1988.

Wild-Schedlbauer, Roswitha. "Einleitung." August Ferdinand Bernhardi, *Anfangsgründe der Sprachwissenschaft. Faksimile-Neudruck der Ausgabe Berlin 1805,* pp. vii–lvi. Stuttgart-Bad Cannstatt: Frommann-Holzboog, 1990.

————. "Reflexionen über A. F. Bernhardis Leben und sprachwissenschaftliches Werk." *Neuere Forschungen zur Wortbildung und Historiographie der Linguistik. Festgabe für Herbert E. Brekle,* ed. Brigitte Asbach-Schnitker and Johannes Roggenhofer, pp. 367–385. Tübingen: Gunter Narr, 1987.

Wittkowski, Wolfgang, "*Der zerbrochne Krug*: Juggling of Authorities." *Heinrich von Kleist Studien,* ed. Alexej Ugrinsky, pp. 69–79. Berlin: Erich Schmidt, 1980.

Index

213

When God portrays himself as a tree, with fruit, which in metaphorical language, that we can see, feel, taste, and know, he is saying that his nature, the essence of his own being, is accessible to human senses, and can be known by these senses.

When he permits us to eat the fruit, we take his nature into ourselves, truly experiencing, to assimilate, and become. When we experience the fruit as most desirable, most sweet above all things, it is not just the fruit, but our response to the fruit - what we are.